45 00

||||| |||| D0793552 |||||

Birth

marcus Afon steall this book

Encyclopedia of Mind Enhancing
Foods, Drugs and Nutritional Substances

ENCYCLOPEDIA OF MIND ENHANCING FOODS, DRUGS AND NUTRITIONAL SUBSTANCES

David W. Group

McFarland & Company, Inc., Publishers
Jefferson, North Carolina, and London

Though every attempt has been made to insure that the information contained in this book is accurate, it is not a substitute for consultation with a physician or health care provider. Any attempt at self-diagnosis or treatment is strongly discouraged. The publisher and author are not responsible for any adverse affects or unforeseen consequences as a result of following any of the advice or procedures in this book. Should there be any questions or concerns about any of the information in this book, it is always advisable to consult with a knowledgeable physician or health care provider first.

Library of Congress Cataloguing-in-Publication Data

Group, David W., 1959–
Encyclopedia of mind enhancing foods, drugs and nutritional substances / David W. Group.
p.   cm.
Includes bibliographical references and index.
ISBN 0-7864-0853-7 (illustrated case binding : 50# alkaline paper) ∞
1. Nootropic agents.   2. Dietary supplements.   I. Title.
RM334.G76   2001   615'.78 — dc21   00-58678

British Library cataloguing data are available

Cover image ©2000 PhotoDisc

Manufactured in the United States of America

McFarland & Company, Inc., Publishers
Box 611, Jefferson, North Carolina 28640
www.mcfarlandpub.com

Contents

Preface

The brain is a physical organ just like the heart or lungs or liver and, as such, its functioning can be affected by our environment, particularly the substances we put in our bodies. I first became aware of smart drugs from an article in *Omni* magazine some twenty years ago while I was attending college. It was also at that time that I was becoming aware of health foods, and the article so impressed me that, while other students were taking speed and No-Doz to cram for exams, I was gobbling handfuls of vitamins. While my approach was undoubtedly too haphazard and belated to have had much effect, it certainly set me on the right path.

But it wasn't until a few years ago that a number of books began coming out extolling the virtues of synthetic drugs that could actually reverse aging, prevent Alzheimer's, or improve the functioning of the brain. I began taking notes, thinking the information, when summarized, would amount to no more than a few dozen pages. Even though I only worked on it occasionally and in my spare time, it didn't take long for the research to swell to its current size.

My enthusiasm for the project was tempered by the fact that many of these books downplayed or ignored the side effects of these drugs, some of which were quite serious. Compounding my frustration was the fact that none was very comprehensive and none could be used for easy reference by the reader. I vowed to remedy that situation. The result is this book, which deals with over 400 various substances ranging from basic foods to the newest wonder drugs, from the most commonplace substances to the most obscure — by far the most complete work on the subject.

The chapters are arranged progressively, beginning with the safest and most natural substances and ending with synthetic drugs and additives that are experimental and potentially hazardous.

The entries for the substances are alphabetized by popular name within the appropriate chapter, and include such information as alternative names and forms (scientific, brand names, and so forth), sources (such as foods), effects (benefits), precautions (side effects, interactions, overdosage, medical conditions that may render the substance ineffective or toxic), and dosage. In the interest of brevity, I have eliminated much of the history, folklore, background, and detailed analysis of individual studies, dealing only with that information that can help the reader evaluate each substance.

This book does not contain a discussion of how the brain works and the various theories of aging. Neither does it deal with all the vitamins and nutritional supplements required by the human body — only those that have more-or-less direct effects on the brain. It should also be noted that all of the substances mentioned in this book are secondary to the two most important brain-boosters: physical exercise and mental exercise. It is essential to keep

challenging yourself throughout life so that the mind and body remain in peak condition.

It seems rather ironic that, with new strides in medical and nutritional science enabling us to live longer and more productive lives, most people would rather not live to a ripe old age. This fear of old age is based on a basic misconception — that the elderly are invariably frail in mind and body. Too often, however, the ravages of age are no more than the accumulated results of a lifetime of poor health habits. Though some decline in abilities is inevitable, the picture is not as dire as it was once thought.

Though smart-drug proponents and the media will often tout a particular substance as a new "wonder drug," the truth is that there is probably no such thing. The human mind — not to mention the human body and the process of aging — is too complex for any single pill to be considered a cure-all, as there are inevitable side effects of any medicine, natural or man-made. The Fountain of Youth is not so much a single herb, or vitamin, or pill, but a way of life, a holistic view that takes into account all aspects of nutrition and health.

CHAPTER 1

Foods

CARBOHYDRATES

Carbohydrates are the principal source of the body's energy and are divided into two types — simple and complex. Simple carbohydrates include the various sugars found in fruit (fructose), milk (lactose), and table sugar (sucrose). Complex carbohydrates are found in vegetables, whole grains, and legumes. Complex carbohydrates are preferable, as it takes longer for the body to break them down, releasing the sugar into the bloodstream slowly. Simple carbohydrates, especially table sugar, can flood the body and trigger an oversecretion of insulin by the isles of Langerhans, resulting in an initial surge of energy from the sugar followed by lethargy caused by the sudden rush of insulin. Foods should be unrefined, fresh, and natural; refined foods, canned goods, and snack foods should be avoided.

Food Sources: Fruits, whole grains, vegetables.

Effects: Carbohydrates help relax the brain and are necessary for good mental functioning. They act as an antidepressant for people with less sugar-induced serotonin in the brain than normal (such as those who suffer from seasonal affective disorder [SAD]), possibly by amplifying serotonergic neurotransmission. If consumption is timed right, they can increase the brain's energy levels, as they are readily broken down into glucose, a simple sugar found in nature that is necessary for the brain's functioning.

Precautions: Fructose does not have this calming effect. Simple sugars (table sugar, brown sugar, and honey, for instance) have no nutritional value except for calories, and can promote cavities, cause rapid changes in blood sugar and insulin, and lead to obesity, hypoglycemia, and diabetes, among other disorders. Some people are "carbohydrate cravers," and need them to prevent drowsiness, restlessness, or boredom; instead of becoming sleepy, these people become more focused and alert, and better sustain concentration. Carbohydrates are safe and, to quote Dr. Stuart Berger, "They are the only food category not linked to any killer diseases."

Dosage: 300 to 400 g/day from complex carbohydrates, or about 1200 to 1600 kilocalories/day (out of an average total of 1800 to 2200 kilocalories/day). Ideally, 65 percent of a person's caloric intake should be carbohydrates — 55 percent from complex carbohydrates and starches and 10 percent from natural sugars such as those found in fruit. A minimum of 50 g/day are needed to prevent ketosis, an acidic condition of the blood. For best effect, carbohydrates should be taken with as little protein and fat as possible, as these slow down or hinder serotonin on its way to the brain.

HONEY

Effects: Contains anti-oxidants. The darker the honey, the more the anti-oxidants; for instance, honey made from Illinois buckwheat flowers has 20 times the anti-oxidants as honey made from California sage. Tupelo honey has the most fructose of any of the honeys and doesn't cause the insulin rush that others do.

Precautions: For the most health benefits, the honey should be unfiltered, unheated, and unprocessed. Despite the claims of some health advocates, the vitamin and mineral content of honey is minimal, and any derived benefits negligible. Honey also has the highest sugar content of all the natural sweeteners, and even has more sugar content than refined sugar; in fact, it can rot teeth faster than table sugar, possibly because of its stickiness and the fact that its vitamin and mineral content, however small, may provide a favorable environment for bacteria.

Compounding the problem is the fact that manufacturers may feed bees sugar water or add sugar syrup to the honey to increase the sweetness (a tip-off is inexpensive brands that pour easily). Further, the honey is heated to high temperatures, destroying much of the protein and nutritional content. Honey could also contain carcinogens that bees have inadvertently picked up from flowers sprayed with pesticides, or traces of penicillin and sulfite, which could pose a threat to susceptible individuals. Honey should never be fed to infants under one year of age, as it contains spores of *Clostridium botulinum*, the organism that causes botulism; while adults and older children have stomach acid that can kill the bacterium, infants do not, leaving them susceptible to sickness or even death.

MICROALGAE AND SEAWEED

AKA: *Aphanizomenon flos-aquae,* chlorella, cyanobacteria, nori, SBGA, seaweed, spirulina, Super Blue Green Algae.

Microalgae are single-celled plants that grow in fresh water or bacteria. The most common types used for food are chlorella and spirulina, though seaweed could probably be placed in this category also.

Effects: Super Blue Green Algae (SBGA) is said to increase energy and give feelings of euphoria. All forms of microalgae and seaweed are excellent sources of amino acids, chlorophyll, protein (higher than meats or soybeans), unsaturated fats, vitamins A, B-12, C, and E, and anti-oxidants.

Precautions: Microalgae and seaweed are good sources of amino acids and some vitamins but, beyond that, claims of their nutritional or therapeutic value are overstated. According to Dr. Andrew Weil, M.D., there is no evidence SBGA strengthens the immune system, and Sheldon Saul Hendler, M.D., Ph.D., states there is no scientific evidence for the salubrious effects attributed to these organisms, except for one report that spirulina is a good source of gamma-linolenic acid (GLA).

Super Blue Green Algae can cause abdominal distress, diarrhea, dizziness, gastrointestinal problems, headaches, heart palpitations, nausea, skin rashes, vomiting, and women may even experience uterine bleeding. Adverse side effects may result from an allergy or intolerance, either to contaminants in harvesting or possible natural toxins in the SBGA itself. *Aphanizomenon flos-aquae*, used in the making of SBGA, is capable of producing two toxins, one of which affects the liver and the other the nervous system; it could also contain any number of naturally occurring toxins that are as yet undiscovered.

Spirulina is high in phenylalanine, and so should not be taken by anyone with phenylketonuria (PKU) or skin cancer. There is no way of controlling the purity or potency of spirulina — consider the fact that Elliot Shubert, Ph.D., professor of biology at the University of North Dakota at Grand Forks, has found that every sample tested had significant levels of the toxic metals mercury and lead. Not only that, Harvard researchers have discovered that some components of this microalga may encourage the growth of cancerous tumors. And the fact that no one knows what the pharmacological agent is that provides the stimulant effect worries Dr. Andrew Weil, as it may cause dependency.

NEW ZEALAND
GREEN–LIPPED MUSSEL

AKA: *Perna canaliculus*, sea mussel.

The oil of this shellfish is rich in amino acids, enzymes, and essential trace elements, and is said to be similar to Omega-3, but more potent in its health benefits.

Effects: Reputed to prevent heart disease and relieve joint and muscle pains.

ROYAL JELLY

Royal jelly is made from bee pollen, saliva secretions of worker bees, and honey, and has a thick, milky texture.

Effects: Protects against bacteria, viruses, and funguses. It contains many vitamins, minerals, amino acids, fatty acids, enzymes, and testosterone, and is one of the richest natural sources of B-5, as well as the sole natural source of pure acetylcholine.

Precautions: It is more stable when mixed with honey, and it loses some of its nutritional value when exposed to air, room temperature, or sunlight. It should never be used in hot drinks, nor should anything hot be consumed immediately after taking it. Some avoid the freeze-dried form, as the chemical structure is said to be altered in the process. Pure royal jelly, the most potent form, is extremely unstable and should always be kept refrigerated.

John H. Renner, M.D., president of the Consumer Health Information Research Institute, asserts that any health benefits of bee pollen are a myth, and that it can even be harmful, as it may contain harmful bacteria, or trigger an allergic reaction from the variety of pollens it may contain. The few studies that have been conducted bear out this statement.

Dosage: Approximately ⅓ of a teaspoon daily; in capsule form, some recommend 150 mg/day, others 600 mg/day. Manufacturers say several weeks may pass before the beneficial effects of improved mental functioning and concentration are evident. It is available in sealed capsules, frozen, freeze-dried, or mixed with honey.

CHAPTER 2

Herbs

Individual herbs may have several active ingredients that enhance each other's effects. Other herbs may be added in a blend that increases the absorption, transport, and effectiveness of the main herb. Preparing herbs from extracts insures the standardization of the level of the active ingredients, as the ingredients in the plants themselves can vary according to soil conditions, climate, when the plant is harvested, and the method of preparation (the word *standardized* should be on any herbal product). Stick with brand-name herbal products made in the U.S., where qualitative standards are higher than in other countries. Care should be taken when using herbs, even teas, for medicinal purposes, as some of them (comfrey, aconite, pennyroyal, and ephedra are some examples), including ones sold in health food stores, are very powerful, even deadly, if used indiscriminately

self-diagnosis and self-treatment are not encouraged. A doctor should always be informed of what herbs are being taken, because some can interact with medications and prescription drugs. Pregnant or nursing women should avoid herbs as a general rule.

ANISE

AKA: Aniseed, common anise, *Pimpinella anisum.*

Effects: Contains several estrogen-like compounds. It has traditionally been used to treat respiratory ailments, though according to James A. Duke, Ph.D., many other herbs work better. It purportedly has antiviral properties, can freshen bad breath, get rid of phlegm and bronchial congestion, and suppress coughing. It is said to increase male libido, though there is no scientific evidence for this. Herbalists have used it to treat cramps, nausea, and gas, and it is said to improve digestion and appetite.

Precautions: None known.

Dosage: James Duke recommends adding 1 to 2 teaspoons of crushed seed per cup of boiling water, steeping for 10 to 15 minutes, then straining. Take once in the morning and once in the evening.

ASTRAGALUS

AKA: *Astragalus hoantchy, Astragalus membranaceous*, huang chi, huang qi.

Effects: An adaptogen that may provide energy and stamina, boost the immune system, detoxify various drugs and metals, have anti-viral properties, improve peripheral circulation, balance the bodily systems, counteract stress, and improve mental functioning. It is said to be a potent anti-cancer agent and may be useful in fighting off the flu and other respiratory infections. Evidence suggests it might be useful in the treatment of colds, flu, high cholesterol, chronic lung weakness, HIV, cancer, and tumors.

Works synergistically with schizandra berry.

Precautions: It should not be taken by those running a fever.

Dosage: In China, the usual dose of a decoction is 9 to 16 g/day, or 9 g/day of a powder composed of 15 to 20 percent astragalus. Cancer patients are generally given up to 30 g/day. Earl Mindell, R.Ph., Ph.D., recommends 400 mg 1 to 3 times a day.

ASHWAGANDHA

AKA: Winter cherry, *Withania somnifera*.

Sometimes referred to as the "Indian ginseng," Ashwagandha is a member of the nightshade family, along with potatoes, tomatoes, and eggplants.

Effects: According to traditional Indian medicine, it is said to reduce stress and anxiety and to improve vitality, learning, and memory. It has been used to treat arthritis and help heal broken bones, and may inhibit cancer, as well. There have been few studies, but those conducted have yielded encouraging results: it enhanced mood and improved hemoglobin and blood plasma protein levels in a 1993 study, was shown to alleviate withdrawal symptoms in morphine addiction in a 1995 study, and showed positive results for patients with anxiety neurosis in a 1997 study.

Works synergistically with gotu kola, shatavari (Indian asparagus), and Siberian ginseng to relieve stress.

Precautions: It can cause mild gastrointestinal problems, but this can be prevented by taking it with meals. Exceeding the recommended dose is not advised, as it may contain some compounds that are harmful when taken in significant quantities. Herbal products from India may be contaminated with mold, insects, and animal feces.

Dosage: One to two cups of tea a day.

BALM OF GILEAD

AKA: Balsam poplar, *Populus balsamifera, Populus candicans, Populus gileadensis, Populus tacamahaca*.

Balm of Gilead is a North American poplar that is different from the biblical plant (*Commiphora meccanensis*) of the same name.

Effects: May have anti-oxidant properties. Taken internally, it is used for coughs and chest conditions; applied externally it is used for rheumatoid arthritis and sore muscles.

Precautions: Common side effects include skin rashes and allergic reactions.

BILBERRY

AKA: Black whortleberry, blueberry, burren myrtle, dyeberry, huckleberry, hurtleberry, *Vaccinium corybosum*, *Vaccinium myrtillus*, whineberry, whortleberry, wineberry.

Effects: A natural anti-oxidant. It is used in Europe to treat varicose veins, problems with blood circulation to the brain, and a variety of eye problems, including night blindness, photophobia, glaucoma, diabetic retinopathy, and — in combination with vitamin E — cortical cataracts. Also used as an antiseptic, astringent, and anti-diarrhea medication. Eating the fresh berries can reportedly regulate bowel action, stimulate the appetite, and reduce intestinal gas. As a tea, it is said to treat coughs, vomiting, stomach cramps, and catarrhal enteritis.

Works synergistically with citrus fruits.

Precautions: Though the fresh berries can stop diarrhea in some people, they can cause it in others. Use of the leaves over an extended period of time can cause poisoning.

It can interfere with the absorption of iron.

Dosage: As a tincture, 15–40 drops in water 3 times a day.

BLACK COHOSH

AKA: Black snakeroot, bugbane, bugwort, cimicifuga, *Cimicifuga racemosa*, rattleroot, rattleweed, richweed, squawroot.

Effects: May be a mild relaxant. It contains estrogen-like substances which may be helpful in treating symptoms associated with menstruation and menopause. Various extracts have displayed anti-inflammatory, sedative, and blood pressure-lowering effects in animals. It has traditionally been used by Native Americans to treat chronic fatigue, malaria, rheumatism, kidney problems, sore throat, and female disorders. Herbalists have used it for bronchitis, fever, itching, high blood pressure, anxiety, menstrual cramps, and symptoms of menopause.

Precautions: It should not be used by anyone suffering from a chronic disease. No scientific studies of its effects have been done on humans. It may have a stimulating effect on the cardiac system. Consumption of large amounts could cause nausea (though mild nausea may just be a response to its bitter taste), vomiting, sweating, and dizziness.

BLESSED THISTLE

AKA: *Cerbenia benedicta*.

Effects: According to James Balch, Ph.D., and Phyllis Balch, C.N.C., it "may act as brain food." It is used by herbalists as a tonic for the stomach and heart, increasing circulation, and treating liver problems. According to James A. Duke, Ph.D., it can reportedly help combat HIV.

Precautions: Handling the plant can cause toxic skin reactions.

Dosage: One ounce of herb in one pint of boiling water taken 1 cup at a time, 3 times a day between meals. James Duke recommends 5 teaspoons of the herb in a cup of boiling water 2 or 3 times a day, presumably for HIV.

Brahmi

AKA: *Hydrocetyle asiatica.*
Effects: Said to relieve anxiety. It has been used to treat epilepsy and leprosy.

Buplerum

AKA: Ch'ai hu.
Effects: Said to reduce anxiety. It has been used to treat nausea, fever, and pain.

Butcher's broom

AKA: Box holly, knee holly, *Ruscus aculeatus*, sweet broom.
Butcher's Broom is an evergreen shrub in the lily family that is closely related to asparagus.
Effects: Said to increase blood flow to the brain. It may relieve inflammation and prove beneficial to the bladder and kidneys. It has been used to treat hemorrhoids, varicose veins, and other circulatory problems, as well as carpal tunnel syndrome, edema, Meniere's disease, obesity, Raynaud's syndrome, thrombophlebitis, and vertigo.
Works synergistically with vitamin C.
Precautions: May increase blood pressure in some individuals. It should not be used as a substitute for anti-coagulant medication.
Dosage: Earl Mindell, R.Ph., Ph.D., recommends 400 mg/day.

California poppy

AKA: *Eschscholtzia californica*, golden poppy.
Though its alkaloids are nowhere near as powerful, the California poppy is related to the opium poppy. Despite this, it is perfectly legal to grow and, in fact, is the state flower of California.
Effects: May relieve insomnia and anxiety. It may also be used to treat nervous tension and muscle tics. The alkaloids are different from those of the opium poppy and, though they have not been thoroughly studied, are not known to be narcotic or addictive.
Works synergistically with such sedative herbs as valerian.
Precautions: Overdose symptoms include headaches, hangover-like effects the next day, and other minor side effects. As with poppy seeds, use can cause a urine test to read positive for opiates.
It should not be combined with alcohol, prescription sedatives, or other depressants.
Dosage: The usual dose is 30 drops of tincture, or a spoonful of whole dried herb in a cup of tea 2 to 3 times a day.

Cardamom

AKA: Bastard cardamom, cardamon, *Elettaria cardamomum*, Malabar cardamom.
Effects: Contains cineole, a mild central nervous system stimulant, which may account for its reputation in Arab cultures as a male aphrodisiac. Cineole also kills bacteria that cause bad breath, and cardamom has been used to treat asthma, emphysema, gas, heartburn, acid indigestion, laryngitis, and vaginitis. Cardamom also contains the compound borneol, which is helpful in treating gallstones. In addition, herbalists have used it to treat colic, diarrhea, and headaches.

Catnip

AKA: Catmint, catnep, catrup, catswort, field balm, *Nepeta cataria.*

A member of the mint family, one active ingredient is similar to an ingredient in valerian. It has a similar effect to marijuana, but much milder.

Effects: A mild sedative used in the treatment of insomnia, it reportedly also relieves stress and anxiety and stimulates the appetite. It is high in vitamin C and is good for colds, flu inflammation, and pain.

Precautions: Used as a folk remedy for a variety of conditions, though scientific evidence is lacking. Some claim that smoking the leaves results in a mild marijuana-like high; this is not recommended.

Dosage: Up to 3 cups of tea a day (one ounce of herb per pint of water).

Cat's claw

AKA: Una de gato, *Uncaria* species.

Effects: An anti-oxidant. It also has anti-inflammatory properties, cleanses the intestinal tract, and stimulates the white blood cells.

Precautions: There is only one documented case of an individual having suffered any adverse reactions.

Cayenne

AKA: Africa pepper, America pepper, bird pepper, capsicum, *Capsicum anuum, Capsicum frutescens*, chili pepper, cockspur pepper, goat's pepper, hot pepper, pod pepper, red pepper, Spanish pepper, Zanzibar pepper.

Effects: May improve blood circulation and help prevent blood clots. Cayenne is also said to help the body utilize other herbs more effectively, stimulate appetite and digestion, normalize blood pressure, and it has been used to treat asthma. It may help prevent colds, flu, depression, arthritis, headaches, heart attacks, and strokes. Capsicum cream reportedly relieves the intense pain following an attack of herpes zoster (shingles) when applied to the affected areas.

Precautions: Those with duodenal ulcers, bleeding problems, or who are taking anti-coagulants should consult a physician before using cayenne. Over-consumption can lead to gastroenteritis, kidney damage, nerve damage, and permanent loss of the sense of taste; some may experience a burning sensation during defecation. Prolonged skin application (for treating arthritis, pericarditis, pleuritis, and rheumatism) can result in dermatitis and blisters, and it can be very irritating to the mucous membranes if inhaled.

Dosage: ¼ teaspoon 3 times a day.

Celery

AKA: *Apium graveolens*, garden celery, wild celery.

Effects: Contains apigenin, which dilates the blood vessels, and several anti-oxidant vitamins. It can be used to treat amenorrhea, angina, cardiac arrhythmia, dizziness, gout, high blood pressure, and high cholesterol. Herbalists have also used it for dropsy, obesity, flatulence, skin problems, and lack of appetite.

Precautions: It is high in sodium. It is also a strong diuretic, and should not be used by those with kidney problems.

Dosage: At least one celery stalk a day. As a tea, ½ teaspoon of seeds in ½ cup of boiling water and strain. As a juice, one tablespoon two or three times a day an hour before meals.

CHAMOMILE

AKA: *Anthemis nobilis* (Roman chamomile), camomile, *Chamaemelum nobile* (Roman chamomile), Kamillosan, *Matricaria chamomilla* (German chamomile), *Matricaria recutita* (German chamomile), Perkamillon.

Effects: Chamomile is said to stimulate the brain, dispel weariness, calm the nerves, counteract insomnia, aid in digestion, break up mucus in the throat and lungs, and aid the immune system. Further, it has anti-bacterial and anti-fungal properties and may inhibit the growth of the polio virus and certain tumors, alleviate the pain and joint inflammation of arthritis, and prevent and heal ulcers. Kamillosan and Perkamillon are German pharmaceutical brands used to treat indigestion and ulcers.

Works synergistically with other sedative herbs.

Precautions: Can cause reactions in those allergic to ragweed, aster, or chrysanthemums. There have also been reports of asthma, hay fever, and hives in susceptible individuals. Overdosing can cause nausea and vomiting. An overdose of the tincture may cause diarrhea.

Dosage: The tea contains only 10 percent of the sedative-inducing chemicals of the herb.

CHAPARRAL

AKA: *Larrea divaricata, Larrea tridentata*.

Effects: Contains nordihydroguaiaretic acid (NDGA), a chemical which has shown anti-oxidant and antiseptic qualities. Traditionally used by Native Americans to treat various cancers, arthritis, bruises, eczema, rheumatism, snake bites, venereal diseases, and wounds. Herbalists have used it as an antibiotic, treating bacteria, viruses, and parasites. Used as a mouthwash, it can reduce cavities by up to 75 percent, though all of it should be spit out immediately after rinsing the mouth, as swallowing could produce side effects.

Precautions: Scientific evidence for any claims is lacking. The plant could cause inflammation of the skin if touched. Internal use may cause damage to the liver, especially if taken in large doses or for prolonged periods of time.

CHICKWEED

AKA: Adder's mouth, *Cerastium vulgatum* (mouse-ear chickweed), Indian chickweed, satin flower, starweed, starwort, *Stellaria media* (common chickweed), *Stellaria pubera* (star chickweed), stitchwort, tongue-grass, winterweed.

Effects: It is high in vitamin C. Herbalists have used it to treat arthritis, asthma, cancer, blood disorders, constipation, eczema, fever, gout, hemorrhoids, infection, inflammation, obesity, tuberculosis, bruises, nosebleeds, abscesses, and boils.

Precautions: There is no scientific evidence for any of its supposed health benefits, though it is generally considered very safe.

Dosage: It is best used sparingly as a vegetable or salad green.

CHINESE CLUB MOSS

AKA: Club moss, foxtail, *Huperzia serrata*, lycopod, *Lycopodium calvatum*, staghorn, vegetable sulfur, wolf claw.

Effects: Contains hyperzine, which inhibits the breakdown of acetylcholine, which may aid in the alleviation of symptoms of Alzheimer's disease. Used by herbalists as a diuretic for kidney disorders and as a treatment for nervous disorders and epilepsy.

Precautions: Only the spores should be used, as the plant itself is poisonous.

Dosage: One to two cups of tea a day.

CLOVE

AKA: *Caryophyllus aromaticus, Eugenia aromatica, Syzygium aromaticum.*

Effects: An anti-oxidant. It increases circulation and thins the blood. It also aids digestion and is used in the treatment of flatulence, vomiting, and nausea. The oil has anti-fungal and anti-bacterial properties.

Precautions: May cause a numbing effect on the tongue, as it contains eugenol, a strong anesthetic. Clove oil is toxic in large amounts.

COLA

AKA: *Cola nitida.*

Cola soft drinks do not contain the herb, but they do share the stimulating compound caffeine.

Effects: Contains the compounds theobromine, kolanin, and caffeine, all of which are stimulants. It is used as a female aphrodisiac in Jamaican and West African societies.

CORDYCEPS

AKA: Caterpillar fungus.

Effects: A mushroom that is used in China as a tonic to increase energy and stamina, either as a tea or an extract.

Precautions: It is said to be non-toxic.

COUNTRY MALLOW

AKA: *Sida cordifolia.*

Effects: Contains the stimulant compound ephedrine, which may explain its reputation as an aphrodisiac. It has been used to treat bronchial congestion and narcolepsy. Herbalists have used it to treat muscular and nervous system problems such as sciatica, and it may also have antiseptic properties.

Dosage: James A. Duke, Ph.D., recommends five teaspoons of the herb in a cup of boiling water.

DAMIANA

AKA: *Turnera aphrodisiaca, Turnera diffusa.*

Popular in Mexico, it is used to make both a tea and a liqueur.

Effects: It may have a calming or sleep-inducing effect. It is traditionally thought of as an aphrodisiac, and has been used to treat impotence and sterility, not to mention diabetes, kidney disease, bladder infections, asthma, bronchitis, chronic fatigue, and anxiety.

Precautions: It can interfere with the absorption of iron. Evidence for its supposed aphrodisiac qualities is only anecdotal, though it is generally considered a safe herb. There appear to be no reports of toxicity.

Dosage: James A Duke, Ph.D., recommends a tablespoon of dried herb in a cup of boiling water.

DANDELION

AKA: Blowball, cankerwort, lion's tooth, priest's crown, puffball, pu gong ying, swine snout, *Taraxacum officinale*, white endive, wild endive.

Effects: A good source of lecithin and choline, both of which are beneficial to memory, plus the anti-oxidant carotenoids lutein and violaxanthin. It may be helpful in treating constipation, fever, gout, hepatitis, insomnia, stiff joints, liver disorders, and chronic rheumatism.

Precautions: It appears to be a safe herb with no apparent side effects.

Dosage: One cup of tea a day.

DA T'SAO

AKA: Jujube date.

Effects: Da t'sao is said to promote calmness and is used in China to treat insomnia and dizziness.

DEVIL'S CLAW

AKA: *Harpagophytum procumbens.*

Effects: In Europe, it has been used to treat senility, as well as allergies, arthritis, and diabetes. In Africa, it is used to treat fever, indigestion, malaria, and skin cancer.

Precautions: There is no scientific evidence for any of its claims. Studies which have shown it relieves the symptoms of gout through anti-inflammatory properties and by lowering uric acid levels have employed injections; it is not known if ingesting this herb would have the same effects.

DONG QUAI

AKA: *Angelica sinensis*, Chinese angelica, dang quai, tang keui, tang kwei.

Don quai is similar to western angelica (*Angelica archangelica*), though its effects are milder and slightly different.

Effects: Known as an anti-aging herb. It is also used to treat menstrual problems, the symptoms of menopause, heart disease, insomnia, high blood pressure, cirrhosis of the liver, herpes zoster (shingles), anemia, and diabetes.

Dosage: Three cups of tea a day, or four tablets or capsules a day in two divided doses.

DON SEN

AKA: *Campanumaea pilosula*, don shen, tang shen.

Effects: Considered similar in effect to ginseng, though milder. It is said to restore energy and improve digestion, and is used to treat heartburn.

Works synergistically with astragalus.

EPHEDRA AND MA-HUANG

AKA: Dymetadrine 25, *Ephedra gerardiana* (Pakistani ephedra), *Ephedra nevadensis* (American ephedra, Brigham Young weed, cowboy tea, desert herb, Mormon tea, squaw tea, teamster's tea, whorehouse tea), *Ephedra sinica* (Chinese ephedra, ma-huang), epitonin.

Effects: Chinese and Pakistani ephedra contain ephedrine, a strong central nervous system stimulant. American ephedra contains norpseudo-ephedrine, which may be even more powerful. It increases adrenaline production, heart rate, and blood pressure.

It is said to be useful in the treatment of asthma (by dilating the bronchioles), narcolepsy, nasal congestion, and allergies. Some claim it helps to burn off fat and contribute to weight loss. Ephedra sinica may contain a substance that prevents the growth of the Influenza B virus. Dymetadrine 25 is an over-the-counter drug that is pure ephedrine.

Traditional Chinese medicine has used it in conjunction with other herbs.

Precautions: It should not be used by persons who suffer from anxiety attacks (panic disorder), diabetes, elevated thyroid, glaucoma, heart disease, hypertension, or high blood pressure, or by those who have a history of abusing stimulant drugs. Those who are underweight, sedentary, subsisting on a poor diet, recovering from an illness, suffering from extreme stress, have sleep problems, or who have a weak digestive system may find that ma huang may make them feel more stressed out and run down.

The effects wear off rapidly, so that larger and larger doses are needed to achieve the same effect. Large doses can cause headache, nervousness, nausea, palpitations, dizziness, difficult urination, insomnia, and chest pain. Overuse may also lead to a condition called the serotonin syndrome, where serotonin levels in the body are too high, and which is characterized by restlessness, confusion, sweating, diarrhea, excessive salivation, high blood pressure, increased body temperature, rapid heart rate, tremors, and seizures. There are twenty reported cases of ephedrine psychosis attributed to overuse, and attempts by individuals to obtain a high have led to a few deaths. Its use in treating allergies, asthma, and congestion has largely been replaced by more effective drugs that exhibit fewer side effects. Ephedra could cause a positive response on a drug test for amphetamine use.

It should not be combined with MAO inhibitor drugs or 5-HTP. Bodybuilders often take 100 mg of caffeine, 50 mg of ephedrine, and one aspirin three times a day for "cutting up" (reducing fat and increasing muscle definition), though this is not recommended, as the caffeine-ephedra combination may have been responsible for almost two dozen deaths in recent years. Proponents of ephedra say the evidence is inconclusive, particularly since ephedra has been used for much of recorded history, and ephedra-based alkaloids are found in numerous over-the-counter remedies that have been used by millions, many of whom also regularly drink caffeinated beverages.

Dosage: James A. Duke, Ph.D., recommends one level teaspoon of the dried herb or one-half to one teaspoon of the tincture, though he cautions that this should only be done after consultation with a doctor. The FDA does not recommend more than 24 mg of ephedrine a day.

FENUGREEK

AKA: Greek hayseed, *Trigonella foenum-graecum.*

Effects: A good source of choline and beta-carotene, both of which are useful in the treatment of Alzheimer's disease. It has also been used in the treatment of gout, neuralgia, respiratory ailments, sciatica, skin irritations, sores, swollen glands, and tumors.

Dosage: Two teaspoons of seeds per cup of water for up to two to three cups a day.

Frankincense

Effects: An anti-oxidant.

Fu Ling

AKA: Muk sheng (red fu ling), *Poria cocos.*

Effects: Said to be useful in treating insomnia and "emotional imbalances" such as apprehension, fear, instability, and insecurity. It is also one of the most powerful diuretics known. Herbalists have also used it to treat kidney problems and lung congestion.

Garlic

AKA: *Allium canadense, Allium sativum,* hu suan.

Effects: Garlic inhibits the formations of nitrosamines, compounds which lead to the development of cancer, especially digestive and colon cancers, and has been used to treat diabetes, heart disease, high blood pressure, high cholesterol, allergies, arthritis, arteriosclerosis, cancer, hypoglycemia, gastrointestinal disorders, asthma, bronchitis, candidiasis, and pneumonia. Because it contains sulfhydryl compounds (which regulate immune function) and the minerals selenium and germanium, it can fight infection by stimulating the immune system, and has been shown to have anti-bacterial, anti-microbial, and anti-fungal properties. Studies have revealed that garlic destroys the *Helicobacter pylori* bug, a bacteria that plays a role in the development of stomach ulcers and possibly even stomach cancer. Garlic can also trigger enzymes in the liver to deactivate aflatoxin, a strong carcinogen found on mold in peanuts and grains. One study

has shown that those who took supplements of 300 mg/day of garlic had aortas that were 15 percent more supple than those who didn't.

Precautions: Very large doses of garlic may cause gastrointestinal problems; even in moderate amounts, it can aggravate gastroesophageal reflux disease, or acid reflux, by relaxing the lower esophageal sphincter muscle. Garlic's effectiveness depends on its allicin production, which occurs as a result of a reaction between the compound alliin — a sulfur amino acid — and the enzyme allinase. Fresh, whole garlic is the only effective form, as the allicin breaks down quickly after it is cut or sliced; allicin is not activated in garlic that has been aged or dried, though Dr. Isadore Rosenfeld states that sanitized capsules are also effective, and these are recommended for those concerned about the odor. On the other hand, Joe and Teresa Graedon, Ph.D., recommend that a clove of garlic should be crushed at least ten minutes before heating to obtain the full cancer-fighting benefits. Recently, a process developed by the Japanese ages garlic for a year, enhancing its anti-oxidant effects by fully metabolizing allicin into other biologically active sulfur compounds while eliminating its odor. Garlic supplements should be stopped about two weeks before surgery, as it could cause excessive bleeding.

Garlic will increase the blood thinning properties of aspirin and other anticoagulants, so caution should be exercised when combining them.

Dosage: A clove of garlic a day (about 4 grams). Supplements should provide at least 10 mg/day of alliin or a total allicin potential of 4000 mcg/day (equivalent to roughly 4000 mg of fresh garlic). A recommended dose of aged extract is 600 to 1200 mg/day, or 2 to 5 mg/day of garlic oil.

GAY GEE

AKA: Lycii, *Lycium chinenses*, lycium chinese, wolfberry.

Effects: It is believed that this herb can contribute to a long life span and a sunny disposition. It is high in antioxidants and carotenoids, and is known to increase testosterone levels in men who are deficient. It has been used to treat high blood pressure, kidney disease, fever, bronchial inflammation, diabetes, and some types of cancer.

GENTIAN

AKA: Bitter root, bitterwort, *Gentiana catesbaei* (blue gentian, American gentian), *Gentiana crinita* (fringed gentian), *Gentiana lutea* (yellow gentian), *Gentiana officinalis*, *Gentiana quinquefolia* (stiff gentian, gallweed), gentian root, pale gentian.

Effects: Gentian may increase circulation, aid digestion, and stimulate the appetite. It has been used to treat earaches, heartburn, hypothyroidism, and ulcers.

Dosage: One teaspoon in one or two cups of water, simmered for 30 minutes.

GINGER

AKA: African ginger, *Asarum canadense*, black ginger, Canada snakeroot, gan jiang, Indian ginger, race ginger, wild ginger, *Zingiberis officianalis*, *Zingiber officinale*.

Effects: Has been used to treat anxiety and depression. A stimulant, it is said to benefit the stomach, intestines, and circulation, and has been used to treat cramps, indigestion, gas, motion sickness, and nausea. It is said to help cleanse the body through sweating, to stimulate the appetite, and to relieve the symptoms of colds.

Precautions: Large doses can cause stomach upset. Use of the whole plant causes liver damage in animals. In the 1930s, Jamaican ginger used in an alcoholic beverage caused major neurological symptoms in some people.

GINKGO BILOBA

AKA: EGb 761, Ginkgold, maidenhair tree, Rokan, Tanakan, Tebonin.

Effects: Acts as a vasodilator, improving circulation in the medium and small capillaries in the brain and extremities (it also increases the circulation of the microcapillaries, something no other known substance is known to do), prevents free radical damage in cell membranes (and repairs lesions caused by free radicals), protects nerve tissue from damage resulting from hypoxia (lack of oxygen), helps the brain to metabolize glucose better, facilitates nerve transmission, and increases alertness (by reducing theta brainwaves, the presence of which indicates inattention and lack of concentration), short-term memory, and overall brain functioning.

It has been used to treat age-related dementia in Europe for years, as it has been found to produce the same consistent EEG changes as those produced by drugs prescribed for dementia, though it may take six months before changes become apparent. It may have no memory- or brain-enhancement effect in healthy people with no brain impairment. It may inhibit mental deterioration in the early stages of Alzheimer's disease for six to twelve months, though some dispute this.

Ginkgo biloba contains ginkgolides, molecules that are antagonistic to Platelet Activating Factor (PAF), a major component of asthma, allergies, and inflammatory conditions. It may also be helpful in relieving the symptoms of such conditions as bronchial and cardiac asthma, cold extremities, diabetes, eczema, glaucoma, inner ear dysfunction, macular degeneration, migraine headaches, multiple sclerosis, neuralgia and neuropathy, retinopathy, tinnitus, vascular fragility, and vertigo. There is no evidence it can help sustain male erections.

Precautions: It has been found to reduce the ability of sperm to penetrate eggs, and individuals should exceed the average daily dose only under a physician's care. Because of the relationship to PAF, it can be a problem for those with clotting disorders. High doses may cause diarrhea, headaches, irritability, nausea, restlessness, skin irritations, and vomiting. The fruit can cause severe allergic reactions much like poison ivy and poison oak. Though commercially sold ginkgo biloba products are tannin-free, there may be a chance that some extracts are not, and these tannins, or astringent chemicals, may cause gastrointestinal disorders.

It may interact with such blood thinners as Warfarin (coumadin) and aspirin.

Dosage: From 120 to 160 mg/day of flavonoid extract in three divided doses (Dr. Isadore Rosenfeld recommends half that, while James A. Duke, Ph.D., considers 60 to 240 mg/day safe); it has a half-life of three hours, and it is pretty much gone after 6 hours. The extract must be at least a 50-to-1 concentration (50 pounds of leaves used to make 1 pound of extract), along with 24 percent active ingredients (gingkoflavonglycosides, also referred to as flavoglycosides, flavone glycosides, or ginkgoheterosides); quite a few products available are lower in concentration and are taken in doses as high as 1000 mg/day. Improvements should be seen within three to six months.

GINSENG

AKA: *Eleutherococcus senticosus* (Siberian ginseng), *Panax notoginseng* (Tienchi ginseng), *Panax quinquefolium* (American ginseng, five fingers, five-leafed ginseng, redberry), *Panax schinseng* (Asiatic ginseng, Chinese ginseng, Wonder-of-the-world), *Panax trifolius* (dwarf ginseng), ren shen.

It has been used as a general health tonic in China for the past forty centuries.

Effects: Works as an adaptogen, a non-toxic substance that normalizes body functions and protects against various stressors on the body. Many people believe Ginseng stimulates the brain and improves concentration, memory and learning, visual acuity, color perception, and aural acuity; works as a general stimulant to combat fatigue and stress; fights free radicals; reduces cholesterol; improves brain circulation; reduces heart rate; normalizes blood pressure; normalizes blood sugar; stimulates endocrine activity and metabolic functions; aids circulation and digestion; helps the body resist toxins, chemotherapy, alcohol, and drugs; boosts athletic performance and recovery from workouts; helps reduce insomnia and sleep disturbances; stimulates macrophage activity in the immune system; normalizes body functions; and improves sexual performance (though it is not an aphrodisiac). It has also been used to treat arthritis, tuberculosis, indigestion, cancer, and the symptoms of menopause.

Precautions: Solid research of its benefits is lacking. Quality can vary widely, and good ginseng is very expensive. Unfortunately, most of what is available is cheap and offers very little in the way of active ingredients: one study in the 1980s found that 50 to 70 percent of the products sold were diluted or adulterated, and a 1997 study by the Bureau of Alcohol, Tobacco, and Firearms found that most liquid ginseng contains alcohol, some as much as 34 percent. Many commercial products which contain ginseng, such as soft drinks, contain too little of the herb to provide any health benefits. Further, there are over two hundred different varieties, and experts cannot come to a consensus on what is the best type. Even within each variety, the quality can vary widely. Koreans routinely strip the bark during processing, the part of the plant which contains the highest amount of the active ingredients; red ginseng always has an intact bark, but white may or may not be stripped. Products should only be made with six-year-old roots, as it should not be harvested before then.

Some prefer American ginseng because it is a milder form than its Asian counterpart and avoids some of the side effects. Those suffering from acute inflammatory disease, anxiety disorder, bipolar disorder (manic-depression), heart palpitations, asthma, emphysema, or bronchitis should avoid American and Asian ginseng. Panax ginseng contains an estrogen-like compound that could cause problems in some individuals. Siberian ginseng is, strictly speaking, not ginseng at all, even though it comes from the same plant family; it has fewer side effects and more consistent results, but since it creates heat in the body, it should be avoided by those suffering from hot dry eyes, rashes, chronic sore throats, or high blood pressure.

Ginseng may cause allergy symptoms, increased blood pressure, diarrhea, gastrointestinal problems, headaches, heart palpitations, hypertension, insomnia, nervousness, tissue swelling, skin eruptions, weakness, tremors, masculinizaton in women and feminization in men, and skin rash, especially if taken at high doses for prolonged periods of time. Large doses should not be taken during an acute infection, as that may suppress the immune system.

There should be at least a three-hour span between taking ginseng and taking vitamin C, as some of the ginseng may be neutralized.

Dosage: From 500 to 3000 mg/day in divided doses. Extracts produce the most consistent results. Taking higher doses should be done only under the supervision of a health professional, and avoided as a general rule. Thomas H. Crook III, Ph.D., and Brenda Adderly, M.H.A., do not recommend taking it, based on many of the precautions cited above, while Dharma Singh Khalsa, M.D., recommends taking four to eight tablets a day of the Chinese medicine Ching Chun Bao, which contains, among other things, Royal Manchurian ginseng, the strongest and most effective form of ginseng.

GOTU-KOLA AND FO-TI-TIENG

AKA (Gotu-kola)**:** Brahmi, *Centella asiatica*, gota-kola, Indian pennywort.

AKA (Fo-ti-tieng): Asian marsh pennywort, fleeceflower, fo-ti, Ho shou wu, *Hydrocotyle asiatica minor, Polygonum multiflorium.*

Gotu-kola is a plant found throughout Africa and the East and, like ginseng, is considered an adaptogen. Fo-ti-tieng is so similar that botanists think it may be a geographic variant.

Effects: Both Gotu-kola and fo-ti-tieng have been used to treat obesity, varicose veins, wounds, and some skin conditions. They may improve attention and concentration, have an anti-stress tranquilizing effect, stimulate the brain by increasing blood flow, detoxify the body, and energize the cells. They are said to increase longevity.

Taken with calamus root, they may improve memory and mental clarity.

Precautions: Solid scientific evidence is lacking for many of their benefits, but they appear to be safe herbs. They should not be taken by those with an overactive thyroid. Gotu-kola can cause dermatitis if applied to the skin.

Dosage: One-half cup of tea using one ounce of gotu-kola per pint of water, taken three times a day.

GRASS, WHEAT AND BARLEY

AKA: Green Kamut, Green Magma.

Effects: Wheat grass is an excellent source of such anti-oxidant vitamins as A, B, C, and E. Both wheat grass and barley grass contain all the minerals essential for health, especially calcium, cobalt, iron, phosphorus, potassium, sulfur, and zinc. In addition to all the vitamins and minerals, they are high in chlorophyll, which according to some experts helps rid the body of toxins (including pesticides, drugs, and radiation) and discourages the growth of harmful bacteria. Barley also contains the anti-oxidants superoxide dismutase (SOD) and 2-0-GIV.

Precautions: Since these grasses cannot be digested by the human body in their solid state, they must be juiced, and they must be consumed before they go bad (within ten minutes). However, they can be stored in plastic containers in the fridge for up to a week, and even longer frozen, but at the expense of some of their nutritional value.

GREEN TEA

AKA: Bancha tea, *Camellia sinensis*, gunpowder tea, Imperial tea, kukicha tea, matcha tea, sencha tea, Yamashire tea.

Green tea is made from the same plant as black tea, but is processed by steaming before drying, rather than being fermented by "sweating," as is done with black tea. Oolong tea (also known as red tea or yellow tea) stands in the middle, as it is fermented, but not for as long as black tea.

Effects: All teas contain mind-altering alkaloids known as methylxanthines, which are also found in chocolate, coffee, cola, guarana, kola nut, and yerbe mate, and include caffeine, theophylline, and theobromine. Though tea leaves have a higher caffeine content than coffee beans (1 to 4 percent as opposed to 1 to 2 percent), green tea may have a much lower level of caffeine than coffee (20 to 30 mg compared to 75 to 150 mg) because caffeine is more readily leached into coffee than tea, and tea is diluted more with water than coffee is. Tea has a calming effect conducive to mental activity, as opposed to the sudden stimulation of coffee, which is more suitable to physical activity, and lacks the toxic or carcinogenic compounds found in coffee (e.g., caffeol, creosote, phenol, tars). Tea that is brewed for only two to three minutes has about half the caffeine as tea brewed for five or more minutes, and is not as bitter. High quality tea is dependent upon three things: (1) leaves and buds that are young and small, (2) leaves that are whole instead of broken, and (3) the absence of less beneficial parts such as twigs and stems. Gunpowder tea from China and matcha and sencha tea from Japan are examples of such teas. Chinese Imperial and Japanese Yamashire teas, though made from older leaves, are still of good quality, while the Japanese bancha and kukicha teas, being the lowest grade as they contain a high amount of twigs and stems, have the lowest amount of caffeine. Tea also contains polyphenols, compounds which have 25 to 100 times the anti-oxidant properties of vitamins C or E. It has been shown to lower levels of LDL, or "bad" cholesterol, and raise the levels of HDL, or "good" cholesterol. It is also said to prevent the buildup of plaque, prevent tooth decay because of its high fluoride content, and contribute to weight loss because of the metabolism-increasing effects of caffeine and the fat-burning property of the polyphenols. Preliminary research has shown that, when applied to the skin, it is an effective sunscreen.

Works synergistically with red wine, grapeseed, and borage oil.

Precautions: Caffeine may be both physically and psychologically addicting, and consuming high amounts could cause restlessness, anxiety, tremors, insomnia, abdominal pain, high blood pressure, and heart palpitations. Women who drink more than four-and-a-half cups of green tea a day are much more likely to suffer from PMS. Studies on whether green tea or black tea causes esophageal cancer are inconclusive, leading some to conclude that the disease may be due more to the habit of drinking tea scalding hot than to any particular ingredient in the tea.

Adding milk to green tea may prevent the absorption of at least some of the polyphenols.

Dosage: Five cups or more a day for at least six months have been shown to significantly lower the risk of pancreatic and colorectal cancers. Five to ten cups a day is believed to normalize blood sugar by regulating insulin production, and 100 to 150 mg/day of caffeine may be necessary for weight loss. Extracts may have lower levels of caffeine and higher levels of polyphenols than the tea.

Guarana

AKA: Brazilian chocolate, Brazilian cocoa, Energy Elixir, Guarana Tai (soft drink), Hit Energy, Josta (soft drink), *Paullinia cupana*, Super Pep, Zoom.

Effects: Traditionally used as a stimulant, aphrodisiac, and appetite suppressant, and used by herbalists to treat diarrhea, fever, and headaches. It does not cause the caffeine "jitters" that coffee normally does, possibly because the fats and oils in the seeds allow the caffeine to be digested much more slowly, resulting in a milder and longer-lasting high, though research has, as yet, not borne this out. The various saponins in guarana may enhance the health benefits of this herb.

Precautions: Has a higher caffeine level than tea or coffee, though the caffeine content may sometimes be misleadingly referred to as guaranine, a name bestowed upon it by early researchers who did not realize the two alkaloids were identical. Guarana sodas have, at most, 0.3 to 0.6 percent of the herb. More unfortunately, however, modern processing grinds the seeds at high temperatures, which oxidizes some of the compounds and produces a product that is both bitter-tasting and potentially irritating to the stomach.

GUAYUSA

AKA: *Ilex guayusa.*

A member of the holly family, it is related to yaupon and yerbe mate.

Effects: One of the richest plant sources of caffeine (up to 7.6 percent), it has traditionally been used by the indigenous peoples of South America as a stimulant, a headache remedy, and as a purgative in ceremonial rituals.

GUGGULU

AKA: Guggul.

A tree resin similar to myrrh.

Effects: A strong anti-oxidant that is said to relieve arthritis and other inflammatory diseases. It has been shown to lower LDL cholesterol and triglycerides and raise HDL cholesterol.

HAWTHORN

AKA: *Crataegus oxyacantha*, English hawthorn, hagthorn, May bush, May tree, quickset, thorn-apple tree, whitethorn.

Effects: May relieve anxiety and insomnia and improve circulation. It contains many bioflavonoids and is used by herbalists for various heart conditions — such as high blood pressure, myocarditis, arrhythmic heartbeat, and arteriosclerosis — digestive problems, and kidney disorders.

Precautions: Its concentrated form should be used only under the guidance of a physician.

Dosage: One teaspoon of flowers steeped in one-half cup of water, for up to one and one-half cups a day, or three capsules a day in three divided doses.

HOPS

AKA: *Humulus lupulus.*

A member of the hemp family, it is used to add flavor to beer.

Effects: May have a relaxing, sedative effect that promotes restful sleep. It also stimulates the appetite, reduces flatulence, and relieves intestinal cramps. Some of its compounds show promise as anti-cancer agents.

Works synergistically with skullcap.

Precautions: It cannot be stored for long, as it deteriorates rapidly and becomes very unstable when exposed to light and air. Those suffering from depression should not take high doses. Because of its sedative effect, it should be taken just before sleep. No significant side effects have been reported.

HORSEBALM

AKA: American horsemint, English horsemint, horsemint, *Mentha sylvestris*, monarda, *Monarda didyma* (bee balm, blue balm, high balm, low balm, mountain balm, mountain mint, Oswego tea), *Monarda fistulosa* (wild bergamot), *Monarda punctata.*

Effects: Contains carvacrol and thymol, both of which prevent the breakdown of acetylcholine, which may aid in the alleviation of symptoms of Alzheimer's disease. These compounds may be able to cross the blood-brain barrier, so it may be beneficial even when used externally. It has been used to relieve the symptoms of various digestive, respiratory, and cold-related ailments.

Dosage: One teaspoon of leaves or tops per cup of water, up to one to two cups a day.

JASMINE

AKA: *Jasminum officinale.*

Effects: Jasmine is believed to promote relaxation and is a possible aphrodisiac.

JATOBA BARK

A plant used as a tea in the rain forests of Brazil and Peru.

Effects: Has an energy-boosting effect. May aid the respiratory and urinary systems and help in weight loss.

KAVA AND KAWAIN

AKA: Ava, awa, kasa, kava kava, Kavaform, Kaviase, kawa, kawa kawa, keu, Laitan, lewena, *Piper methysticum*, *Piper wichmannii*, sakau, seka, waka, wati, yagona, yaqona.

A Polynesian herb used by native peoples to make an alcoholic drink. The practice of preparing the root and stem for the drink by having a designated person chew on them is no longer done because of health risks. Kava contains several active compounds called kavalactones, also known as kava alphapyrones or kava-pyrones, which include kawain (or kavain), dihydrokawain, methysticin, dihydromethysticin, and yangonin; each kavalactone has a different effect on the body, and the effects of different plants may vary according to the levels of the various kavalactones. It's uncertain whether the leaves and stems produce different effects from the roots, or whether older plants are more potent than younger ones.

Effects: May induce a sense of well-being in small doses, and relaxation, lethargy, and drowsiness in larger doses. The effects begin after twenty or thirty minutes and generally last two to three hours. According to Dr. Harold Bloomfield, "Medical studies have shown that kava can often relieve mild to moderate anxiety as effectively as benzodiazepine tranquilizers." It has been found to improve digestion, memory, reaction time, and vigilance, relax muscles, and decrease anxiety, chest pain, dizziness, gastric irritation, headaches, heart palpitations, muscle spasms, and symptoms of menopause and PMS. It also has local anesthetic properties and can be used to treat urinary tract infections and bladder disorders. Unlike other psychoactive plants (e.g., mushrooms and peyote), it does not enhance intellect or produce altered states of consciousness, though anecdotal evidence indicates it may enhance visual and auditory perception as well as produce more vivid dreams. How the kavalactones work is still not known, though it is believed they pass through the blood-brain barrier and affect certain neurotransmitters.

Kawain, a resinous pyrone extracted from the root of the kava plant, has been shown to control lipofuscin deposits. *Waka* is a Fijian term that refers to the kava taken from the plant's lateral roots, and *waka* is the most expensive and potent form. *Lewena*, the rootstock, and *kasa*, the lower stems, are cheaper and less potent forms.

Kava works synergistically with chamomile, hops, licorice, and valerian.

Precautions: Kava should not be taken by those with Parkinson's disease (it could worsen muscular weakness and twitching), by those who are severely depressed, or by those allergic to it. The elderly or ill should take smaller doses, and then only under the care of a physician. Kava is not advisable when driving or operating heavy machinery. It can be habit-forming. No clinical studies have been done in the U.S., and some are concerned that it might be abused as it has psychotropic properties similar to opium and cocaine. It probably should not be used for severe anxiety or for long-term treatment. Neither should it be used as a substitute for benzodiazepines, as it is not as effective in inducing sleep; is not as effective for severe agitation, severe anxiety, or convulsions; is slower to take effect; and does not remain effective for as long a period as the prescription drug.

A pungent and numbing aftertaste deters the drinker from consuming too much. Tea made from the dried and powdered root bark may not have the pleasant lilac aroma and flavor of freshly made kava. Stronger effects may be achieved by chewing the root, though this is something even the indigenous population of the South Seas do not engage in, as the taste and thick fibers of the root make this an unappealing alternative.

Extended use of doses equal to 400 mg/day of kavalactones and higher could result in a buildup of toxins in the liver, damage to the heart and lungs, and skin that is pigmented or darkened, dry, and covered with scales, particularly on the palms, soles, forearms, back, and shins (which may clear up when use is discontinued). Other symptoms include numbness of the tongue, dizziness, gastrointestinal distress, grogginess, inflammation of the skin and eyes, insomnia, sudden muscle spasms, nausea, biochemical abnormalities, vision disturbances, and shortness of breath.

There is one documented case of a man who lapsed into a brief coma after combining kava with the drug Xanax. It is recommended that kava not be combined with benzodiapezine tranquilizers, alcohol, antidepressants, or sleeping pills.

Dosage: The most effective method of consumption is by eating the dried root, as saliva activates the kavalactones. An acceptable dosage is 1.5 to 3 mg/day in divided doses. Probably the least effective method of consumption is as a tea, as water does not release the kavalactones the way oil does. An acceptable compromise is liquid extract formulas or standardized extract capsules. Generally, kava root of high quality will contain approximately 5 to 8 percent kavalactones. Though kavalactones are not, for the most part, water soluble, a water-soluble extract can be made; it differs from the usual fat-soluble extract in that it does not induce sleep, but it does have some pain-killing properties. Fat-soluble kava, on which most of the studies have been done, induces sleep and has much greater pain-killing abilities. If taking a tincture with a 1:2 ratio, dosage should be between 3 to 6 ml/day in divided doses. The initial dose should be about 70 mg of kavalactones, which should be gradually increased to about 100 mg. Reports indicate that 150 to 210 mg/day of kavalactones relieves anxiety, while one daily dose of this amount taken a half hour before bedtime induces sleep. It is more effective when taken on an empty stomach. Kava should not be taken on a daily basis for more than four to six months.

LAVENDER

AKA: *Lavandula officinalis, Lavandula vera.*

Effects: Lavender may relieve stress, depression, and insomnia because of its ability to slow nerve impulses, producing an anesthetic effect. It may also be good for the skin, and has been used in the treatment of amenorrhea, burns, carpal tunnel syndrome, fainting, pain, psoriasis, and vaginitis, and by herbalists in the treatment of dizziness, flatulence, headaches, and skin problems. According to James A. Duke, Ph.D., the sedative compounds can be absorbed in the skin, and tossing a handful in bathwater is a good way to relax.

Precautions: Some species, such as Spanish lavender, are stimulating rather than tranquilizing.

Dosage: One teaspoon of leaves in one-half cup of water, for a maximum of one cup a day.

LICORICE

AKA: Gan cao, *Glycyrrhiza glabra,* licorice root, sweet licorice, sweet wood.

Most licorice candy does not contain any trace of the herb but, instead, anise; some European licorice candies, however, may contain dangerously high levels of licorice. Licorice is a legume, part of the same family as beans and peas.

Effects: Licorice has been used to treat depression, as well as digestive, respiratory, kidney, and bladder ailments. In Japan, it has been used to treat chronic hepatitis B and C. It can also inhibit tooth decay, inhibit the growth of cancer *in vitro* and in mice, is helpful in the treatment of sore throats and coughs, and may aid in the treatment of Addison's disease. An extract, glycyrrhizin, has been used to treat such viruses as herpes zoster (shingles), herpes simplex 1, polio type 1, and vaccinia *in vitro*, and to inhibit HIV. Derivatives have also led to such drugs as Carbenoxolone, used in the treatment of various types of ulcers. Used by herbalists to treat allergies, asthma, chronic fatigue, emphysema, fever, hypoglycemia, and inflammation of the bowels.

Precautions: Licorice should not be used by those with hypertension (it could raise the blood pressure even more), depression (it can elevate blood cortisol and deepen the depression), severe menstrual problems, heart disease, diabetes, or glaucoma.

Overdosage or constant use (i.e., on a daily basis for more than a week) can result in headache, high blood pressure, hypertension, lethargy, retention of water and salt, and excessive loss of potassium. One man suffered congestive heart failure after eating a pound and a half of the herb for a week, and one woman suffered cardiac arrest (among other side effects) after consuming four pounds a week over an unknown period of time.

At least eight compounds in licorice are MAO inhibitors, so it should not be combined with certain drugs.

Dosage: One teaspoon of rootstock in one cup of water for up to three cups a day.

LIGUSTRUM

AKA: *Ligustrum lucidium.*

Effects: Its medicinal qualities are said to be similar to astragalus; it contains two potentially immune-regulating ingredients, syringin and a terpene compound. In China, it has been used to treat fatigue and prevent aging, in addition to being prescribed for infections, heart disease, body aches, dizziness, and tinnitus.

Dosage: From 6 to 15 g/day of a decoction made from the berries.

MEXICAN WILD YAM

AKA: *Dioscorea barbasco, Dioscorea composita, Dioscorea mexicanan, Dioscorea villosa.*

Effects: Contains DHEA and diosgenin, or steroid saponins, which are the precursor to the hormone progesterone. Said by herbalists to be good for estrogen imbalances in women and in relieving the symptoms of diverticulitis; some even claim that a salve made from it can enlarge women's breasts.

Precautions: There is little scientific evidence to back up any of its supposed benefits.

Only whole yam will provide benefits. Synthetic progesterone, called progestins or prestrogens, or products containing wild yam may be lacking in essential nutrients and may have many side effects, including depression, kidney problems, and increased risk of cancer.

MILK THISTLE

AKA: *Carduus marianus,* holy thistle, Marythistle, St. Mary's thistle, *Silybum marianum,* wild artichoke.

Effects: Contains the bioflavonoid mixture silymarin, which protects the liver against hepatitis, cirrhosis, and toxins such as carbon tetrachloride, alcohol, and the poisonous Amanita mushroom. It may also help protect the liver from otherwise beneficial pharmaceuticals such as anti-anxiety drugs, antidepressants, cholesterol-lowering drugs such as Zocor (simvastatin) and Mevacor (lovastatin), and high doses of Tylenol (acetaminophen) and iron. Milk thistle may even reverse damage that has already occurred. Studies published in the *Journal of the American Medical Association* have revealed that at least three-quarters of all adult Americans show at least some sign of chronic liver damage — which could manifest itself as irritability, fatigue, malaise, anxiety, depression, and mild intellectual impairment — possibly indicating that this may be an important herb to add to the diet. This bioflavonoid mixture may also be useful in preventing or treating gallstones and in relieving the symptoms of psoriasis. It has shown promise in treating liver disorders and hepatitis (including chronic hepatitis). Silymarin and its basic component silybin may protect cell membranes from free radicals through anti-oxidant properties.

Precautions: Those taking any medication or suffering from liver damage should consult a physician first.

There appears to be little chance of any side effects with moderate use: studies have shown that less than one percent of users have suffered side effects — and then only gastrointestinal discomfort and loose stools.

Dosage: The common dosage is a 200 mg pill containing a standardized extract of 80 percent silymarin (160 mg of silymarin) taken one to three times a day.

MUGWORT

AKA: *Artemisia vulgaris,* common mugwort, felon herb, sailor's tobacco.

Effects: Has been used to reduce nervousness and insomnia. May relieve mental fatigue and improve memory.

Precautions: High doses can lead to poisoning, but normal usage reportedly produces no adverse symptoms.

Dosage: One tablespoon of dried herb steeped in half a cup of water or one-half teaspoon of powdered rootstock with water twice a day.

MURIA PUAMA

AKA: *Ptychopetalum olacoides.*

Effects: Used as a stimulant in Brazil. Also used as a stomach tonic and to treat rheumatism. It is said to be an aphrodisiac.

MYRRH

AKA: *Commiphora myrrha*, gum myrrh tree.

Effects: An anti-oxidant. Herbalists have used it to treat bad breath, periodontal disease, and skin disorders, and the tincture is used to treat mouth and throat ulcers.

Precautions: It is toxic in large amounts.

Dosage: One teaspoon steeped in one pint of boiling water for a few minutes before straining, or two to five drops of tincture at a time as needed.

NETTLE

AKA: Common nettle, common stinging nettle, dwarf nettle, great stinging nettle, stinging nettle, *Urtica dioica, Urtica urens.*

Effects: Contains high levels of boron, which can increase the body's estrogen levels, improving mood and short-term memory in those with Alzheimer's. It is also a rich source of vitamins A, C, and E, protein, and minerals. Nettle has been used by herbalists to treat anemia, cancer, goiter, kidney problems, liver disease, constipation, asthma, worms, arthritis, gout, tuberculosis, and gonorrhea.

Precautions: Scientific evidence is lacking in its treatment for the above disorders, and effectiveness in such cases is very doubtful. Eating old, uncooked plants can cause kidney damage and poisoning. Side effects from the tea include upset stomach, a burning sensation on the skin, difficult urination (even though it is normally a mild diuretic), and bloating.

Dosage: Two to three tablespoons of leaves or plants in one cup of water.

OAT

AKA: *Avena sativa.*

Effects: Said to have anti-depressant and aphrodisiac properties. Preliminary studies have shown that extracts have some success in helping individuals overcome opiate and nicotine (from cigarette smoking) addiction. It is well-known that oat bran lowers cholesterol. According to James A. Duke, Ph.D., a few handfuls of oatmeal in a warm bath can relieve the itching of hives.

Precautions: Evidence of its anti-depressant and aphrodisiac qualities is lacking.

OREGANO

AKA: Marjoram, mountain mint, *Origanum majorana, Origanum vulgare*, wild marjoram, winter marjoram, wintersweet.

Effects: An anti-oxidant. It may have a calming effect, and a pillow made from the bruised leaves may help insomnia.

Dosage: Two or three teaspoons of herb in one cup of water once or twice a day.

Passion Flower

AKA: Maypops, *Passiflora incarnata*, passion vine, purple passion flower.

Effects: Passion flower is said to relieve depression and anxiety and promote restful sleep. It has been used to treat anxiety, convulsions, and neuralgia, though scientific evidence is lacking.

Works synergistically with other sedative herbs.

Precautions: It should only be taken an hour or two before sleep. No significant side effects have been reported.

Dosage: From 200 to 300 mg of extract one hour before bedtime, containing 3.5 to 4 percent isovitexin (flavonoids). The fruit, though low in nutrition, may be eaten when ripe, simmered for 5 minutes to make a tea, or made into a jelly.

Peppermint

AKA: American mint, brandy mint, lamb mint, *Mentha piperita*, mint.

Effects: An anti-oxidant. It is said to be good for abdominal pains, chills, colic, coughs, cramps, diarrhea, gastrointestinal problems, headache, heartburn, indigestion, insomnia, migraine headaches, nausea, nervousness, poor appetite, rheumatism, and spasms.

Precautions: It can worsen heartburn and gastroesophageal reflux disease, or acid reflux. Overdosage may cause heart problems.

It may interfere with the absorption of iron.

Dosage: Two to three teaspoons of leaves per cup of water, not to exceed one and a half to two cups a day for eight to twelve days.

Polynesian Noni

AKA: *Morinda* species.

Effects: Reportedly aids cell regeneration, strengthens the immune system, and slows aging.

Purslane

AKA: Portulaca, *Portulaca oleracea*, pussley.

Effects: Rich in anti-oxidants, including glutathione and vitamins A, C, and E. It also contains high levels of Omega-3 fatty acids, magnesium and potassium, along with calcium, folate, and lithium, all of which may help relieve depression. Purslane has been used to treat asthma, angina, bursitis, cardiac arrhythmia, chronic fatigue syndrome, gingivitis, headache, high blood pressure, intermittent claudication, multiple sclerosis, psoriasis, shingles, skin problems, tendinitis, wrinkles, and yeast infections. It may also help prevent cataracts and heart disease. It has been used by herbalists as a tonic for the kidneys, bladder, and urinary tract.

Dosage: The fresh stems and leaves can be used as salad greens.

Rauwolfia

AKA: Indian snakeroot, *Rauwolfia serpentaria*, *Rauwolfia serpentina*, serpentwood.

Effects: Dilates the blood vessels and contains the alkaloid reserpine, which has a tranquilizing effect. It is used to treat insomnia and Raynaud's disease. Though it contains some yohimbine, it should not be considered a substitute for yohimbe.

Precautions: It should not be taken by anyone who suffers from an allergy to rauwolfia alkaloids, depression, peptic ulcers, or ulcerative colitis. Those who suffer from epilepsy or who have had surgery in the past two months requiring general or spinal anesthesia should consult a physician first. Those over age sixty may suffer increased adverse reactions or side effects. Performing isometric exercises while on rauwolfia may cause the blood pressure to rise too high.

Common side effects to prescription rauwolfia alkaloids include depression, dizziness, headache, faintness, drowsiness, lethargy, red eyes, stuffy nose, impotence, reduced sex drive, diarrhea, and dry mouth. Less common side effects include black stools, bloody vomit, chest pain, shortness of breath, heartbeat that is irregular or slow, stiffness (muscles, bones, and joints), trembling in the hands, and swelling in the feet and legs. Rare side effects include a rash or itchy skin, sore throat, fever, abdominal pain, nausea, vomiting, unusual bruising or bleeding, jaundice, painful urination, and nightmares.

Overdose symptoms include drowsiness, a pulse that is slow and weak, breathing that is slow and shallow, diarrhea, flushing, coma, lowered body temperature, and pupils contracted to pinpoints.

The effects of rauwolfia alkaloids may be increased by other antihypertensives, beta-adrenergic blocking agents, Carteolol, and Lisinopril, and decreased by Sotalol. Rauwolfia alkaloids can increase the effects of antide-pressants, antihistamines, central nervous system depressants, Ethinamate, and Methyprylon, and decrease the effects of aspirin, levodopa, Pergolide, and terazosin. The effects of both rauwolfia alkaloids and Dronabinol, Fluoxetine, Guanfacine, Loxapine, or Sertraline are increased when combined. When combined with oral anticoagulants, it can result in an unpredictable increase or decrease in the anticoagulant effect; with anticonvulsants, it can result in changes in the seizure pattern; with Clozapine, the two could be toxic to the central nervous system; with digitalis preparations, it could result in an irregular heartbeat; with Leucovorin's high alcohol content, it could cause some side effects; with any mind-altering drug, it could cause excessive sedation; with MAO inhibitors, it could cause severe depression; with Nabilone it could cause increased depression of the central nervous sytem; with Nicardipine or Nimodipine, it could result in a drop in blood pressure; and with Procarbazine, there could be a marked increase in blood pressure.

Combining rauwolfia alkaloids with alcohol can lead to greater intoxication, while carbonated beverages can decrease the rauwolfia effect, cocaine can increase the risk of heart block and high blood pressure, spicy foods can cause an upset stomach, and marijuana can cause drowsiness, low blood pressure, and depression.

REISHI

AKA: Ganoderma, *Ganoderma lucidum*, ling-chih-tsao, ling-zhi, wu-ling-chih.

Reishi is a mushroom that grows in the mountains of Asia.

Effects: An adaptogen that boosts the immune system, balances the bodily systems, counteracts stress, and improves mental functioning. It may reduce symptoms of altitude sickness by thinning the blood. It has been used to treat viral hepatitis, may protect the liver from various toxins, and may be useful in treating chronic bronchitis, peptic ulcer disease, hypertension, insomnia, and high cholesterol.

Precautions: It should not be taken by hemophiliacs because it is high in adenosine. It should not be taken for longer than two or three months on a daily basis, as long-term effects are unknown. Side effects include achiness, more frequent bowel movements in the first few days, vertigo, itchiness, and skin eruptions.

Reishi can interact with Thorazine and barbiturates.

Dosage: Between 750 and 1000 mg/day of extract in three divided doses.

ROSEMARY

AKA: Compass plant, incensier, mi die xiang, *Rosemarinus officinalis*.

Effects: An anti-oxidant which also prevents the breakdown of acetylcholine. It acts as a stimulant and improves blood circulation, and may relieve mental fatigue, insomnia, and depression, and improve memory. It can protect the liver against toxins, and is also used by herbalists to treat colic, fevers, gas, headaches, high or low blood pressure, indigestion, menstrual cramps, and nausea.

Precautions: Raises blood pressure. Excessive amounts taken internally can be fatal.

Dosage: One teaspoon in half a cup of water once or twice a day, or 5 to 20 drops of tincture a day.

SAFFRON

AKA: Autumn crocus, *Crocus sativus*, Spanish saffron.

Effects: Contains crocetin, which lowers blood pressure. It has been used by herbalists to treat amenorrhea, coughs, whooping cough, stomach gas, colic, and insomnia. Saffron oil, or safrol, can be processed to make the narcotic MDA (methylenedioxyamphetamine).

Precautions: It contains a poison that can affect the central nervous system and damage the kidneys. It can be fatal at doses of 10 to 12 grams.

SAGE

AKA: Garden sage, *Salvia officinalis*.

Effects: Sage is anti-oxidant, a central nervous system stimulant, and a producer of estrogen-like effects. It may help oxygenate the brain, and may also be helpful in treating nervous conditions and depression. It is also used by herbalists in the treatment of bladder infections, colds and flus, diarrhea, dysentery, inflammatory conditions, mouth and throat disorders, night sweats, excessive perspiration, and sinus conditions.

Precautions: It should not be taken by those with seizure disorders or in large quantities because it contains thujone, which can cause convulsions in high doses. Prolonged use or overuse can lead to poisoning.

It can interfere with the absorption of iron and other minerals.

Dosage: One teaspoon of leaves steeped in one-half cup of water for 30 minutes and taken one tablespoonful at a time, for up to one cup a day.

One-quarter to one-half teaspoon of powdered leaves at a time. Fifteen to 40 drops of tincture three or four times a day.

St. John's Wort

AKA: Amber, goatweed, hypericum, *Hypericum perforatum*, Johnswort, Klamath weed, Tipton weed.

Effects: Probably the most effective natural anti-depressant known (it is used extensively throughout Europe), working much like Prozac and similar drugs, but with fewer side effects. It enhances three important neurotransmitters — serotonin, norepinephrine, and dopamine — the first substance known to do so. Benefits may include longer and deeper sleep, improved mood, greater energy, and increased appetite. It has been used to treat exhaustion, headaches, and insomnia. It may have anti-viral properties and be useful against herpes, HIV, chronic fatigue syndrome, and Seasonal Affective Disorder (SAD).

Works synergistically with kava.

Precautions: It may cause the skin to be sensitive to light, and can cause cataracts if the individual is exposed to bright light. It has a very mild MAO inhibitor effect, but not enough to warrant food restrictions. Recent evidence has shown that it can completely prevent the ability of sperm to penetrate eggs and may cause a genetic mutation which, if found in adult women, is correlated with an increased risk of breast and ovarian cancer. Less common side effects include gastrointestinal irritation, dizziness, dry mouth, and mild allergic reactions. Overdose symptoms, which can occur at dosages of 900 mg/day or more, include depression, gastrointestinal problems, nervousness, irritability, mild anxiety, restlessness, insomnia, headaches, cardiac symptoms, and sweating. It should not be used for serious depression.

In 1998, a study commissioned by the *Los Angeles Times* found that seven out of ten of the leading brands of St. John's Wort had only 20 to 90 percent of the potency listed on the label.

It can interfere with the absorption of iron and other minerals. It should not be taken with any tyramine-rich foods or drugs, and high doses should not be combined with high doses of 5-HTP. It should not be combined with Prozac, Paxil, or other anti-depressants, as it could cause dangerously high blood pressure, hypertension, severe anxiety, fever, muscle tension, and confusion; there should be at least a four week interval between taking an MAO inhibitor and taking St. John's wort.

Dosage: From 600 to 900 mg/day in three divided doses of 0.3 percent hypericin strength (Rosenfeld recommends 300 mg/day). Extracts must be at least 0.3 percent hypericin to be effective. Just 300 mg/day has proven effective against Seasonal Affective Disorder (SAD). Standardized extracts are more likely to have active ingredients, and extracts using the whole plant are more effective than extracts derived solely from the hypericin compound. Dr. Isadore Rosenfeld does not recommend using it for more than eight weeks at a time; others recommend not using it for more than six to eight months at a time. St. John's wort as a tea is not very effective, as just 10 to 20 percent of the active ingredients are dissolved in water. It may take three to six weeks for it to fully take effect.

SARSAPARILLA

AKA: *Aralia hispida* (bristly sarsaparilla), *Aralia nudicaulis* (wild sarsaparilla), *Aralia racemosa* (spikenard), Chinese root, life-of-man, small spikenard, *Smilax officinalis*.

Effects: Sarsaparilla is said to increase energy, regulate hormonal activity and protect against radiation. Herbalists have used it for catarrhal problems, colds, fever, flatulence, frigidity, gout, hives, impotence, infertility, nervous system disorders, PMS, rheumatism, and certain blood disorders.

Dosage: One teaspoon of rootstock in one cup of water for one to two cups a day.

SCHIZANDRA BERRY

AKA: *Schizandra chinensis*, *Schizandra fructus*, wu-wei-tzu.

Effects: An adaptogen that reportedly boosts the immune system, balances the bodily systems, counteracts stress, and improves mental functioning. It has proven beneficial in treating some liver disorders and appears to have some cortisone-like effects. In China, it has been used to treat dry cough, asthma, night sweats, nocturnal emissions, and chronic diarrhea, though evidence is no more than anecdotal.

Works synergistically with astragalus.

SHANKA PUSPI

AKA: *Convolvulus mycrophyllus*.

Effects: An herb used in India to relieve anxiety.

SKULLCAP

AKA: Blue skullcap, blue pimpernel, helmet flower, hoodwort, mad-dog-weed, scullcap, *Scutellaria baikalensis* (Chinese skullcap), *Scutellaria laterifolia*, *Scutellaria lateriflora*, side-flowering skullcap, Virginia skullcap.

Effects: Reported to reduce insomnia and anxiety. Bioflavonoids in Chinese skullcap have anti-inflammatory and anti-allergic properties. It may be useful in treating muscle cramps, rheumatism, neuralgia, delirium tremens, and barbiturate addiction.

Works synergistically with hops.

Precautions: Scientific evidence is lacking for many of its claims, including its ability to reduce insomnia and anxiety. An overdose of the tincture can cause confusion, giddiness, stupor, twitching, and other neurological problems. There are a few recorded cases where high doses have caused liver damage.

SUMA

AKA: Para todo, *Pfaffia paniculata*.

Effects: Promotes energy and stamina. Has been used to treat exhaustion resulting from Epstein-Barr disease and chronic fatigue syndrome.

Dosage: Three to six capsules a day in three divided doses.

SWEET FLAG

AKA: *Acorus calamus*, calamus, flag root, grass myrtle, myrtle flag, rat root, sweet calomel, sweet cinnamon, sweet grass, sweet myrtle, sweet root, sweet rush, vacha.

Effects: Relieves anxiety. It can kill lice when applied directly to the affected parts, and it was used by Indians in the Northwest to increase endurance and stamina. It is said to stimulate the appetite, relieve various stomach problems, and be an aphrodisiac.

Precautions: When chewed, the dried root can cause nausea in smokers, a property which leads some to promote it as an aid for those wishing to quit. The species native to India, Europe, and North America may each have very different pharmacological properties.

Dosage: One teaspoon of rootstock in one-half cup of water, for up to one cup a day.

TARRAGON

AKA: *Artemisia dracunculus,* estragon.

Effects: When taken as a tea just before bedtime, it may help relieve insomnia. It may also prove useful in treating amenorrhea and high blood pressure, and herbalists have used it for treating digestive problems.

Precautions: Contains a weak carcinogen.

Dosage: One-half teaspoon of dried plant in one-half cup of water, for up to one cup a day.

TURMERIC

AKA: *Curcuma longa,* curcumin.

Effects: A strong anti-oxidant. It may be beneficial to those with atherosclerosis, cancer, gallbladder disease, indigestion, inflammation, liver disease, obesity, osteoarthritis, and rheumatoid arthritis.

Works synergistically with artichoke, dandelion root, licorice, and milk thistle.

Dosage: It could cause problems when used in large quantities.

VALERIAN

AKA: All-heal, Biral, Euvegal, moon root, Nutrasleep, phu, setwall, Undine's herb, Valdispert forte, *Valeriana officinalis,* Valmane.

The most widely-used sedative in Europe.

Effects: Reduces anxiety and insomnia to a moderate degree, possibly because of chemicals called valepotriates and an as yet poorly understood ability to interact with either of the neurotransmitters serotonin and GABA. It may be used as a treatment for headaches, high blood pressure, altitude sickness, convulsions, seizures, stomach cramps, irritable bowels, menstrual cramps, and tense muscles.

Works synergistically with other sedative herbs.

Precautions: Though it is said to be safe, it should not be used by those with impaired kidney or liver function or those with chronic insomnia; a few individuals may experience paradoxical reactions, finding that it makes them more alert. The plant has a strong unpleasant odor which some liken to smelly socks. Its daily use should be limited to a few weeks, and definitely no more than six months, as a tolerance toward the herb could develop, and long-term effects are not known. It should not be taken during the day, as it produces lethargy. Some of its components are very unstable, making accurate dosage difficult. Some studies indicate that valepotriates may cause cancer, but other studies do not bear this out. Claims by herbalists that it is good for chest congestion, digestive problems, menstrual pains, sores, wounds, epilepsy, convulsions, and the plague are unproven.

Rare side effects include restless legs during sleep and stomach upset. Overdose symptoms in susceptible individuals include tiredness the following day, restlessness, lethargy, mild confusion upon awakening, heart palpitations, and headaches. There is one case on record of an 18-year-old college student who took approximately 20 grams of powdered valerian root in capsule form and experienced fatigue, abdominal cramps, tightness of the chest, tremors in the hands and feet, and mild pupil dilation; her EKG, blood, and liver enzymes were all normal and, after treatment in a hospital, she fully recovered within 24 hours.

It should not be used with alcohol, some antihistamines, sedatives, muscle relaxants, psychotropic drugs, or narcotics, unless under the guidance of a physician.

Dosage: Two teaspoons of powdered root in one cup of hot water (the herb should not be put in boiling water, as that will destroy some of its beneficial oils).

Sheldon Saul Hendler, M.D., Ph.D., recommends no more than two cups of tea or two capsules of 500 mg each per day. Ray Sahelian, M.D., recommends 300 to 500 mg/day of concentrated root extract containing 0.5 to 1 percent of essential oils about one-half to two hours before sleep, and 100 mg/day to reduce anxiety. Valepotriates are very unstable, and their levels |in products may decline after a few months. With the dried root, the potency is directly related to the strength of its smell.

VANILLA

AKA: *Vanilla planifolia.*

Effects: An anti-oxidant. It has been traditionally used in Mexico for gastrointestinal disorders and as a mild brain stimulant.

WILLOW

AKA: *Salix alba* (salicin willow, white willow, withe, withy), *Salix caprea* (goat willow, sallow), *Salix nigra* (black willow, catkins willow, pussywillow), *Salix purpurea* (purple osier, purple willow).

Willow is the herbal origin of aspirin.

Effects: May aid in the prevention of Alzheimer's disease much in the same manner that anti-inflammatory drugs for arthritis seem to, as studies of those individuals taking the drugs seem to show a lower incidence of that disease. It may also be good for backache, headache, nerve pain, and toothache.

Precautions: It should not be taken by anyone allergic to aspirin.

It could interfere with the absorption of iron and other minerals. Taking it on a regular basis with large doses of vitamin C could cause it to build up to dangerous levels in the body.

WORMWOOD

AKA: Absinthe, *Artemisia absinthium.*

Effects: A mild sedative. Has been used by herbalists to treat fever, flatulence, heartburn, indigestion, lack of appetite, vascular disorders such as migraines, and intestinal parasites.

Precautions: May be habit-forming if used for a prolonged period of time or cause poisoning if taken in large quantities; the pure oil is a strong poison.

Dosage: Two teaspoons of leaves or tops in one cup of water for one-half cup a day to be taken in one teaspoonful doses.

YAUPON

AKA: Black drink plant, cassene, cassina, emetic holly, *Ilex vomitoria*, Indian black drink, Indian Black Tea, yaupon holly.

A rare North American shrub, it is related to yerbe mate and guayusa, and is the only plant native to the U.S. to contain caffeine.

Effects: A mild stimulant because of its caffeine content, which is rather small (0.1 percent). Indians have used it to induce ecstasy and visions.

Precautions: As its Latin name suggests, it can readily induce vomiting. The berries are slightly poisonous and can cause vomiting and diarrhea.

Dosage: The plant can be made into a tea by drying in the oven until black and then steeping in hot water.

YERBE MATE

AKA: Holly, *Ilex paraguariensis*, *Ilex paraguayensis*, mate, mate yerba, Morning Thunder (tea), Mucho Mate (tea), Paraguay tea, South American holly, yerba, yerba mate.

Effects: A caffeine-like stimulant reputed to relieve fatigue and insomnia, it may also cleanse the blood, control the appetite, benefit the nervous system, encourage the production of cortisone, and work synergistically with other healing herbs. Herbalists use Yerbe mate for allergies, coffee addiction, constipation, and inflammatory bowel disorders.

Precautions: Excessive consumption can lead to a feeling of exhaustion, overstimulation, insomnia, and dehydration. An overdose may cause nausea. Researchers have noted a correlation between mate drinkers and cancer of the esophagus, though other factors such as

the steaming hot temperature at which the tea is sometimes consumed, tobacco consumption, and alcohol consumption may also play a role. James A. Duke, Ph.D., does not recommend it for treating chronic fatigue syndrome.

Dosage: One cup of tea or one dropperful of extract.

YOHIMBE AND YOHIMBINE

AKA: Actibine, Aphrodyne, Baron-X, *Corynanthe yohimbe*, Dayto Himbin, lizard tail, *Pausinystalia yohimbe*, Prohim, Thybine, yerba del pasmo, yerba mansa, Yocon, Yohimar, yohimbine hydrochloride, Yohimex, Yoman, Yovital.

Effects: Yohimbe is said to produce a tingling feeling along the spine, followed by a mild, pleasant, and euphoric high lasting four to six hours. In high enough doses, it can produce mild hallucinogenic-like effects. It contains a number of psychoactive alkaloids, including yohimbine, and has shown positive results in treating both psychological and physiological impotence; it even increases the sex drive of men with normal libido. It may have the same effects on women, with the added benefit of helping them lose weight. According to Ward Dean, M.D., it "is the only substance with a specific FDA-approved indication as an aphrodisiac." The active compound, called yohimbine or yohimbine hydrochloride, is isolated and sold as a prescription medication, and is much safer.

Works synergistically with 500 to 1000 mg of vitamin C, which quickens its effects and reduces the nausea.

Precautions: It should not be used by those with an allergy to yohimbine or any of the Rauwolfia alkaloids, angina pectoris, hepatitis, hypoglycemia, blood pressure disorders, ulcers, diabetes, kidney disease, liver disease, heart disease, panic attacks, bipolar disorder, or schizophrenia. Those suffering from or being treated for depression, any psychiatric disorder, any other allergy, or those taking any drugs that interfere with norepinephrine's neuronal uptake or metabolism (including Selegiline) should use yohimbe only under a physician's guidance; in fact, many herbalists caution that the potent herb should never be used without the advice of a physician or herbalist.

According to James A. Duke, Ph.D., using the herb in its natural form (dried bark) is dangerous. The amount of yohimbine in herbal products can vary considerably.

There are no known life-threatening or common side effects. Less common side effects include anxiety, rapid heart rate, lack of coordination, overstimulation, increased blood pressure, dizziness, salivation, hallucinations, panic attacks, and headache. Rare side effects include nausea, vomiting, flushed skin, sweating, and tremors. There are no known overdose symptoms; an overdose is not generally considered life-threatening, though a trip to the hospital or doctor is recommended in such cases. The doses needed to produce the hallucinogen-like effects are very high and potentially toxic. It is not physically addictive, but can create a psychological dependence. The whole herb is a complex combination of adrenergics, cholin-

ergics, yohimbine alkaloids, and reserpine alkaloids, substances which act counter to each other and which could cause serious health risks.

While yohimbine is not an MAO inhibitor, yohimbe is, and so should not be combined with tyramine-rich foods or MAO inhibitors. The effects of yohimbe can be decreased by alcohol. Yohimbe can decrease the effects of antidepressant and antihypertensive drugs. It should also not be combined with antihistamines, tranquilizers, diet pills, narcotics, amphetamines, cocaine, marijuana, or any mood-altering drug. W. Nathaniel Phillips does not recommend taking it with meals.

Some supplements may contain little or no active yohimbine.

Dosage: Six to ten teaspoons of shaved bark boiled in a pint of water for five minutes. Mark Mayell recommends 15 to 20 drops of tincture, 250 to 500 mg of the dried herb in capsules, or one cup of tea a day. Sheldon Saul Hendler, M.D., Ph.D. recommends one 5.4 mg tablet three times a day for up to ten weeks, with the dosage cut in half and gradually built up to a full dose if side effects occur. It may take two to three weeks for any effects to occur.

ZIZYPHUS

Effects: Induces relaxation and sleep. In traditional Chinese medicine, it is often combined with other herbs for a sedative effect, which could be useful in cases of insomnia.

Chapter 3

Vitamins, Minerals, and Related Nutrients

VITAMIN A, BETA-CAROTENE, CAROTENOIDS

AKA: Acon, Afaxin, Alphalin, Aquasol A, carotene, Dispatabs, pro-vitamin A, retinol, retin A, Sust-A, vitamin A acetate, vitamin A acid, vitamin A palmitate.

Beta carotene (sometimes called carotene or pro-vitamin A) is found almost exclusively in plant foods and is a precursor to vitamin A, which, after it is converted by the body, works as an anti-oxidant (prevents vitamin C from oxidizing). Carotenoids, of which there are over 600, are also found in plant foods, but are not as plentiful or important. Retinol is the form of vitamin A found in animal foods. Vitamin A acetate and vitamin A palmitate are synthetic forms found in fortified foods.

Food Sources (vitamin A): Beef, butter, chicken, egg yolk, fish, fish liver, fish liver oils, heart, kidney, liver, milk, sea food.

Food Sources (Beta-carotene): Some fruits, dark-green and orange vegetables, tomatoes.

Food Sources (carotenoids): egg yolks, pink grapefruit, oranges, parsley, red palm oil, shellfish, spinach, tomatoes.

Effects: Vitamin A is essential for the skin, hair, nails, and vision; helps the immune system work better; helps fight infections and speeds up healing; shields the skin from the harmful effects of the sun's UV rays; and protects the membranes of brain cells, which have lots of fat and thus are readily damaged by free radicals. Both beta-carotene and vitamin A each have their own specific anti-oxidant properties. A recent study by the Salk Institute for Biological Studies indicates vitamin A may be an important factor in memory and learning.

Beta-carotene appears to prevent lung cancer and tumors of the mouth and throat, and recent research has shown that it may protect against memory loss and other forms of cognitive impairment.

The carotenoids lutein and zeaxanthin, found in spinach and collard greens, may help prevent macular degeneration, one of the main causes of blindness in old people. Other carotenoids could lower the chance of heart attack in men with high blood pressure by 60 to 70 percent. Astaxanthin, which exists in some plants, yeasts, and marine animals, has 5 to 20 times the antioxidant activity of beta-carotene.

Deficiency is rare, as the liver can store enough for months or even years before it is depleted, even if none is consumed in the diet. A deficiency can result in dry skin, eyes, and mucous membranes; loss of vitamin C; impaired night vision; degeneration of tooth enamel and gums; problems with bone growth; sinus trouble; loss of smell; and increased susceptibility to infections.

Precautions: Daily doses of vitamin A higher than 25,000 IU taken over an extended period of time can result in abdominal pain, loss of appetite, blurred vision, bone pain, confusion, diarrhea, dizziness, drowsiness, fatigue, hair loss, headaches, irritabilty, joint swelling, dry cracked lips, sensitivity to light, liver enlargement, irregular menses, muscle pains, nausea, rashes, restlessness, dry rough or scaly skin, swelling over the long bones, vomiting, weight loss, and liver and eye damage (the main storage

sites in the body for vitamin A). These disappear when the dosage is reduced. There are some reports that large doses of vitamin C can prevent these problems. Those with kidney disorders should consult a physician before increasing intake of vitamin C.

Individual needs vary widely, and what might be a low dose for one person could be toxic to another. Beta-carotene, on the other hand, is non-toxic, as the body only converts it into vitamin A when it is needed; excessive amounts may cause a yellowing of the skin (carotenosis), which is harmless and disappears when the dosage is reduced.

There are other common precautions that should be kept in mind: polyunsaturated fatty acids with carotene can work against vitamin A if antioxidants are not present; women on oral contraceptives have a decreased need for vitamin A; at least 10,000 international units (IU) of A are needed if more than 400 IU/day of vitamin E are taken; and vitamin A can interfere with the effectiveness of phenytoin. If more than 10,000 IU/day are taken, it will increase the effect of anticoagulants.

Antacids, aspirin, barbituates, pollution, stress, and various prescription drugs can all take their toll on the body's supply of vitamin A. The absorption of vitamin A can be inhibited by alcohol, coffee, mineral oil, an excess of iron, a deficiency of vitamin D, calcium supplements, and the drugs cholestyramine, colestipol, and neomycin. The cholesterol-reducing drug Questran (cholestyramine) may interfere with the absorption of vitamin A to such an extent that supplementation may be needed. If taking a broad-spectrum antibiotic, do not take high doses of vitamin A. And vitamin A should not be taken with the acne drug Accutane (isotretinoin). The fat substitute Olestra can interfere with the absorption of carotenoids, a situation which alarms some because the average American diet is already deficient in this important class of nutrients.

Paradoxically, beta-carotene has been found to increase the death rate of smokers due to lung cancer if their levels of vitamin C are low, resulting in an increase of free radicals rather than a reduction.

Dosage: The RDA for vitamin A is 5000 IU/day; the majority of health professionals recommend 10,000 to 35,000 IU daily for maximum health. Nutritionists recommend taking more beta-carotene than vitamin A, though Dr. Stuart Berger recommends a maximum daily dosage of 17,500 IU/day. About 20 to 25 mg of zinc may be needed to help utilize vitamin A that is stored in the liver, along with adequate supplies of the B vitamins, vitamin C, vitamin D, vitamin E, calcium, choline, and phosphorus. Both vitamin A and beta-carotene are absorbed more readily if consumed with foods containing fat and any hard physical activity is avoided for four hours afterwards. Carotenoids are more effective if taken in combination — for instance, alpha and beta carotenes from carrots, spirulina (an algae), dimallela salina (a marine plant), lycopene from tomatoes, and lutein from spinach.

Those with poor health habits — such as smokers — and those with specific problems that inhibit absorption of vitamin A and beta-carotene — such as those with gastrointestinal or liver diseases, gall bladder problems, or diabetes — may require a higher dosage; in the latter case, higher dosages should only be taken under the careful eye of a qualified professional.

Mycelized vitamin A can be at least five times as powerful as oil-based supplements, due to its higher degree of absorption. Retin A, or vitamin A acid, is commonly used in prescription doses of 10,000 to 25,000 IU/day.

VITAMIN B-1

AKA: Betalin S, Betaxin, Bewon, Biamine, Thiamine.

Food Sources: Asparagus, beans, bran, broccoli, brown rice, fish, kelp, lima beans, liver, lean pork, milk, nuts, oatmeal, split peas, poultry, soybeans, sunflower seeds, fresh green vegetables, wheat germ, whole-grain cereals, yeast.

Effects: A strong anti-oxidant, vitamin B-1 also helps in stabilizes the brain and nervous system's energy production from glucose, stabilizing the appetite, aids in the functioning of the nervous system, helps repair cell damage, helps relieve air- and seasickness, and is used in the treatment of herpes zoster (shingles), alcoholism, cirrhosis, overactive thyroid, infection, absorption diseases, prolonged diarrhea, and burns.

A deficiency (dosages below the minimum daily requirement of 1 mg/day) known as beriberi often results in physical and mental deterioration, manifesting itself in anxiety, neurosis, depression, loss of manual dexterity, shortness of breath, numbness in hands and feet, weakness, fatigue, sensitivity to noise, loss of appetite, vision problems, irritability, confusion, poor memory, sleep disturbances, and gastrointestinal disturbances.

Precautions: There is a wide variation in the amount individuals need; some people seem to be able to manufacture it from their intestinal bacteria, though antibiotics may disturb the natural balance of these bacteria. High doses can result in deficiencies of other B vitamins, which can be prevented by increasing the intake of other B vitamins accordingly, such as with a B-complex supplement. Overdosages can also affect thyroid and insulin production, and symptoms — though rare, and usually resulting from injections of B-1 — include allergic reactions, edema, faintness, headache, herpes, hives, insomnia, irritability, severe itching, muscle tremors, nervousness, rapid pulse and heartbeat, rash, weakness, and wheezing.

Antibiotics, oral contraceptives, chronic heavy drinking, antacids, barbituates, caffeine, carbonated citrates in food and drinks, estrogen, fever, stress, sulfa drugs, tobacco, and eating fish, clams, eggs, brussel sprouts, and red cabbage in their raw state can destroy or inhibit the absorption of B-1. Cooking, food processing, and marinating meat in soy sauce, vinegar, or wine can also contribute to the destruction of this vitamin in foods. Vitamin B-1 should be taken with carbohydrates, as it helps metabolize them, though a diet too high in carbohydrates may increase the need for B-1. Its benefits are enhanced when taken with adequate amounts of other B vitamins, vitamins C and E, manganese, and sulphur.

It may enhance the effects of neuromuscular blocking agents, a class of drugs used with anesthesia to relax the muscles during surgery. It should not be taken in high doses in combination with vitamin C and the amino acid L-cysteine except under the supervision of a doctor, as these can render insulin inactive. High doses can produce false positive results in tests for uric acid and urobilinogen; it can also produce a false reading in a test for the level of theophylline (a drug used for the treatment of bronchial asthma) in the blood.

Dosage: The RDA is 1.4 mg/day for men, 1 mg/day for women. Recommended dosage is 50 to 1000 mg/day, though 100 to 300 mg/day is probably the optimal range. It is best taken with the other B vitamins, including pantothenic acid, folic acid, B-12, and the equivalent amounts of B-2 and B-6. Should be taken in 3 or 4 divided doses with meals.

VITAMIN B-3

AKA: Niacin, niacinamide, nicotinic acid, nicotinamide.

L-tryptophan can be converted by the body into B-3, though it takes 60 parts tryptophan to make one part niacin, and a person who is deficient in B-1, B-2, and B-6 may not be able to produce niacin in this manner.

Food Sources: Avocados, brewer's yeast, dates, eggs, figs, fish, lima beans, liver, lean meat, milk, roasted peanuts, poultry (white meat), prunes, wheat germ, whole wheat products.

Effects: Improves memory and other mental functions, protects against stress, reduces blood clotting, and improves the oxygen-carrying ability of red blood cells. Drs. Humphry Osmond and Abram Hoffer contend that B-3 is an effective treatment for schizophrenia, though other researchers have not been able to duplicate their success. Vitamin B-3 is a histamine releaser, which can cause a flushing, tingling, and redness of the skin in some people, effects which can heighten sexual pleasure. It is also necessary for the synthesis of cortisone, throxine, and insulin, as well as the sex hormones estrogen, progesterone, and testosterone. The vitamin can relieve gastrointestinal problems, maintain the health of the skin, ease the severity of (or even prevent) migraines, fight canker sores and bad breath, and lower cholesterol and triglyceride levels. It is used to treat vertigo, ringing in the ears, premenstrual headaches, reduced levels of cholesterol and triglycerides in the blood, and pellegra.

The active co-enzymatic form, and a natural metabolite, of B-3, called variously niacinamide adenine dinucleotide, nicotinamide adenine dinucleotide, NAD, or NADH (the reduced form), has shown promise in mental enhancement, though only recently has a process been developed that can stabilize this nutrient so that it can be taken orally, and one admittedly flawed study using 17 subjects suggests that 5 mg twice daily can improve the symptoms of Alzheimer's. Much more research is needed.

A deficiency is known as pellegra, and is characterized by gastrointestinal disturbances leading to a redness of the skin and inflammation, inability to recall recent events, apprehension, depression, emotional instability, and hyperirritability. An unusual sensitivity of the skin to sunlight may be an early warning sign. The victims of pellegra suffer from dermatitis, diarrhea, dementia, and some cases lead even to death.

Precautions: It should not be taken by those sensitive to niacin or who have liver disease, stomach ulcers, very low blood pressure, gout, or hemorrhaging. It should be taken only under the guidance of a physician if any of the following conditions are present: diabetes, gall bladder or liver disease, glaucoma, gout, high blood pressure, impaired liver function, porphyria, sensitivity to tartrazine dye, or ulcers. Those with ulcers may have to take an antacid to prevent aggravating their condition, and those with gout may find their symptoms increasing because of increased uric acid levels in the blood. Individuals with allergies may have problems, as nicotinic acid reportedly raises the histamine level in the body. Some may also find that they have an abnormal glucose tolerance such as found in diabetics.

In some cases, extremely high doses — over 750 mg/day — can cause abdominal cramps, diarrhea, fainting, body flush, jaundice, lightheadedness, liver damage, nausea, sweating, vomiting, weakness, and "niacin hepatitis," though the latter is not life-threatening. In doses larger than 50 mg (the RDA is 18 mg/day for men, 13 mg/day for women), it may cause dry skin, a flushing or redness of the skin accompanied by a tingling, dizziness, itching, or headaches for about 10 to 20 minutes when first starting supplementation; the flushing usually occurs on an empty stomach, is reportedly harmless, and should go away within two months. Some say this only occurs with pure niacin, and that taking aspirin an hour before taking B-3 or drinking a glass of water with the vitamin can prevent these symptoms, while others say that this only occurs with nicotinic acid. It should be noted that there is good evidence that toxicity can result from long-term intake of as low as two and one-half times the RDA. There are time-release niacin tablets that avoid the flush, but some evidence indicates that the continuous release of niacin may be detrimental to the liver. Other uncommon side effects may include abdominal pain, bloating, low blood pressure, diarrhea, fainting, gas, rapid or irregular heartbeat, heartburn, and hunger pains. Even rarer are incidents of nervousness and panic caused by high doses of nicotinic acid, blurred vision and related eye problems, and apparently one case of hypothyroidism. "Nicotinic analogues" or "niacin analogues" are drugs used to treat specific conditions, and have no value as vitamin supplements. Similarly, niacinimide, which avoids the niacin flush, lacks many of the beneficial effects of niacin, and can also cause liver damage and, in some people, depression.

Nicotinic acid can also interact with ganglionic blocking drugs, enhancing their blood pressure–lowering effect. Isoniazid, used to treat tuberculosis, can increase the need for niacin. Nicotinic acid can also interfere with the Benedict's reagent test for sugar in the urine, the measurement of catecholamines in the blood or urine, and — in one case — it has decreased the liver's uptake of the chemical used to make that organ visible for a liver scan. Niacin can reduce the effectiveness of antidiabetic drugs, probenecid, and sulfinpyrazone. Combining with beta-andrenergic blocking agents, mecamylamine, methyldopa, or alcohol could result in excessively low blood pressure. Combining with HMG-CoA reductase inhibitors could increase the risk of heart or kidney problems. With cocaine, it could cause an increased flushing of the skin.

Niacin can be destroyed by alcohol, antacids, aspirin, estrogen, food processing, sleeping pills, sulfa drugs, and water. Its effectiveness can be reduced by tobacco and obesity.

Dosage: Start at low doses and gradually increase to 100 to 200 mg/day. It should be taken in 3 to 4 divided doses, preferably with meals. A high-protein diet with meat, eggs, enriched cereals, and other foods high in B-3 can provide adequate amounts.

VITAMIN B-5

AKA: Calcium pantothenate, Dexol T.D., pantothenic acid, panthenol.

Food Sources: Avocados, broccoli, chicken, egg yolks, lentils, liver and other organ meats, nuts, oats, fresh vegetables, and yeast are the best sources. Vitamin B-5 occurs in such a wide variety of foods that a deficiency is rare and, if it does occur, indicates a diet so poor that deficiency symptoms of other vitamins are also likely to be present.

Effects: A strong anti-oxidant, stamina enhancer, and protector against stress. It helps in the synthesis of acetylcholine, is essential for the synthesis of antibodies, and is needed for the utilization of PABA and choline. Among the other benefits are the healing of wounds and minimizing the side effects of many antibiotics. According to Earl Mindell, 1000 mg twice a day with meals helps relieve the suffering from allergies. It may help promote sleep when combined with inositol.

A naturally occurring deficiency is probably extremely rare, and is characterized by blood and skin disorders, duodenal ulcers, and hypoglycemia.

Precautions: It can cause heartburn or, less frequently, cramps. Rare symptoms include hives, rash, and difficult breathing. There are no known overdose symptoms, though initial large doses can cause temporary diarrhea. Taken by itself over an extended period of time may increase the need for B-1, leading to neuritis. There is no known toxicity. It should not be taken by those who are allergic to pantothenic acid, and those with hemophilia should consult a physician first.

Vitamin B-5 can be destroyed by alcohol, caffeine, canning, cooking, estrogen, food processing, heat, sleeping pills, sulfa drugs, and tobacco. It can reduce the effectiveness of levodopa (but not carbidopa-levodopa). Chloramphenicol, cycloserine, ethionamide, hydralazine, immunosuppressants, isoniazid, and penicillamine can all reduce the absorption of B-5 and cause anemia and tingling or numbness in the hands and feet.

Dosage: It is generally recommended that initial doses should be 100 mg/day, gradually increasing to 250 to 1000 mg/day in 3 to 4 divided doses.

VITAMIN B-6

AKA: Beesix, Hexa-Betalin, Pyridoxine, Pyroxine, Rodex, Vitabec 6.

Vitamin B-6 is actually a trio of very similar substances — pyridoxine, pyridoxinal, and pyridoxamine — working together. Though it is a water-soluble vitamin that needs to be supplied every day, there is some evidence that it can be manufactured by intestinal bacteria, possibly by the cellulose in a largely vegetarian diet.

Food Sources: Bananas, beef, blackstrap molasses, bran, brewer's yeast, brown rice, cabbage, cantaloupe, carrots, diary products, eggs, fish, grapes, kidney, lamb, liver, meat, milk, nuts, peas, pork, potatoes, poultry, prunes, wheat bran, wheat germ, whole grains.

Effects: Vitamin B-6 protects against stress and is needed by the brain for transporting and metabolizing amino acids to develop various neurotransmitters (such as norepinephrine,

serotonin, and dopamine) needed for mental energy and memory. The vitamin also helps the immune system by producing antibodies and red blood cells. Necessary for the proper functioning of the thymus, spleen, and sexual organs. Those on a high-protein diet will need more B-6. It may play a key role in fat metabolism, so a diet rich in animal fats may be more likely to result in cholesterol plaques if there is insufficient B-6. Diabetics may find that B-6 can be used to decrease their need for insulin, though experimenting with supplements could be risky. It may also help in relieving the symptoms of depression and sickle-cell anemia. Research has shown that women can cut their risk of heart disease in half by consuming at least 400 mcg/day of folic acid and 3 mg/day of B-6; it is believed men can enjoy similar benefits from such an increase.

A deficiency can be similar to thiamin and niacin deficiencies, resulting in acne, anemia, arthritis, brain-wave abnormalities, convulsions, depression, glossitis, hair loss, headaches, inflammation of the mouth and tongue, irritability, learning disabilities, mental confusion, nausea, malfunctioning of the nervous system, nervousness, seborrheic dermatitis, and possible cardiovascular disease. A deficiency of both B-6 and folic acid is correlated with a high level of the amino acid homocysteine, which plays a role in heart disease.

Precautions: Too much B-6 in the body can result in night restlessness and very vivid dream recall. Taking more than 200 mg/day can cause peripheral neuropathy and such high dosages should be administered only under the guidance of a physician. Doses higher than 500 mg/day may be toxic, leading to serious central nervous system problems, with such symptoms as pain in the arms and legs, a numbness or tingling in the hands and feet, clumsiness, loss of balance, and difficulty in walking. Chronic megadoses of 2 to 6 grams/day used to treat carpal tunnel syndrome have led to vitamin toxicity and sensory neuropathy, which go away once the dosage is reduced, though some permanent nerve damage (such as loss of sense of touch) may remain. High doses of B-6 can lead to increased susceptibility to cadmium toxicity. High protein diets increase the need for B-6.

Vitamin B-6 can be destroyed by alcohol, birth control pills, canning, estrogen, food processing (up to half the B-6 in flour may be lost in the refining process), roasting or stewing of meat, radiation, and tobacco.

The following drugs may increase the need for B-6: birth control pills, chloramphenicol, cycloserine (Seromycin), estrogens, ethionamide, the ingredient Hydralazine (contained in such blood pressure medications as Apresazide, Apresoline, Rezide, Ser-Ap-Es, Serpasil-Apresoline, and Unipres), Isoniazid, and Penicillamine (a drug unrelated to penicillin which is used to treat rheumatoid arthritis and rare genetic diseases), and immuno-suppressants. The vitamin can interfere with the effects of hypnotic barbiturates, L-dopa (though the drug Sinemet may be able to bypass this interaction, and a carbidopa-levodopa combination does not have this problem), phenobarbital, and phenytoin.

Dosage: Some suggest 10 to 75 mg/day; others, 50 to 200 mg/day in 3 to 4 divided doses. Do not exceed 500 mg/day. Best taken with vitamins B-1, B-2, pantothenic acid, C, and magnesium.

VITAMIN B-12

AKA: Acti-B-12, Alphamin, Alpha Redisol, Anocobin, Bedoc, Berubigen, Betalin 12, Cobalamin, Codroxomin, Cyanabin, cyanocobalamin, Droxomin, hydroxocobalamin, Kaybovite, Kaybovite-1000, Redisol, Rubion, Rubramin, Rubramin-PC.

The only B vitamin that can be stored by the body (the liver can store three to five years worth).

Food Sources: Beef, brewer's yeast, cheese, dairy products, egg yolk, fish, kidney, liver, milk, pork, seaweed, soybeans and soy products, yeast, yogurt.

Effects: Encourages RNA and DNA synthesis in nerve cells, is needed for the transportation and storage of folic acid, helps stabilize the brain's metabolism of carbohydrates and proteins and its synthesis of myelin in the nerves, plays an indirect role in making choline available for the synthesis of neurotransmitters, protects against stress and fatigue (promotes the release of energy in foods), and is an essential growth factor needed for healthy brain and nerve function. Lab rats experience an increase in their rate of learning, and it has been used to treat depression, insomnia, and memory loss. Preliminary studies have shown that supplementation of B-12 and folic acid may prevent or delay the onset of Alzheimer's. According to Pearson and Shaw, a dose of approximately 1000 micrograms taken immediately before sleep has about a 50% chance of creating dreams in color. Combined with folic acid and methionine, it can help manufacture choline in the body.

Because the body can recycle the vitamin, deficiency is rare, and years of chronic inadequate intake may precede the onset of symptoms. Those at risk include smokers, heavy drinkers, pregnant women, vegans, those who do not produce enough intrinsic factor in the stomach to help utilize it, those with chronic malabsorption problems, those who have undergone stomach surgery, and those taking estrogen, potassium supplements, sleeping pills, and anticoagulant drugs. A deficiency is known as pernicious anemia, and symptoms include poor appetite, a tingling in the hands and feet, depression, nervousness, nerve disorders, fatigue, weakness, digestive disorders, memory loss, moodiness, difficulty walking and maintaining balance. The effects of pernicious anemia may include nerve transmission problems, severe psychosis, brain damage, and death. Deficiency symptoms of B-12 can be masked by taking more than 1000 mcg/day of folic acid.

Precautions: It should not be taken by those with Leber's disease (optic nerve atrophy). Those with gout should consult a physician before taking supplements. The RDA for adults is 3 micrograms, yet no toxicity was observed in tests where individuals took 500 to 1000 micrograms (0.5 to 1 mg) for up to five years, or took 100,000 micrograms in a single dose. Allergies to this vitamin are rare, and reactions (the symptoms for which include acne, eczema, and a swelling or crusting of skin around the lips) usually occur with injections, rather than tablets. Rare side effects consist of itchy skin, wheezing, and diarrhea. Life-threatening symptoms, usually resulting from overdose, consist of faintness (from anaphylaxis), hives, itching, and rash.

Dilantin can deplete the body's stores of B-12, and an underactive thyroid gland can interfere with the absorption of this vitamin. It can also be destroyed or have absorption interfered with by acids and alkalies, alcohol, anticonvulsants, chloramphenicol, cholestyramine, cimetidine, coffee, colchicine, estrogen, famotidine, laxatives, neomycin, nizatidine, oral contraceptives, potassium (extended-release forms), ranitidine, sleeping pills, stomach medications (such as Prevacid, Prilosec, Pepcid, Tagamet, and Zantac), sunlight, tobacco, vitamin C (if taken within two hours of each other), and water. As it is only found in meat and dairy products, strict vegetarians may not get enough, though lack of deficiency in non-meat eaters leads some to speculate that some vegetables may contain bacteria that produce B-12. The vitamin needs to be taken with calcium to be properly absorbed and utilized by the body.

Dosage: 3 mcg/day. It is absorbed best when taken with meals that contain calcium. It is recommended that those age 51 and over take 4 mcg/day; however, recent evidence suggests that some older people who have less stomach acid and more digestive bacteria may need to take as much as 25 mcg/day. Some tablets sold contain the B-12 intrinsic factor, a mucoprotein secreted in the stomach which aids in the absorption of this vitamin, overcoming deficiency. Vitamin B-12 injections are generally regarded as worthless.

VITAMIN B-15 AND DIMETHYLGLYCINE

AKA: Calcium pangamate and pangamic acid.

Effects: Prevents oxygen deprivation in the body's tissues, while reducing oxidation within cells. The active ingredient is dimethylglycine (DMG), a metabolic brain enhancer said to detoxify the body, lower cholesterol, and protect the liver. Its advocates contend that DMG increases energy, endurance, and strength (mainly by reducing the lactic acid in the muscles), improves the immune system (mainly be creating phosphocreatine, which also helps the muscles contract), and maximizes blood transport from the blood to the heart and brain.

Precautions: Though it is non-toxic, sale of B-15 is illegal. It is not a vitamin, as there is no evidence that the body has a need for it. None of the benefits claimed for it or DMG have any basis in fact. In fact, there is evidence that DMG and another component, diisopropylamine-dichloracetate (DIPA-DCA), are potential carcinogens.

Dosage: Approximately 150 to 250 mg/day, according to John Mann. Sheldon Saul Hendler, M.D., Ph.D., does not recommend supplementation under any circumstances.

BORON

Food sources: Most fruits and vegetables, particularly dried fruits.

Effects: Boron helps keep the brain alert and able to perform simple functions. It also helps keep the bones strong and metabolizes calcium, magnesium, and phosphorus.

Deficiency is rare.

Precautions: While there appear to be no adverse effects with doses as high as 6 mg/day, dosage should not exceed 10 mg/day.

Dosage: There is no RDA. The recommended dose is 3 mg/day. It is best if taken with a multi-vitamin which includes calcium, magnesium, manganese, and riboflavin.

VITAMIN C AND BIOFLAVONOIDS

AKA (Vitamin C): Ascorbic acid, Ascorbicap, ascorbyl palmitate, calcium ascorbate, Cecon, Cemill, Cenolate, Cetane, Cevalin, Cevi-Bid, Ce-Vi-Sol, Cevita, cevitamin acid, C-Span, Ester C, Flavorcee, magnesium ascorbate, Redoxon, sodium ascorbate, Sunkist.

AKA (Bioflavonoids): Flavonoids, vitamin P.

Man is the only animal that cannot synthesize vitamin C in the body (apes and guinea pigs have a similar problem in that their bodies cannot synthesize it fast enough), though some research indicates that human placentas and nursing mothers may have this ability.

There are two new forms of vitamin C. One, Ester C, has a higher level of bioavailability — patients given this form of the vitamin only need 20 to 30 percent of the usual dose of vitamin C, as it enters the body tissues faster and remains there longer than regular vitamin C. The other, ascorbyl palmitate, is a fat-soluble form (vitamin C is basically water-soluble): it remains in the fat tissues until used by the body and is not wasted through excretion. The dosage is about 250 mg/day.

Bioflavonoids, which include rutin and hesperidin, are part of the C complex of vitamins, and work synergistically with C. They give plants their color, and researchers have identified over 500 of them.

Food Sources: Bean sprouts, berries, cauliflower, citrus fruits, liver, potatoes, sweet potatoes, tomatoes, green leafy vegetables.

Effects: Works as an anti-oxidant (unlike anti-oxidants vitamin E, beta-carotene, and CoEnzyme Q10, which reduce oxidation damage, vitamin C works pre-emptively, intercepting the oxidants that initiate the free-radical cycle) is needed for the manufacture of neurotransmitters and cell structures, helps preserve the elasticity of the skin and capillaries, protects the lungs by preventing oxygen from converting into peroxides, boosts the immune system, helps wounds heal faster, helps the intestine absorb iron, lowers blood cholesterol, protects the body against the effects of pollutants (particularly the metals lead, mercury, and aluminum) and chemical toxins (such as formaldehyde, organic solvents, and pesticides), protects against bacteria and viruses, protects against heart and blood diseases, protects against heart attacks, reduces anxiety, and aids in restful sleep. Additionally, vitamin C, a natural antihistamine, increases alertness and mental functioning, may help safeguard against and reduce the symptoms of colds and flu, helps build collagen (the connective tissue in the body), and diminishes the duration and severity of herpes blister outbreaks. It also helps regenerate vitamin E after the latter has done its own job of eliminating free radicals. With vitamin E, it can counteract the effects of a fatty meal, especially damage done to blood vessels from high cholesterol. According to some studies, students with high vitamin C levels did better on IQ tests than those with lower levels.

A deficiency is known as scurvy which, though rare, may be the end result of long-term deprivation of vitamin C. Symptoms include bleeding gums, hemorrhaging, loose teeth, emotional disturbances, and poor healing of wounds. Some contend that the U.S. RDA of 60 mg/day prevents these obvious symptoms, but does not prevent the occurrence of subclinical deficiency, a slight deficiency which may have no readily identifiable symptoms and which may lead to health problems years down the line. The only deficiency symptom of bioflavonoids that has been identified is bleeding gums.

Precautions: Supplements should not be taken by those with increased iron absorption (caused by such conditions as hemochromatosis), diabetes, folic acid deficiency (from such conditions as alcoholism), serious kidney disease or kidney failure, leukemia, polycythemia (an increase in the blood's total cell mass), thalassemia (hereditary anemia), thrombosis, or an allergy to vitamin C. It can also cause problems in people with sickle cell anemia, G-6PD deficiency, kidney stones, or gout. Some brands contain tartrazine dye, and should be avoided by those who are allergic.

With too high a dose, diarrhea, dizziness, gastritis, gas, headaches, lightheadedness, nausea, and vomiting can occur, though these may be just temporary. Rare symptoms include abdominal pain and anemia. Lowering the dosage or using a buffered form (such as sodium ascorbate, calcium ascorbate, and Ester C) can stop these symptoms. In fact, the first sign of diarrhea (called the "bowel tolerance") is a sign that the body's optimal dosage of vitamin C has been surpassed.

Daily dosages above 500 mg/day may deplete the level of copper in the blood of males, leading to anemia; whether this also occurs in females is unknown. Vitamin C may also deplete the sulfur reserves in the body, placing vegetarians at risk, as this mineral is mainly found in eggs. Women taking 2000 mg or more a day may experience fertility problems; individuals taking 2000 mg or more a day may lower the resistance of their white blood cells to fight one common form of bacteria, and may need to take a folic acid supplement, as such a high dose of C will deplete this B vitamin. Those taking 3000 mg or more a day may experience reduced levels of the amino acid cysteine in the blood (though this condition is not serious) and lowered resistance to high altitude conditions. Dosages above 4000 mg/day can increase kidney stone formation in those already susceptible (though magnesium supplements may prevent this problem). Deficiency symptoms related to scurvy that accompany a sudden withdrawal of high dosages are rare.

Vitamin C should not be taken in large doses in conjunction with vitamins B-1 and the amino acid L-cysteine, as they can render insulin ineffective. In doses above 200 mg/day, vitamin C by itself may reduce the effectiveness of warfarin and other oral anti-coagulants, dicoumarol, amphetamines, anticholinergics, mexiletine, quinidine, tranquilizers such as phenotiazine, and a class of drugs called tricyclic antidepressants, including Amitriptyline (also known as Elavil, Endep, Etrafron, Limbitrol, Triavil), Amoxapine (also known as Asendin), Desipramine (also known as Norpramin, Pertofrane), Doxepin (also known as Adapin, Sinequan), Imipramine (also known as Tofranil), Nortriptyline (also known as Aventyl, Pamelor), Protriptyline (also known as Vivactil), Trimipramine (also known as Surmontil). It can also slow down the metabolizing of aspirin by the body, which can lead to a toxic buildup after several doses. Vitamin C can increase the effect of barbiturates, increase the iron absorp-

tion from iron supplements, increase the side effects from estrogens (if vitamin C taken is more than 1 g/day), and lead to salicylate toxicity if such supplements are taken.

Drugs whose long-term use may increase the need for vitamin C include barbiturates, birth control pills, cellulose sodium phosphate, cortisones, levodopa, phenacetin, salicylates, sulfonamides, and tetracycline. More than eight aspirin a day for more than a week can cause the body to excrete more vitamin C; even a few can cause the body to excrete it at up to three times the normal rate.

Vitamin C can give false readings for the following blood and urine lab tests: blood bilirubin, blood glucose, creatinine, LDH, occult blood test for colon cancer, SGOT, uric acid, and urinary glucose.

Chewable vitamin C can lead to severe dental erosion. Extra care should be taken when using the powdered form, mixing it fresh each time, as C will readily oxidise to the toxic form dehydroascorbate. Those who experience stomach problems or heartburn from taking ascorbic acid may eliminate these problems by taking calcium ascorbate, magnesium ascorbate, or sodium ascorbate. Contrary to earlier beliefs, large doses of C does not destroy B-12 (if taken more than two hours apart) or contribute to the formation of kidney stones in those not already susceptible.

Alcohol, antibiotics, aspirin, baking soda, cooking, copper pots, cortisone, heat, high fever, light, oxygen, smoking (each cigarette can destroy 25 to 100 mg), stress, vitamin A deficiency, and water can all contribute to the loss or reduced effectiveness of this vitamin. Vegetables should be washed, but not soaked, to prevent vitamin loss, and fruits and vegetables should be cut with a sharp knife immediately before consumption, as bruising with a dull knife and letting cut food stand can destroy vitamin C. Fresh fruits and vegetables should be eaten within a few days, and frozen vegetables should not be thawed before cooking. There should be at least a three-hour span between taking vitamin C and taking ginseng, as some of the ginseng may be neutralized.

Dosage: The current RDA is 60 mg/day, though a 1999 research paper in the *Journal of the American Medical Association* recommends that this be increased to 200 mg/day. Some recommend 1000 to 3000 mg/day, others 2000 to 5000 mg/day, in 3 or 4 divided doses. It has often been taken in doses up to 10,000 mg/day without serious consequences; it encourages the production of other enzymes that utilize C and is water-soluble, so it is readily excreted by the body. Smart drug expert Michael Hutchison even states that dosages of 10 to 20 grams are not unheard of! In fact, one would probably have to ingest several pounds a day to reach toxic levels. It is more effectively utilized by the body if taken with bioflavonoids, plus the minerals calcium and magnesium. Earl Mindell recommends 100 mg of bioflavonoids for every 500 mg of C, with the ideal balance of ten parts bioflavonoids to one part rutin and hesperidin. Dr. Stuart Berger states that bioflavonoids, or the so-called vitamin P, is not a vitamin at all, but a growth factor needed by certain organisms, excluding man. Moreover, Sheldon Saul Hendler, M.D., Ph.D., states that there is no solid evidence that bioflavonoids help the body utilize vitamin C better; in fact, one study shows that synthetic vitamin C is absorbed more fully than "natural" vitamin C from orange juice or vitamin C with rutin.

CHROMIUM AND CHROMIUM PICOLINATE

Food Sources: Beef, beer, black pepper, bran, brewer's yeast, cheese, chicken, clams, corn oil, liver, meat, mushrooms, poultry, shellfish, thyme, wheat germ, whole-grain cereals.

Effects: Chromium assists in the breakdown and distribution of proteins and carbohydrates in the body. It is also essential for the production of an enzyme-like substance called Glucose Tolerance Factor or GTF (chromium combined with nicotinic acid and amino acids), which aids in the making and proper utilization of insulin; this insulin, in turn, takes carbohydrates from the blood and gets them to the brain cells, which use them for energy. It is believed that sufficient amounts keep the blood sugar on a consistent level, preventing mood swings, depression, and adult-onset diabetes, and providing energy throughout the day. Chromium picolinate is a scientifically developed form which appears to be more efficient than regular chromium; it may also have a mild muscle-building effect on people with a regular exercise program. Chromium picolinate, as well as chromium polynicotinate and chromium chloride, can inhibit sugar-induced high blood pressure. The picolinate and polynicotinate forms (the latter sold under the brand name Chrome-Mate) also act as antioxidants.

Deficiency (which may be very widespread in the U.S. population) can lead to diabetes mellitus (though this condition may result from a chromium-poor diet that is deficient in other minerals, too) and arteriosclerosis (though chromium's exact role in this is not yet clear). Refined sugar should be avoided for three reasons: it has been stripped of its chromium (along with the magnesium), it requires chromium to metabolize it, and it causes a loss of chromium through the urine.

Precautions: Some people cannot convert chromium chloride or chromium from chelated supplements into the "biologically active" form, or GTF, that the body can use, in which case chromium should only be taken under a doctor's supervision, especially in cases of those who are diabetic. Chromium salts, which are an inorganic form of chromium, do not seem to be absorbed by the body very well and so are of little use as supplements. As people get older, they retain less of this mineral in their bodies. A few more things should be kept in mind: cases of allergies to this mineral have been reported; and the chromium content of brewer's yeast, though often high, varies among brands. There are no known symptoms of toxicity, attributable, perhaps, to the low absorption rate (about 2 percent of intake); however, ulceration of the nasal tissues and toxic levels can occur with long-time exposure in workers who deal with chromium in metal plating or making dyes. There is one case of a false-positive reading for a test of porphyria in a man who took one-third of an ounce a day. Chromium supplements should not be taken at the same time as vanadium supplements, as there could be a negative interaction between them. Chromium picolinate's reputation as a muscle-building nutrient may be overrated, its effect possibly due to the fact that subjects may have been deficient in

chromium to begin with. One study in 1996 showed that chromium picolinate caused chromosome damage in cells that had been grown in a laboratory; what this means for individuals taking the supplement is, as yet, undetermined.

Dosage: The RDA has not yet been established. Studies seem to indicate that 200 mcg/day for women is a good dose; athletes and those who exercise heavily — male or female — may need up to 400 mcg/day (though Dr. Stuart Berger recommends only 40 mcg/day for those who exercise at least 5 times a week). Some recommend no more than 200 mcg/day on the basis that no adequate research has been conducted on levels higher than that. Studies on lab animals have shown, however, that it might take a dose of several thousand times the recommended dosage to produce adverse side effects.

DMAE

AKA: Acumen, Atrol, Bimanol, Cervoxan, dimethylaminoethanol p-acetamidobenzoate, Deaner, deanol, Diforene, Dimethaen, Dimethylaminoethanol, DMAE-H3, Elevan, Pabenol, Paxanol, Risatarun, Tonibral, Varesal.

Food Sources: DMAE exists in tiny amounts in the brain and is found in such seafoods as anchovies, herring, and sardines. The prescription drug Deaner (deanol) is chemically similar.

Effects: When combined with phosphatidyl choline and vitamin B-5, it produces acetylcholine, the neurotransmitter essential for short-term memory. It also removes the cellular aging pigment called lipofuscin, a waste product that may inhibit nerve cell functioning. There is some evidence it stabilizes the cell membranes of neurons, preventing one of the major factors of aging, the breakdown of neuronal membranes. It is similar in effect to centrophenoxine or Lucidril, in that it elevates mood, strengthens memory and learning, improves intelligence, lengthens the life span of lab animals (in one study, it lengthened the life span of mice 33–50 percent), reduces fatigue, produces sounder sleep, and decreases the amount of sleep needed. It can cross the blood/brain barrier more readily than choline or lecithin, so an effective dosage is much lower than for the other two supplements, and it has a mild, steady stimulant effect which is said to lead to no letdown or side effects. No letdown or depression is experienced if use is discontinued.

Works synergistically with choline, Hydergine, Piracetam, Selegiline, and vasopressin, so lower doses should be taken if any of these supplements are also being taken.

Precautions: People with manic-depression should not take DMAE, as it can worsen the depressive phase; those with epilepsy or seizure disorders should only do so under a physician's guidance. Too high a dosage (at least 500 mg/day in some cases) can cause anxiety, nervousness, increased blood pressure, insomnia, dull headaches, or muscle tension (especially in the jaw, neck, and legs), which disappear if dosage is reduced. There are no known serious side effects or contraindications.

Dosage: Gradually increase the dosage until it is around 500 to 1000 mg/day, though many people may respond well to lower dosages; one study recommends oral doses as low as 10 to 30 mg/day, which is enough to produce the desired effects. In general, older people can tolerate higher doses, either

because they have lower levels of acetylcholine, they may have reduced receptor sensitivity to acetylcholine, or they may have altered feedback in their brain metabolism. It may take up to three weeks before the effects are noticed. It should be stored in a cool, dark place, as it can deteriorate rapidly.

VITAMIN E

AKA: Aquasol E, Chew-E, d-alpha-tocopherol, d-alpha-tocopheryl acid succinate, dl-alpha-tocopherol, dl-alpha-tocopheryl, Eprolin, Epsilan-M, Pheryl-E, Viterra E.

Eight different forms of vitamin E molecules, or vitamers, are found in nature (alpha, beta, gamma, delta, epsilon, zeta, eta, and theta), each of which is absorbed differently in the body and stays in the body for varying amounts of time. As yet, there is no evidence that each of these forms serves a specific purpose. Even so, some recommend switching back and forth between these mixed tocopherols and D-alpha-tocopherol, both in their natural forms.

Controversy has arisen over the efficacy of natural versus synthetic forms of vitamin E. While most synthetic vitamins are just as effective as the natural forms, such is not the case with E. Vitamin E exists in two forms, each a mirror image of the other, the d-tocopherol (right-handed) form and l-tocopherol (left-handed) form. Only the "d" forms are produced in nature, while the synthetic products are a mixture of both "d" and "l" forms, therefore d-alpha-tocopherol would be a natural vitamin whereas dl-alpha-tocopherol would be synthetic. Synthetics are only 50 to 70 percent as effective as naturals. Still, synthetic and natural are equally as effective in preventing heart disease and inhibiting the oxidation of LDL cholesterol. According to one study, doses of 400 to 800 IU/day can reduce heart attacks by 77 percent in those already suffering from heart disease.

Though vitamin E is fat-soluble, it acts more like a water-soluble vitamin, as it is excreted by the body rather quickly.

Food Sources: Eggs, nuts and oils of nuts, seeds, soybeans, soybean oils (cold-pressed and unrefined only), fresh wheat germ, wheat germ oil, whole grains; smaller amounts are found in asparagus, broccoli, brussel sprouts, cabbage and other dark leafy vegetables, molasses, and sweet potatoes.

Effects: Vitamin E is a strong antioxidant, especially when taken in conjunction with selenium. It also strengthens the immune system; enhances the ability of brain cells to use oxygen; increases the ability of cells to make energy; helps preserve the lung function of elderly people; and it may slow the aging process by protecting the skin and brain cells (which have high percentages of fat compared to the rest of the body's cells) from free radicals (as people age, their ability to absorb E decreases). It has been used by NASA astronauts to fight the breakdown of red blood cells from radiation. In the past few decades in the U.S., there seems to be a direct correlation between the decline in the amount of vitamin E in the diet and the rise in heart attacks, but hard evidence is still lacking. Recent evidence indicates that an optimum level of 200 IU/day can protect the elderly from heart disease and dementia, as well as boost the immune system; higher doses have not led to greater protection. When given in doses of 2000 IU/day, it may slow the progress

of Alzheimer's to a moderate degree, though it is still not known whether it can protect healthy people from getting the disease. A dosage of as little as 50 IU/day, or five times the minimum daily recommended intake for men, can help protect against lung, colorectal, and — especially — prostate cancers. Regular supplementation has also been proven to protect against exercise-induced DNA damage that may lead to cancer. In lab rats, it has been shown to prevent liver damage and liver cancer caused by DHEA.

It also helps the body utilize vitamin A better, and raises the levels of HDLs, the "good" cholesterol. It is reported to extend the life of red blood cells, dilate the blood vessels, and thin the blood. It can even halt, and sometimes reverse, nerve damage caused by such neurological disorders as cystic fibrosis and chronic liver disease.

Vitamin E breaks down sodium nitrate, a food additive and suspected carcinogen; blocks the formation of nitrosamine, another carcinogen; prevents lung damage from nitrogen oxides; and can counteract the effects of a fatty meal, especially damage done to blood vessels from high cholesterol.

Works synergistically with the steroid DHEA.

Deficiency symptoms include gastrointestinal problems, dry dull hair, heart disease, impotency, miscarriages, enlarged prostate, and sterility.

Precautions: No known toxicity up to 3200 IU, though it should not be taken by those who are allergic to vitamin E. Those with thrombophlebitis (blood clots in the leg veins) or liver disease should consult a physician first. Evidence indicates that it may suppress the immune system when taken in doses of 100 IU or more. It can elevate blood pressure when first taken, so those with high blood pressure or heart disease should not take more than 200 IU without consulting a physician first. Dosages above 600 IU/day should not be taken by those with high blood triglyceride levels or a thyroid condition. Vitamin E prolongs the clotting of blood, which can lead to problems such as bleeding-type strokes, cerebral hemorrhage, internal bleeding or ecchymoses (discoloration of the skin due to blood leaching into body tissues) if there is a deficiency of vitamin K, certain rare medical conditions are present, or if a person is taking coumarin-type drugs or drugs with anti-clotting properties, such as Warfarin (Coumadin) or aspirin. Vitamin E supplementation should be stopped about two weeks before surgery, as it could cause excessive bleeding. Paradoxically, vitamin E may *cause* blood clots if taken in doses above 800 IU/day. Common side effects include breast enlargement, dizziness, and headaches. It may also cause abdominal pain, diarrhea, fever, gas, hives, chapped lips, muscle aches, nausea, upset stomach, fatigue, weakness, and blurred vision, though these are rare. Allergies can also occur when vitamin E is used in skin preparations, but these are extremely rare. Overdose symptoms consist of fatigue, nausea, and vomiting. Lab animals given extremely high doses have experienced adverse effects on their adrenal, thyroid, and sex glands.

Recent evidence indicates that the pill form may be harmful, as most only contain alpha-tocopherol, and may do an incomplete job of neutralizing some harmful compounds. Only gamma-tocopherol can eliminate peroxynitrite, a very destructive nitric oxide radical found at sites of inflammation which can lead to cancer and heart disease, and remove nitrogen oxide, a component of air pollution. High levels of alpha-tocopherol can suppress levels of gamma-tocopherol in the blood. Unfortunately, it is impossible to maintain adequate levels, even from a healthy diet; some, however, say a healthy diet can offset this deficiency.

Vitamin E can increase the effect of oral anticoagulants, decrease the effect of iron supplements in those with iron-deficiency anemia, and deplete the body of vitamin A if vitamin E is taken in excessive amounts (and yet, in recommended doses, E can increase the benefits and decrease the side effects of A). When high dosages are combined with high dosages of BHA, BHT, or 2-MEA, it may shorten the life span.

Beyond this, researchers are evenly divided on whether vitamin E is harmful or not. One study indicates that, in some people, doses in the 800 IU/day range may cause weakness and fatigue — symptoms which disappear a day or so after supplementation is stopped — and damage to the skeletal muscles. The findings are supported by the fact that excessive amounts of creatinine, an end product of muscle metabolism, was found in subjects' urine. Claims that it is a causative factor in phlebitis, breast tumors, and breast enlargement (in men as well as women) are unsupported by hard evidence.

Vitamin E can be destroyed or rendered ineffective by birth control pills, chlorine (including chlorinated drinking water, which is common in most communities), cholestyramine, colestipol, cooking in copper pots, food processing, estrogen, freezing, heat, inorganic iron (ferrous sulfate; organic iron, such as ferrous gluconate, peptonate, citrate, or fumarate has no known adverse effect), iron supplements (in healthy individuals), mineral oil, neomycin, rancid fat and oil, Olestra, and oxygen. Individuals using mineral oil on a frequent basis may need more vitamin E, as do those eating a lot of polyunsaturated vegetable oils. If taking a multi-vitamin supplement with iron, make sure there is at least a six- to eight-hour span between taking the supplement and vitamin E.

In 1998, the University of Arizona found that microbiologist Dr. Marguerite Kay had published erroneous research papers on aging, including one study that concluded that vitamin E had some positive effects on aging.

Dosage: Some suggest 100 to 1000 IU/day, others 800 to 1200 IU/day, with daily doses not to exceed 1600 IU/day. A dose of 400 IU/day, however, is reportedly enough to protect against heart disease (the RDA is only 30 IU/day). To increase potency, it is recommended that 25 micrograms of selenium be taken with each 200 IU of vitamin E; adequate amounts of inositol and choline should also be present in the diet. It also works synergistically with French maritime pine bark extract, another antioxidant. Those engaged in regular strenuous exercise have a greater need for this vitamin than most people. It is recommended that those who are elderly or who have digestive problems take the dry or succinate form.

FOLIC ACID

AKA: Folacin, folate, vitamin Bc, vitamin B-9, vitamin M, vitamin U.

Folic acid is considered one of the B vitamins.

Food Sources: Almonds, apricots, avocados, beans, brewer's yeast, cantaloupe, carrots, egg yolk, flour (whole wheat and dark rye), fresh fruits, liver, milk, mushrooms, peas, peanuts, pumpkins, salmon, green leafy vegetables (such as collard greens, kale, lettuce, and spinach).

Effects: Needed for synthesis of RNA and other molecules in the brain, the manufacture of DNA coding in the cells, and helps maintain brain's protein metabolism. Preliminary studies have shown that supplementation of B-12 and folic acid may prevent or delay the onset of Alzheimer's. Combined with vitamin B-12 and methionine, it can manufacture choline in the body. According to John Mann, it may increase life span when combined with the sulfhydryl drug 4-thiazolidine carboxylic acid, and may restore hair to its original color when 5 mg of folic acid are combined with 300 mg each of pantothenic acid and PABA, along with sufficient amounts of the other B vitamins (the addition of 1500 mg of inositol, 50 to 100 mg of B-6, and sufficient amounts of protein may restore hair growth).

Deficiency symptoms include bleeding gums, forgetfulness, graying hair, irritability, sore tongue and throat, occasional diarrhea and constipation, gas and abdominal discomfort, weight loss, lack of development of red blood cells, and infertility. A chronic deficiency may lead to a condition called megaloblastic folic-acid-deficiency anemia. A deficiency of both B-6 and folic acid is correlated with a high level of the amino acid homocysteine, which plays a role in heart disease.

Precautions: It should not be taken by those who are allergic to any of the B vitamins, and those with liver disease and pernicious anemia should consult a physician first. A common side effect is yellow urine; rare side effects include rash, itching, and bronchospasm. In one preliminary study dosages above 400 micrograms/day blocked the absorption of zinc in the body, though zinc levels remained within the normal range. Dosages above 1000 micrograms/day range may block the absorption of vitamin B-12, and the symptoms may include anorexia, nausea, abdominal bloating, insomnia, nightmares, malaise, irritability, impaired concentration, pernicious anemia. Permanent nerve damage may result. Supplements should not be taken by anyone with hormone-related cancer. Too high a dosage can mask symptoms of pernicious anemia.

Folic acid can interact with the anti-convulsant drugs (such as sodium phenytoin) used to treat epilepsy, and may, in dosages above 1000 micrograms/day, interact with anti-psychotic medication. It can also inhibit the effectiveness of sulfonamides like Gantrisin. Those with chronic liver disease may be candidates for a folic acid deficiency. Those taking methotrexate as part of a chemotherapy treatment are advised not to take folic acid supplements, as it will interfere with the effectiveness of the drug. Cases of allergies to this vitamin are extremely rare.

Folic acid in the body can be destroyed or inhibited by alcohol, analgesics, antibacterial drugs, anticancer drugs (e.g., methotrexate), anticonvulsant drugs, antituberculosis drugs, aspirin, barbiturates, birth control pills, blood pressure pills such as Dyazide (triamterene and hydrochlorothiazide), chloramphenicol, coffee, cortisone, estrogen, food processing, heat, para-aminosalicylic acid (PAS), pyrimethamine, stress, sulfa drugs, sulfasalazine, sunlight, tobacco, trimethoprim, vita-min C (in dosages above 2000 mg/day), and water. It can also be destroyed by cooking, especially cooking with copper pots.

Dosage: Supplements are generally in the 100 to 800 mcg/day range.

FRENCH MARITIME PINE BARK EXTRACT

AKA: Pine bark extract, Pinus maritima, Pinus pinaster, Pycnogenol.

A complex of some 40 anti-oxidant flavonoids and organic acids working together synergistically, it is one of the polyphenol extracts known as oligomeric proanthocyanidins (OPCs), which also include grape seed extract.

Effects: One of the most potent anti-oxidants available (it is 50 times more powerful than vitamin E and 20 times more powerful than vitamin C), it can extend the effectiveness of vitamin C over a longer period of time and can effectively protect against the hydroxyl free radical, which can directly damage DNA. The extract can also cross the blood/brain barrier and protect brain cells from harmful compounds in the body. It also aids the immune system, strengthens and repairs connective tissue, helps prevent heart disease, strengthens the capillaries, and has anti-inflammatory properties that protect against such ailments as arthritis and allergic reactions. Studies have also shown that it can protect against stroke, stress-related ulcers, diabetic retinopathy, and some forms of cancer. It may also increase athletic performance because of its anti-oxidant properties, and it can relieve the symptoms of psoriasis and swelling of the lower legs. Its anti-coagulant effect is five times greater than that of aspirin. Current research is attempting to determine whether it has any effect on attention deficit hyperactivity disorder (ADHD).

Works synergistically with vitamin E.

Precautions: No adverse side effects have been found in doses as high as 35,000 mg/day over a six month period.

Dosage: Anti-oxidant expert Laster Packer, Ph.D., recommends 50-100 mg/day.

GERMANIUM

AKA: GE-132, Germanium sesquioxide, PCAGeO, PCAGeS, vitamin O.

Food Sources: Aloe, barley, chlorella, comfrey, garlic, ginseng, onions, shiitake mushrooms, suma.

Effects: Germanium stimulates the immune system, acts as a free radical blocker, and protects against cancers, tumors, and viruses. Improves brain functioning by oxygenating the brain. It may also cure arthritis, and has been used in the treatment of AIDS, chronic fatigue syndrome, candidiasis, Parkinson's disease, cerebral sclerosis, and eye diseases. Much more research needs to be done, however.

GE-132, PCAGeO, and PCAGeS are organic forms which have been shown to inhibit the growth of tumors in mice, but no studies on humans have yet been done.

Precautions: Only the organic form (sesquioxide) of germanium has the beneficial effects.

Rare side effects include skin eruptions, softened stools, and kidney failure.

Dosage: It appears to have low toxicity, even in doses of 10 g/day taken for several months. Sheldon Saul Hendler, M.D., Ph.D., does not recommend

supplementation until more research is done. According to James F. Balch, M.D., and Phyllis A Balch, C.N.C., a beneficial intake of 100 to 300 mg/day can be obtained through dietary means.

GRAPE SEED EXTRACT

AKA: Activin, Resivit.

Effects: Like French maritime pine bark extract, it is one of the polyphenol extracts known as oligomeric proanthocyanidins (OPCs), and is 50 times more powerful than vitamin E and 20 times more powerful than vitamin C in its anti-oxidant properties.

INOSITOL AND IP6

AKA (Inositol): Myo-inositol, phosphatidylinositol, phytic acid.

AKA (IP6): Inositol hexaphosphate, InsP6, myo-inositol hexakisphosphate, phytate, phytic acid.

A sugar-like molecule that exists in large amounts in the brain, inositol is considered part of the B vitamin complex, though it is not, itself, a B vitamin. Myo-inositol is the nutritionally active form, and a component of phosphatidylinositol which, in turn, is a phospholipid molecule that is a small component of cell membranes. Its plant form is known as phytic acid or IP6 (inositol plus six phosphate groups of PO4), and is one component of insoluble fiber.

Food Sources (Inositol): Beans (almost all kinds), brown rice, calf's liver, cantaloupes, chick peas, most citrus fruits (lemons are one exception), lentils, nuts (almost all kinds), oatmeal, pork, veal, wheat germ, and whole-grain flour.

Food Sources (IP6): In descending order: Corn, sesame, wheat beans, rice, peanuts, sunflower seeds, soybeans, barley, peas, oats.

Effects: Inositol acts as a cell membrane stabilizer. It also helps redistribute body fat, keep cholesterol low, prevent eczema, and keep hair healthy. Claims that myo-inositol lowers triglycerides and cholesterol in the blood, protects against cardiovascular disease, promotes sleep, or relieves anxiety are, as yet, unproven, though these last two effects may result from its effects on phosphatidylinositol levels in brain cells. It has been shown to provide some benefit in improving sensory nerve function in those with diabetic peripheral neuropathy, though more research is needed to determine its exact role in this disease.

No definite deficiency symptoms have been identified in humans.

Phytic acid (IP6) is an anti-oxidant. It also fights cancer, protects cells (particularly blood cells) from excess iron by chelating the iron atoms. It may be a more potent cancer-fighter when taken by itself than when taken as part of a high-fiber diet, mainly because it is not bound up in protein, allowing phytase, a food enzyme, to break it down before it can be released. Evidence also indicates it may reduce lung damage from asbestos, prevent kidney stones, reduce the risk of coronary heart disease, reduce heart attacks, prevent some of the damage caused by sickle-cell anemia, and lower cholesterol.

It works synergistically with green tea to reduce colon cancer.

Precautions: Frozen, canned, or salt-free foods contain less myo-inositol than fresh foods. No adverse effects have been reported in those taking supplementation of myo-inositol or phosphatidylinositol, though the former is the one that should be taken, as it is the nutritionally active form.

Consuming large amounts of caffeine (coffee, tea, soft drinks) can deplete the amount of inositol in the body.

Dosage: Inositol has so far been found to be non-toxic in doses as high as 50 grams. Those who have taken it to relieve insomnia or anxiety have generally taken 1 to 2 g/day of myo-inositol, and up to 3 g/day have been taken for short periods of time with no apparent ill effects. The average American diet for adults provides approximately 1 g/day of myo-inositol. Abul Kalam M. Shamsuddin, M.D., Ph.D., recommends 1 to 2 grams of IP6 plus inositol.

MAGNESIUM

AKA: Magnesium ascorbate, magnesium gluconate, magnesium lactate, magnesium orotate, magnesium oxide.

Food Sources: Almonds, apples, apricots, avocados, bananas, blackstrap molasses, Brazil nuts, brown rice, canteloupe, corn, diary products, figs, filberts, grapefruit, lemons, nuts, peaches, seafood, seeds, soy products, sunflower seeds, green leafy vegetables, hard water, whole grains.

Effects: Magnesium provides energy; aids in the metabolism of calcium and vitamin C; enhances the immune system; plays a key role in the chemical reactions of some 325 essential enzymes; plays a role in the manufacture of DNA and RNA coding in cells; and contributes to the formation and growth of cell membranes, nerves, muscles, and the heart. It protects against anxiety, calcium buildup in neurons (a common condition found in those with Alzheimer's), depression, diabetes, fatigue, insomnia (when combined with calcium), kidney stones and gallstones, poor memory, migraines, osteoporosis, heart disease, high blood pressure, tooth decay, the toxic effects of the heart drug digitalis, and — in women — the tension of PMS and postmenopausal bone loss. Most people may not get enough, and athletes should be especially aware of their intake, as exercise depletes the body of this nutrient. In combination with vitamins C and E and choline, it may prevent some of the side effects of vitamin A and D overdoses.

Magnesium orotate may help control lipofuscin deposits.

Deficiency symptoms are vague and ill-defined, but signs of severe deficiency include loss of coordination, loss of appetite, confusion, depression, diarrhea, headaches, high blood pressure, irritability, kidney disease, memory impairment, nausea, nervousness, vomiting, tremors, and sometimes fatal convulsions. Chronic deficiency can result in various cardiovascular problems. Even a mild deficiency can lead to abnormal heart rhythms. Because of its depletion in soil on U.S. croplands, the daily intake of the average American is about one-half to one-third of what it was nearly a century ago.

Precautions: Those with severely impaired kidney function or some types of heart rhythm abnormalities should consult a physician before taking supplements.

Overdose is rare, and usually occurs in individuals with kidney failure. Magnesium salts have a laxative effect in healthy individuals in doses of 3000 to 5000 milligrams/day, and toxicity involving magnesium generally occurs in the 9000 mg range, often resulting in diarrhea. Some over-the-counter products are hidden sources of magnesium, including Bayer Plus, Bufferin, De-Gel, Epsom salts, Maalox, magnesium citrate, Mylanta, and Phillips' milk of magnesia.

Magnesium can be toxic in high dosages if calcium and phosphorus intakes are also high, and it can interfere with calcium absorption if too much or too little is taken (ideally, magnesium and calcium intake should be a 1:1 to 1:2 ratio). Magnesium in foods can be depleted by poor soil conditions, milling (in grains), processing, and cooking. Magnesium absorption can be decreased by a diet high in fats and proteins, foods rich in oxalic acid (almonds, cocoa, spinach, tea), and malabsorption disorders such as Crohn's disease. The magnesium stored in the body can be depleted by the synthetic vitamin D in milk, coffee, tea, alcohol, heart medications such as digitalis and digoxin, antibiotics, anticancer drugs, anticonvulsants, diuretics, oral contraceptives, Premarin, and stress.

Dosage: A maximum intake of 500 to 750 mg/day. Magnesium ascorbate is a combination of the mineral with vitamin C, and should be in the proper proportions of one part magnesium to nine parts vitamin C.

MANGANESE

AKA: Manganese gluconate, manganese sulfate.

Food Sources: Avocados, beans, fruits, milk, nuts, organ meats, dried peas, shellfish, green vegetables, and whole grains.

Manganese is a little-understood mineral, and much more research needs to be done to determine its effects on human metabolism.

Effects: Manganese is involved in the formation of bones and the growth of connective tissue, activates some enzymes and other minerals, helps utilize vitamins B1 and E, aids in cell division and the production of DNA and RNA, and may be an anti-oxidant.

A deficiency, which is virtually unheard of, can cause confusion, convulsions, eye and ear problems, muscle contractions, a rapid pulse, a lowering of serum cholesterol, impaired blood clotting, a reduction in the growth of hair and nails, and scaly dermatitis. Without exception, tumors are deficient in superoxide dismutase, which contains manganese.

Precautions: Overdose through diet is extremely unlikely, though miners in northern Chile exposed to manganese dust have commonly developed a disorder known as "locura manganica," or manganese madness. The first sign is a manic stage characterized by inexplicable laughter, heightened libido, impulsiveness, insomnia, delusions, and hallucinations, followed by a depressive stage of extreme drowsiness, impotence, and slowed speech. The third and final stage is distinguished by symptoms much like those of Parkinson's disease and, like Parkinson's, can be treated by levodopa.

The absorption of manganese may be decreased by high dietary levels of magnesium, calcium, iron, phosphate, antacids, magnesium-containing laxatives, fiber (including bran), phytates in vegetables, tannins in tea, and oxalic acid in spinach.

Dosage: 15 to 25 mg/day, though some recommend 2 to 5 mg/day, not to exceed 10 mg/day.

OPCs

AKA: Oligomeric proanthocyanidins, PCOs, proanthocyanidins, procyanidins, procyanidolic oligomers.

The OPCs are polyphenol extracts derived from plant sources, the most popular being French maritime pine bark extract (Pycnogenol), grape seed extract (Activin and Resivit), and Landes pine bark (Flavan). They have often been mistakenly referred to as bioflavonoids; they share a similar chemical structure, but OPCs are 100 percent bioavailable, non-toxic, colorless, and can bind with proteins, whereas bioflavonoids are, for the most part, not biologically active, sometimes toxic, yellow in color, and unable to bind with proteins.

Effects: The OPCs are anti-oxidants. They can also lower LDL cholesterol levels, reduce the risk of atherosclerosis, improve the strength and elasticity of blood vessels, maintain cardiovascular health, protect against age-related and degenerative diseases by increasing collagen's ability to repair itself, prevent edema and inflammation, relieve the symptoms of varicose veins, relieve the discomfort of PMS and menopause, reduce the probability of developing diabetic retinopathy, and maintain skin health. They are one of the keys to understanding the "French paradox," the fact that the French consume just as much dietary fat and cholesterol as Americans, yet do not suffer the same rate of cardiovascular disease, mainly due to their intake of red wine.

Dosage: Optimal dosage appears to be 100 to 200 mg/day for the average healthy individual. Grape seed extracts are superior to pine bark extracts, as the former contains 92 to 95 percent OPCs, compared to 80 to 85 percent in the latter; grape seed extracts also contain the gallic esters of OPCs, the most effective form for scavenging free radicals, while pine bark extract does not. In addition, a new process (called the phytosome process) also binds grape seed extract OPCs to lecithin, allowing them to be better absorbed by the gastrointestinal tract and more fully utilized by the body, making it preferable to the unbound form.

Selenium

AKA: L-selenomethione, selenium ascorbate, selenocystine, selenomethionine, sodium selenate, sodium selenite.

A trace element that, until recently, was unjustifiably considered a deadly poison. It is one of the most powerful of the anti-oxidant minerals.

Food Sources: Brazil nuts, broccoli, brown rice, cabbage, celery, cucumbers, dairy products, eggs, garlic, herring, organ meats (such as liver and kidneys), mushrooms, onions, poultry, radishes, sardines, shellfish, tomatoes, and tuna can have high levels. Barley, bran, whole-grain breads and cereals, brewer's yeast, and wheat germ may have high levels if grown in soil that is high in selenium, but levels can vary widely.

Effects: Selenium detoxifies heavy metals (such as arsenic, cadmium, lead, and mercury), alcohol, peroxidized fats, and some drugs; reportedly slows down some of the aging processes, and inhibits the oxidation that leads to hardening of the tissues, keeping them more elastic. One study found that 200 micrograms/day can protect against lung, colon, and prostate cancer, but appears to have no effect on skin cancer, though it may help eradicate moles and brown spots. Other studies have correlated high levels of selenium with a low incidence of leukemia and cancers of the rectum, pancreas, breast, ovary, bladder, skin, stomach, esophagus, liver, and gastrointestinal tract. Studies have shown that, when given in doses around 220 micrograms/day, it improves moods and thinking, even in those who are not deficient, indicating most people do not get enough.

Selenium has a synergistic effect when taken with vitamin E, as both are strong anti-oxidants. It strengthens the immune system — some say that when selenium and vitamin E are taken together, the body's antibody defenses experience a thirty-fold increase. When combined with zinc, it can improve mental performance.

The only known deficiency symptom is a heart condition known as Keshan's disease.

Precautions: The FDA's recommended intake is 50 to 200 micrograms/day; an early symptom of overdose is a garlicky scent in the breath, urine, and sweat. Men, especially sexually active men, have a greater need for it than women, as this mineral is lost through semen. Selenium in its natural state is poisonous, though some say organic selenium is three times less toxic than inorganic selenium, and can cause symptoms when approximately 2400 to 3000 micrograms/day is taken over a long period of time. Some studies have found no harmful effects in people whose daily intake averages 1500 micrograms/day. Pearson and Shaw, however, claim that an inorganic form, sodium selenite, is relatively nontoxic, while selenomethionine and selenocystine — two organic forms — are potentially harmful, as the body may mistake these amino acids for sulfur-containing amino acids and make them perform functions they are incapable of carrying out. Overdose symptoms include a metallic taste in the mouth, garlic breath, skin inflammation, loss of hair, brittle or blackened nails, bad teeth, discoloration of skin, dizziness, nausea, fatigue and lethargy, gastrointestinal problems, irritability, jaundice, and progressive paralysis; acute poisoning is evidenced by fever, rapid breathing, upset stomach, inflammation of the spinal cord and bone marrow, anorexia, and death. Permanent side effects are rare, and most adverse effects disappear within a few weeks, even after several months of high dosages. The risk of toxicity is low because selenium is quickly excreted by the body; metal and refinery workers, however, may be exposed to toxic levels, as selenium is used in the processing of some metals, though this occupational poisoning has been characterized as "mostly accidental and rare." Another risk group may be office workers who are at a copy machine all day, as these machines use selenium plates, which release this mineral into the air.

There have been documented cases of cystic fibrosis patients who have become gravely ill or died after taking supplemental doses that would have been well within the safe range for the average person. Despite early reports, there appears to be no link between high selenium levels and amyotropic lateral sclerosis (ALS, otherwise known as Lou Gehrig's disease).

There appear to be no contraindications with any drugs or any other vitamins, though vitamin C may decrease the absorption of inorganic selenium if taken at the same time.

Dosage: The RDA is 70 mcg/day for men and 55 mcg/day for women. There is no consensus on the optimal dose—some say 100 to 300 mcg/day, while others claim good results with doses of up to 3000 mcg/day, though these higher doses should be taken only while under the guidance of a physician. Nutritionist Nicola Reavley sets the toxic dosage at 600 to 750 mcg/day; Dr. Stuart Berger sets the upper limit at 300 mcg/day and Earl Mindell, R.Ph., Ph.D., at 200 mcg/day, though Sheldon Saul Hendler, M.D., Ph.D., suggests 400 to 1000 mcg/day is equivalent to the anticancer doses given to animals, and suggests supplementation of 50 to 200 mcg/day. Organic selenium (made from high-selenium yeast) has a higher nutritional value and is more readily absorbed by the body than inorganic selenium salts (sodium selenite); most multiple vitamin supplements contain the inorganic form.

SULFUR

Food Sources: Dried beans and peas, lean beef, brussel sprouts, cabbage, clams, eggs, fish, garlic, onions, peanuts, wheat germ.

Necessary for good complexion, healthy hair, and strong nails.

Effects: Helps provide the brain with sufficient oxygen, and also helps the blood resist bacterial infections.

Sulfur works synergistically with the B vitamins to maintain basic body metabolism and strong nerves.

There are no known deficiency symptoms.

Precautions: It is not known whether any overdose symptoms are associated with organic sulfur, but inorganic sulfur may pose problems.

Dosage: No RDA has been established, but since sulfur is an important component of many amino acids, those eating sufficient protein are most likely getting adequate amounts of sulfur.

XANTHINOL NICOTINATE

AKA: Androgeron, Angiomanin, Angiomin, Cafardil, Circulan, Clofamin, Complamex, Complamin, Dacilin, Emodinamin, Jupal, Landrina, Niconicol, Sadamin, SK 331 A, Vasoprin, Vedrin, Xanidil, and Xavin.

A form of niacin that passes through cell membranes more readily than niacin.

Effects: Xanthinol nicotinate increases ATP production, dilates blood vessels, and improves short-term memory.

Precautions: People with ulcers, cardiovascular problems, or liver problems (xanthinol nicotinate can cause liver dysfunction) should avoid taking it. There may be minor reactions such as blurred vision, diarrhea, headaches, heartburn, heart palpitations, itchy skin, muscle cramps, nausea, skin flushing or a sense of warmth, skin rash, skin-color changes, or vomiting; these generally disappear with continued use or when use is discontinued. It may cause postural hypotension, or a sudden drop in blood pressure when going from a sitting to a standing position.

Dosage: 300 to 600 mg/day in three divided doses with meals.

ZINC

AKA: Chelated zinc, Egozinc, Orazinc, PMS Egozinc, Verazinc, zinc chloride, zinc acetate, zinc ascorbate, Zincate, zinc gluconate, Zinkaps-220, zinc pyrithione, zinc sulfate, Zinc 220.

A mineral important to many of the brain's enzyme systems, it is a component of 90 essential enzymes, including superoxide dismutase. Most of the medical research has been done with zinc sulfate, which is 22 percent zinc by weight; however, most of the supplements sold to the public are zinc gluconate, which is 14 percent zinc by weight and is not widely researched. There are no studies comparing the two. Likewise, almost nothing is known about chelated zinc. Zinc acetate causes fewer gastrointestinal problems than the other forms, yet is not widely available. Zinc pyrithione is used for shampoos and hair conditioners and is not intended for oral use.

Food Sources: Beef, blackstrap molasses, bran (wheat and rice), egg yolk, fish (particularly herring), lamb, legumes, liver, nonfat dry milk, ground mustard, nuts, organ meats, oysters, pork, poultry, pumpkin seeds, seafood and shellfish, soybeans, sunflower seeds, turkey, wheat germ, whole-grain flour. The zinc content of vegetables is dependent on the soil in which they are grown. More readily available zinc is found in meats than from other sources.

Effects: Zinc is important in protecting cell membranes against free radical damage, essential for the growth and development of the reproductive organs, helps the body get rid of carbon dioxide, helps in the manufacture of DNA and RNA, aids in the smooth contraction of muscles, and boosts the immune system. It also helps the body absorb vitamins (especially the B vitamins), synthesize proteins, metabolize carbohydrates, and form insulin. There are significant amounts of zinc in the brain, which may help protect against lead poisoning from the environment. Additional reported benefits include faster healing of wounds, a restoration of loss of taste, protection against prostate problems, and lower cholesterol deposits. It has been used to treat psoriasis (when used in combination with sulfur), acne (when used in combination with vitamin A), rheumatoid arthritis, impotence, and irregular menses. Zinc gluconate is said to help speed recovery from the common cold.

When combined with selenium, it may improve mental performance. Some say that a combination of zinc and manganese supplements help guard against senility.

Precautions: It should not be taken by anyone with an upper respiratory infection. Rare side effects, which occur with an overdose, consist of chest pain, chills, dizziness, drowsiness, fever, heartburn, indigestion, nausea, shortness of breath, sore throat, extreme fatigue or weakness, ulcers in the throat or mouth, vomiting, and yellow eyes and skin. Any stomach discomfort can usually be avoided by taking zinc after meals or with milk. Some have reported mouth irritation and taste distortions when dissolving lozenges (those made for swallowing) in the mouth for 10 to 20 minutes. Too much zinc, which can even occur from eating too much high-zinc foods or from foods which have been stored in galvanized containers, can interfere with the body's absorption of copper. Dosages above 80 mg/day can cause levels of high-density lipoprotein-cholesterol (the "good" cholesterol) in the blood to fall, possibly leading to heart disease. The dosage normally used for treating acne, 135 mg/day, is very near the toxic level for some individuals, and some may experience the overdose symptoms mentioned above. Dosages above the 50 to 150 mg/day range can cause severe anemia due to iron and copper deficiency (Conversely, a high level of copper can collect in the blood and sap the brain's supply of zinc).

Zinc supplements can also irritate the stomach lining and perforate ulcers. Those involved in smelting operations can suffer from zinc poisoning by inhaling the fumes.

On the other hand, some feel that zinc deficiency is very common in the U.S., and is often characterized by hypogeusia (a loss of taste and smell), scaly skin, slow healing of wounds, depression, fatigue, mental dullness, difficulty in concentration, hair loss, decline in the number of red and white blood cells, diarrhea, lowered resistance to infections, low sperm count and, in severe cases, atrophy of the sex glands. Alcoholics, diabetics, strict vegetarians, and heavy exercisers need higher than normal levels of zinc, as do persons eating high-fiber diets, living in hot climates (heavy sweating depletes the body's supply to a significant extent), or taking vitamin B-6 supplements. Medical conditions associated with insufficient zinc in the body include chronic infections or inflammatory diseases, kidney disease, pancreatic disease, psoriasis, sickle-cell anemia, and thalassemia.

Whole grains and breads that have been prepared without yeast have a high level of phytic acid, a phosphorus compound that prevents the body from absorbing the zinc in the food; this is especially true if extra bran has been added (though phytic acid is now believed to prevent colon cancer). Also, cadmium, a toxic mineral which can be found in food as a result of pollution, can take the place of zinc where both are present. This is a problem with white bread, in particular, because zinc is concentrated in the bran (largely absent from white bread), whereas cadmium is concentrated in the white part of the grain. A zinc deficiency can make a vitamin A deficiency worse (conversely, zinc supplements may increase the need for vitamin A).

Zinc can be destroyed or inhibited by alcohol, bran, cadmium, EDTA (a food additive found in beer, canned foods, soft drinks, and foods high in vegetable oils), fiber, phosphorus-containing additives used in foods, phytic acid (phytates), stress, folic acid supplements, iron supplements, and tobacco.

Decreased absorption of zinc can be caused by tetracycline (Achromycin V, Mysteclin F, Sumycin). Other drugs that inhibit or deplete zinc include penicillamine and the antibiotics chlortetracycline (Aureomycin) and oxytetracycline (Terramycin). There is one case where the anti-cancer drugs mercaptopurine (Purinethol) and methotrexate caused a deficiency. Corticosteroids, or cortisone medications, may cause an excessive amount of zinc to be excreted and may retard wound healing. These medications include dexamethasone (Decadron), prednisone, prednisolone (Deltasone), betamethasone (Celestone), desoxycortisone (Percoten), and methy-

prednisolone (Depo-Medrol, Depo-Predate). Diuretics like chlorthalidone (Combipres, Hygroton, Regreton) and thiazide diuretics may also increase the excretion of zinc. Metal-binding drugs such as penicillamine (Cuprimine) can cause zinc to bind with copper, which can lead to a deficiency in the long run. Birth control pills increase the amount of zinc in the red blood cells but, as yet, the consequences of this have not yet been determined.

Dosage: Doses higher than 15 to 30 mg/day are not recommended, as long-term effects are not known. Zinc sulfate and zinc gluconate are both well tolerated by the body, but the latter is less susceptible to side effects; in both, side effects occur in many individuals in the 100 to 200 mg/day range, but taking frequent small doses throughout the day with meals may prevent some of these. If high doses of vitamin B-6 are taken, there is a greater need for zinc, especially for alcoholics or diabetics. The best supplements to take are those composed of chelated zinc. Individuals taking zinc should take adequate amounts of vitamin A, calcium, and phosphorus for zinc to work with maximum efficiency.

CHAPTER 4

Amino Acids

Though most of the amino acids needed are manufactured by the body, nine are not; these are known as the essential amino acids — L-histidine, L-isoleucine, L-leucine, L-lysine, L-methionine, L-phenylalanine, L-threonine, L-tryptophan, and L-valine — and all are provided by proteins in the diet. The other fifteen not needed in the diet are alanine, arginine, asparginine, aspartic acid, carnitine, cysteine, cystine, glutamic acid, glutamine, glycine, hydroxyproline, ornithine, proline, serine, and tyrosine. The line between essential and non-essential amino acids is fuzzy, as children require arginine for growth and, for adults under such condition as stress to the body (extreme heat, extreme cold, shock, drugs, toxic agents), illness (fever), or pregnancy, any one of the non-essential amino acids, mostly the "branch-chain" ones (leucine, isoleucine, valine), can become essential.

Those with allergies, for example, use an excess of histamine in their bodies, which is manufactured from histidine. Genetic problems can also lead to deficiencies.

Complete proteins provide the proper balance of all the amino acids, and these foods include meats, poultry, seafood, eggs, milk, and cheese. Incomplete proteins — such as those found in beans, grains, nuts, peas, and seeds — lack some essential amino acids and must be eaten in combination for best results.

The functioning of the brain relies on amino acids, as these are the essential components for the development of neurotransmitters. In turn, neurotransmitters are important factors in brain chemistry, as certain deficiencies or excesses of some neurotransmitters can cause mood disorders. Though amino acids play an essential role in brain function, there are some experts, such as Dr. Andrew Weil (author of *Natural Health, Natural Medicine*) and Dr. Stuart Berger, who do not believe they should be taken as supplements, as they can severely disrupt the brain chemistry. Some reference texts, such as the *Psychotropic Drug Handbook*, caution that non-dietary amino acid supplements may produce effects different from those found in food. Also, a highly imbalanced intake of amino acids could have an adverse effect on protein synthesis in children.

Amino acids can be in either the "L" or "D" form. The "L" forms are readily absorbed and utilized by the body as proteins, while the "D" forms must be converted by the body into a usable form first; despite the therapeutic value found in some "D" forms, the FDA bans sale of the latter, so you may not encounter it when buying supplements.

Free-form amino acids are ones that have been taken from complex proteins, and you must be sure that, when buying powdered amino acid supplements, the label specifies the amount of free-form amino acids in the product. Chances are that if the label says only "amino acids," the bottle may contain mostly inexpensive protein filler and not much of any amino acids.

Amino acids should be taken with cofactors — such as vitamins, minerals, or nutrients — that assist the body in metabolizing them; it is also a good idea to take a variety of amino acids together and in their proper proportions to one another.

There is one instance, however, where two amino acids play opposite roles and are not compatible with each other: L-tyrosine, which the brain uses to manufacture the neurotransmitters norepinephrine and dopamine — both of which have a stimulating effect, contributing to clear , fast thinking, long-term memory, and alertness — and L-tryptophan, used by the brain to synthesize the neurotransmitter serotonin — which has a sedative effect on the brain, leading to a slower reaction time, a feeling of fullness after a meal, and sleepiness. To get the mental lift from L-tyrosine, it is necessary to eat the proteins (meat, poultry, seafood, beans, tofu, and lentils) in the meal before the food that contains carbohydrates. To relax or fall asleep, it is necessary to eat the foods high in L-tryptophan (bananas, milk, sunflower seeds) first, along with the foods rich in carbohydrates, because they enhance the effect of L-tryptophan. In order to get an energy boost, it is necessary to eat foods high in L-tyrosine. The reason for this is that, even though L-tryptophan needs carbohydrates to get into the brain, it does so much more readily than L-tyrosine.

ARGININE

AKA: L-arginine.

Arginine is needed for the normal functioning of the pituitary gland.

Food Sources: Carob, cereals, chocolate, gelatin desserts, nuts, oatmeal, popcorn, protein-rich foods, raisins, brown rice, sunflower and sesame seeds, whole wheat bread.

Effects: The body converts it to spermine, found in semen, blood tissue, and brain cells. It is said to help fight cancer by boosting the immune system (more specifically, by stimulating the production of T-cells), protect the liver by detoxifying harmful substances, and increase the sperm count in men. Reduced levels have been found in people with senility and memory loss. Though it does seem to have a stimulating effect on human growth hormone when taken along with lysine, and thus may be of some benefit to bodybuilders, it apparently does not reduce fat to any significant extent.

A deficiency can result in male infertility, premature aging, increased free radical activity, and obesity.

Precautions: Supplements should not be taken by those with schizophrenia, though there is no evidence that it aggravates this condition. Those with any form of liver or kidney failure should take high doses for a prolonged period of time only while under the care of a physician. Supplementary forms should not be taken by children or teenagers, as there is the possibility it could cause bone and skin disorders. Too large a dose can result in diarrhea, nausea, a thickening or coarsening of the skin, and the possible promotion of the herpes virus (though Sheldon Saul Hendler, M.D., Ph.D., says this last has not been proven). In fact, those with herpes should avoid arginine supplements and arginine-rich foods, though sufficient amounts of lysine may help counteract this; in such cases, ornithine may be used in place of arginine. Dosages over 20 to 30 grams a day could lead to enlarged joints and bone deformities.

Dosage: The RDA has not yet been established. The large doses given to sick people are safe only for short periods of time; the safe level for healthy people has not yet been determined, though Leon Chaitow recommends up to 8 g/day and Hendler suggests a more conservative dose of 1.5 g/day.

CARNOSINE

AKA: L-carnosine.

Carnosine is a composite of two amino acids that work synergistically with other anti-oxidants such as vitamin C, E, B-complex, beta-carotene, selenium, and the sulfur-containing amino acids cysteine and methionine.

Food Sources: It is found only in animal foods such as eggs, fish (all kinds), meat (all kinds), and milk.

Effects: Carnosine stabilizes some thirteen important functions of the body and is also an anti-oxidant that fights certain free radicals found in air pollution and second-hand smoke.

CYSTEINE

AKA: Cysteine hydrochloride monohydrate, L-cysteine, NAC, N-acetyl-cysteine, N-acetyl-L-cysteine.

Manufactured from methionine or serine by the liver.

Food Sources: Some cereals, dairy products, eggs, meat.

Effects: Cysteine is a strong anti-oxidant believed to purify the body, removing heavy metals and protecting the blood, lungs, intestinal tract, and liver against the harmful effects of alcohol, smoking, and pollution by detoxifying acetaldehyde. It plays a role in the formation of the skin, helps prevent cataracts, helps offset the effects of iron deficiency, and is used in the treatment of rheumatoid arthritis, bronchitis, cancer, hardening of the arteries, and chronic diseases. It may boost the immune system and help fight liver cancer, and has been used to treat allergies, arthritis, cataracts, diabetes, hypoglycemia, and the adverse consequences of radiation in chemotherapy and

X-rays. It has been proven to extend the life span of mice and guinea pigs, possibly because it contains sulfur, a substance that deactives free radicals; Pearson and Shaw claim that it can restore hair growth and extend a person's life span.

Cysteine helps protect against radiation damage when combined with vitamins C and B1, and also works synergistically with vitamin E and selenium.

N-acetylcysteine (NAC) is form of cysteine more fully utilized by the body. Both NAC and cysteine are helpful in preventing damage to the body and subsequent side effects from radiation, particularly in relation to chemotherapy and radiation treatments.

Precautions: Anyone with diabetes or blood sugar problems should not take supplements in doses above 3000 mg and in combination with large doses of vitamins B-1 and C except under the guidance of a physician, as it can inactive insulin production. On the other hand, Pearson and Shaw recommend taking three times as much vitamin C as the total cysteine intake and plenty of fluids to prevent the formation of kidney and bladder stones.

Anecdotal evidence indicates that it could increase the toxicity of monosodium glutamate (MSG) in those already susceptible.

Dosage: Up to 1 to 3 g/day, along with vitamin C (in doses three times the amount of cysteine so that the body does not produce too much cystine) and vitamin B-6, though Sheldon Saul Hendler, M.D., Ph.D., recommends no more than 1.5 g/day. It should also be taken on an empty stomach and with water. Ray Sahelian, M.D., states that because cysteine cannot cross cell membranes, supplements are useless.

CYSTINE

Effects: Cystine removes heavy metals from the body and is used in the treatment of psoriasis and eczema. It may also help tissue healing after surgery protect the liver against damage from exposure to carbon tetrachloride.

Precautions: Cystine should be used with caution by those susceptible to kidney, liver, or bladder stones.

ETHYLENE DIAMINE TETRAACETIC ACID

AKA: EDTA.

A synthetic amino acid.

Effects: EDTA has been used in chelation therapy to treat Alzheimer's patients. It works by binding to harmful metals in the brain and body and removing them. Subjects in the early stages of Alzheimer's have shown definite improvements in brain-cell function.

5-HTP

AKA: 5-hydroxy tryptophan, 5-hydroxy l-tryptophan, 5-OHT, oxitriptan.

Effects: It is converted by the body into serotonin after it has been converted from the amino acid tryptophan. It induces calmness and reduces insomnia, and has shown some promise as an appetite suppressant and in treating mild depression. It has also shown promise in treating anxiety, obsessive-compulsive disorder (OCD), panic disorder, fibromyalgia, PMS, and migraine headaches. Unlike serotonin, it can cross the blood/brain barrier.

It works synergistically with melatonin.

Precautions: It should not be taken

by anyone with ulcers or other gastrointestinal diseases, Crohn's disease, scleroderma, excess prolactin secretion, or carcinoid syndrome. Those over 60 may need smaller doses.

Nausea and fatigue occur initially, but may eventually disappear. Daytime drowsiness, nightmares, loss of appetite, diarrhea, cramps, upset stomach, gas, vomiting, sweating, and lowered sex drive may also result, generally from higher doses. Rare side effects include long-term fatigue, stuffy or runny nose, and headaches. Daily use can lead to increased tolerance, with the result that higher doses are needed to achieve the same effects, and it can sometimes be hard to determine if 5-HTP will make you alert or drowsy (dosage, time of meals, time of day, supplements or medications, age, and hormonal levels all play a part). Long-term effects are not known.

Overdose symptoms include the serotonin syndrome, where serotonin levels are too high, and which is characterized by restlessness, confusion, sweating, diarrhea, excessive salivation, high blood pressure, increased body temperature, rapid heart rate, tremors, seizures, and — in rare cases — death. Recovery is complete if dosage is stopped.

Some 5-HTP supplements contain vitamin B-6 (pyroxidal phosphate), which helps to convert tryptophan to melatonin. However, there is concern that the vitamin may convert 5-HTP to serotonin in the blood or tissues, which could cause adverse reactions or increase the manufacture of norepinephrine and dopamine, counteracting any sedative effects of 5-HTP. More ominously, while the brain creates 5-HTP and immediately destroys it, the pill distributes it, through the bloodstream, all over the body; the consequences of this are as yet unknown.

It should not be combined with selective serotonin reuptake inhibitors (SSRIs) and other antidepressants, or the diet drug dexfenfluramine (Redux). It should only be combined with MAO inhibitors under the guidance of a physician; combining 200 mg of 5-HTP with MAO inhibitors can result in high blood pressure and emotional instability. When combined with St. John's Wort, both should be taken in smaller doses to prevent the serotonin syndrome.

Dosage: It is about ten times more potent than tryptophan. Ray Sahelian recommends 10 to 50 mg one-half to one hour before sleep. Side effects generally occur in doses above 100 mg. It should be taken no more than once or twice a week. Taking it with 25 to 50 mg of vitamin B-6 may increase the amount converted to serotonin in the brain, and eating it with carbohydrates may help improve the rate at which it enters the brain.

GLUTAMINE

AKA: L-glutamine.

A free-form amino acid that produces glutamic acid, a brain chemical that protects against ammonia metabolic waste.

Effects: Subjects have reported clearer thinking, improved alertness, and better moods. It manufactures GABA, a neurotransmitter which soothes and calms the mind. It has also reportedly helped in the control of obesity (by reducing the craving for carbohydrates) and alcoholism, in reducing the healing time for ulcers, and for the relief of depression, fatigue, and impotence. It has been used to treat schizophrenia and senility, and research has shown that it can offset the adverse effects of immune system suppression caused by intense exercise. Laboratory tests have shown that glutamic acid retards the formation of or dissolves kidney stones.

A deficiency can result in moodiness, ill temper, and a weakened immune system.

Precautions: Glutamic acid, unable to cross the blood-brain barrier, provides no known benefit. Over 2 g/day of glutamine can cause manic behavior. One individual taking high doses of glutamine experienced sleep loss, hyperactivity, and vivid uncontrollable thoughts. In a second reported case, a man taking four grams a day of L-glutamine for three weeks became psychotic, with hallucinations, grandiose delusions, insomnia, and a voracious sex drive. Those with sensitivity to the food additive monosodium glutamate (MSG) may experience an allergic reaction to glutamine.

Dosage: Some suggest starting with 250 to 500 mg/day and increasing to as much as 1 to 2 g/day. Earl Mindell, R.Ph., Ph.D., recommends 1 to 4 g/day in divided doses.

GLUTATHIONE

AKA: Glutaplex, GSH, GSH 250 Master Glutathione Formula.

A stable tripeptide made by the body from the three amino acids L-cysteine, L-glutamic acid, and glycine. It does not break down into the toxic product cystine (which can crystalize and produce kidney stones), but is totally absorbed by the gastrointestinal tract.

Food Sources: Asparagus, avocados, broccoli, cabbage, cauliflower, grapefruit, oranges, peaches, potatoes, purslane, strawberries, tomatoes, watermelon.

Effects: Glutathione is said to protect the brain cells against the cross-linking of proteins — a condition which reduces the efficiency of the brain cells — and increases the flow of oxygen and blood to the brain. It reportedly deactivates free radicals and counters the effect of lipid peroxides, which may be the key to its antiaging effect. The effectiveness of glutathione can be increased by lipoic acid, selenium, and vitamins B-2 and E.

Precautions: Persons with kidney disease, severe liver disease (especially that resulting from cirrhosis or Reye's syndrome), or those with seizure disorders should not take glutathione supplements without first consulting a physician. Those with diabetes or blood sugar problems should avoid doses above 3000 mg except under the care of a physician, as a combination of L-cysteine and large doses of vitamins B1 and C may inactivate insulin. Cysteine may also make some people more sensitive to the food additive MSG.

Dosage: Some suggest 250 to 500 mg/day, though Leon Chaitow recommends 1 to 3 g/day. The precursor N-acetyl-cysteine has been proven a more potent source of glutathione, but the exact dosage needed has not yet been determined. It may be more effective to consume the three amino acids and allow the body to manufacture glutathione on its own, rather than taking supplements.

HISTIDINE

AKA: L-histidine.
Effects: Histadine is converted by

the body into the neurotransmitter histamine, which plays a role in smooth muscle function and the dilation and contraction of blood vessels. It removes heavy metals from the body, helps protect nerves by maintaining the myelin sheath, and helps protect against radiation damage. Additionally, it promotes the manufacture of both red and white blood cells. It has been used in the treatment of rheumatoid arthritis, poor sexual arousal, ulcers in the digestive tract, and nausea during pregnancy.

A deficiency can lead to partial or total deafness and one form of schizophrenia (sufferers are referred to as histapenics).

Precautions: Histidine should not be used by manic-depressives with elevated levels of histamine or by women suffering from premenstrual depression. Whereas a deficiency can lead to one form of schizophrenia, an overdose can lead to another form (sufferers are referred to as histadelics; in some cases, methionine can decrease the level of histamine). Excessive histadine intake in males can lead to premature ejaculation, which can be countered with a supplementation of 500 mg of methionine, 500 mg of magnesium, and 50 mg of vitamin B-6. Dosages of over 4 g/day in women can trigger menstruation.

Dosage: Between 1 to 6 g/day with vitamin C.

L-PROLYL L-LEUCYL GLYCINE AMIDE

A tripeptide formed by three amino acids linked together.

Effects: It has been found to enhance learning.

METHIONINE

AKA: L-methionine.

A sulfur-containing amino acid.

Food sources: Found only in animal foods such as eggs, fish (all kinds), liver, meat (all kinds), milk, and poultry (all kinds).

Effects: Methionin is an antioxidant that is also said to protect against the accumulation of chemicals and heavy metals (e.g., cadmium, mercury) in the brain and body, play a key part in the production of the brain neurotransmitter choline (not to mention adrenaline, lecithin, and vitamin B12), prevent fat from getting into the arteries and liver, render selenium available to the body, and play an important role in the biosynthesis of two other amino acids — cysteine and taurine. Methionine is believed to relieve some cases of schizophrenia by lowering the level of histamine in the blood, and has been useful in the treatment of arthritis, cataracts, high cholesterol, chronic pain, asthma, allergies, and some cases of Parkinson's disease. It may help protect the liver against damage from carbon tetrachloride, and prevent certain tumors when used in combination with choline and folic acid.

Deficiency symptoms include bad skin tone, loss of hair, a buildup of toxic wastes in the body and fat in the liver, anemia, impeded protein synthesis, and atherosclerosis.

Selenomethionine is a variant in which selenium atoms replace the sulfur atoms.

Precautions: Methionine should always be taken with B-6 — to prevent an excess of homocysteine — and magnesium. Capsules are preferable to other forms because they avoid the rotten egg smell that usually accompanies it.

One study suggests that methionine might be destroyed by excessive alcohol consumption.

Dosage: 100 to 250 mg/day. Leon Chaitow, N.D., D.O., recommends 200 to 1000 mg/ day with vitamin B-6 and magnesium; Sheldon Saul Hendler, M.D., Ph.D., advises against supplementation.

PHENYLALANINE

AKA: DL-phenylalanine (DLPA), D-phenylalanine, L-phenylalanine.

Phenylalanine helps create the neurotransmitters, chiefly norepinephrine, epinephrine (or adrenalin), and dopamine, that produce mental arousal, alertness, and a better emotional state. It is often used by those attending raves.

Food sources: Almonds, aspartame (NutraSweet), beef, black beans, chicken, cottage cheese, dairy products, eggs, fish, lima beans, milk, nuts, peanuts, pumpkin and sesame seeds, soybeans, sunflower seeds, watercress. Plants contain mostly the "D" form, while animal proteins contain mostly the "L" form.

Effects: Phenylalanine may contribute to a more positive mental state, alertness, more motivation and ambition, more energy, an increase in learning ability, better memory, and an increased ability to focus and pay attention. (Leon Chaitow, N.D., D.O., claims only the "D" form produces these beneficial results, while Mark Mayell claims that the "L" form stimulates the nervous system and libido, enhances mood and cognition, and suppresses the appetite, whereas the "D" form elevates mood and enhances memory, and DLPA combines the effects of both.) It may help counter jet lag when taken first thing in the morning or right after a long flight, as it helps regulate the body's biological clock. It is believed that DLPA activates the morphine-like endorphins in the body, hormones which act as painkillers.

One study has shown that a significant percentage of individuals suffering from depression exhibited rapid improvements in mood when given 500 mg/day of L-phenylalanine (which was gradually increased to 3 to 4 g/day), along with 100 to 200 mg a day of vitamin B-6 to facilitate the effects of the amino acid. Another study showed significant improvements in those with depression when 250 mg of L-phenylalanine was combined with 5 to 10 mg of Eldepryl. In combination with B-6, it produces the compound phenylethylamine (PEA), which may elevate mood based on its action as a neurotransmitter. There is some evidence that, in combination with other substances, phenylalanine can help suppress addictive behavior and cravings, but there is no evidence that it suppresses appetite or enhances the libido.

A deficiency can result in mood swings, weight gain, and problems with blood circulation.

Precautions: It should not be taken by those with pigmented malignant melanoma cancer, phenylketonuria (or PKU, a genetic metabolic disorder), psychosis, or Wilson's disease (otherwise known as hepatolenticular degeneration, a rare hereditary disease chiefly characterized by a toxic buildup of copper in the organs and tissues of the body). Likewise, those taking MAO-inhibitor drugs should avoid phenylalanine, as should pregnant or lactating women. Early studies seem to indicate that phenylalanine and tyrosine encourage the growth of melanomas (or skin cancers, one of the deadliest forms of cancer), and doctors usually have patients restrict their intake of these amino acids. Those with high blood pressure should only take it under the guidance of a health professional.

Some warn that the daily dosage should not exceed 2.4 grams a day. Too much phenylalanine can result in over-stimulation, nervousness, heart palpitations, high blood pressure, and irritability; if taken later in the day, it may cause insomnia. Mayell says these symptoms only occur with the "L" form, and can be avoided by reducing the dosage, switching to DLPA, or taking it only in the morning. Other symptoms include headaches and nausea.

Dosage: The RDA has not been established. It is recommended that both "D" and "L" forms be used, especially in the treatment of depression or for increased energy. A dose of 1000 to 1500 mg of DLPA may be taken in the morning without food; a second dose may be taken later in the day, this time with 100 mg of B-6, 500 mg of vitamin C, and some fruit or fruit juice to help convert the amino acid to norepinephrine. Hendler, M.D., Ph.D., recommends no more than 1.5 g/day, with 20 to 30 mg/day of vitamin B-6 (not to exceed more than 50 mg/ day). Mayell advocates a more modest dose of 375 to 500 mg of the "L" form or 750 to 1000 mg of DLPA, first thing in the morning and at least 30 minutes before breakfast.

PYROGLUTAMATE

AKA: Adjuvant, Alpha-aminoglutaric acid lactam, Amino Mass, Arginine Pidolate, arginine pyroglutamate, Deep Thought, glutamic acid lactam, glutimic acid, glutiminic acid, Mental Edge, PCA, Piraglutargine, pyroGlu, pyroglutamic acid, pyrrolidon carboxylic acid, 2-oxo-pyrrolidon carboxylic acid.

Pyroglutamate is able to cross the blood/brain barrier, and is found in significant amounts in the brain, the cerebrospinal fluid, and blood. It is used to make various nootropic drugs such as piracetam and oxiracetam. Similar in effect to piracetam, though not as strong.

Food sources: Dairy products, fruits, meats, vegetables.

Effects: Pyroglutamate improves memory, alertness, concentration, and learning, and reduces anxiety and depression. Arginine pyroglutamate also increases muscle mass by stimulating the growth hormone.

Works synergistically with choline, DMAE, and other acetylcholine-enhancing nutrients.

Precautions: None known.

Dosage: 500 to 1000 mg/day for arginine pyroglutamate; a bit less for plain pyroglutamate.

TAURINE

AKA: L-taurine.

Food sources: Eggs, fish (all kinds), lamb, meat (all kinds), milk, pork, shellfish. Though it is not found in any plant foods, it can be manufactured in the human body from cysteine. High levels are found in human milk, but not cow's milk.

Effects: An electrical-charge stabilizer in the nerves of the brain and nervous system (it can decrease or even prevent epileptic seizures, and may even prove beneficial in other brain disorders such as Huntington's chorea), it is important for muscle function, and plays a role in the manufacture of the neurotransmitter glutamate. It is said to help the heart function better by conserving potassium and calcium, and help regulate insulin and blood sugar levels. Since taurine controls the synthesis of glutamate, it acts as a depressant. It may be necessary for proper growth of the human body. Women require taurine more than men because its synthesis is inhibited by the female hormone estradiol.

Taurine has been used in the treatment of congestive heart failure, atherosclerosis, stress, eye problems, immune function disorders, gall bladder disease, and some types of epilepsy, and it may be of some benefit in treating cystic fibrosis.

Individuals deprived of full-spectrum light may suffer a deficiency of taurine in the pineal and pituitary glands, leading to depression and mental impairment. Eye problems may result if a zinc deficiency is also present.

Precautions: There is good evidence that taurine is a central nervous system depressant and that it can impair short-term memory, so supplementation is not advised.

Dosage: 100 to 500 mg/day. Sheldon Saul Hendler, M.D., Ph.D., advises against supplementation.

TRYPTOPHAN

AKA: L-tryptophan.

Food sources: Bananas, unripened cheese, chicken, chicken liver, cottage cheese, evening primrose seeds, fish, lentils, meat, milk, peanuts, pineapple, pumpkin seeds, seaweed, soybeans and soybean products, spirulina, sunflower seeds, turkey, yogurt.

Effects: Tryptophan is necessary for the manufacture of the neurotransmitter serotonin, which regulates mood and sleep patterns. It has proven helpful in the treatment of jet lag, depression, binge eating, obsessive-compulsive disorder, some forms of vascular migraines, panic attacks (when taken with vitamin B-6), and chronic pain, and may help in cases of rheumatoid arthritis and tardive dyskinesia.

A deficiency may be characterized by insomnia, mental disturbances (particularly aggressive behavior), depression, bad skin color and tone, brittle fingernails, indigestion, and a craving for carbohydrates.

Precautions: It forms a harmful interaction when combined with MAO-inhibitor drugs or tricyclics, as it intensifies the side effects of these drugs. Because there are rare cases where tryptophan can cause excitability and insomnia, those who experience such symptoms should cease taking it immediately. It may be harmful to pregnant women, and may worsen the symptoms of bronchial asthma and lupus.

Side effects may include nausea, headaches, gastric discomfort, and constipation. Specific tryptophan metabolites could cause bladder cancer. If the level of tryptophan is high in relation to the other amino acids, fatigue may result. It is not recommended that more than 2 grams a day be taken; nausea and vomiting are likely to occur in doses used to treat depression (6 to 9 grams and higher), though some studies have given subjects as much as 15 grams a day with no serious consequences. Scientists have still not unraveled the complicated process by which tryptophan is converted into serotonin, and some question whether oral doses are effective in this regard.

In 1989, some 5,000 people suffered

debilitating health problems from impurities in a batch of L-tryptophan distributed by Showa Denko, a Japanese firm that did not specialize in drugs or nutritional supplements; 36 of them died and many more were left permanently crippled. As a result, the sale of L-tryptophan supplements was banned in 1990. The FDA contends that the illness suffered by these victims, a blood disease called eosinophilia-myalgia syndrome (EMS), and related illnesses are attributable to L-tryptophan itself. Cases have also been reported for uncontaminated batches and for the similar compound L-5-hydroxytryptophan, but many experts dispute the validity of these reports.

Dosage: For the cure of insomnia, Dr. Stuart Berger recommends 2 grams of tryptophan, 100 mg of vitamin B-6, and 1 gram of vitamin C on an empty stomach before going to bed, though some research indicates that 1 gram of tryptophan may be sufficient for most people (this applies only to late at night; to sleep during the day, the need for tryptophan will be higher); some supplemental B-3 (in a ratio of two parts tryptophan to one part B-3) and magnesium may also be helpful. High-tryptophan foods should be combined with carbohydrate-rich foods such as bread, pasta, or potatoes for best results. Proteins inhibit the brain's ability to absorb this amino acid. Eating sugary snacks can cause wild swings in insulin production and interfere with the body's ability to absorb tryptophan.

TYROSINE

AKA: L-tyrosine.

Food sources: Fish, particularly shellfish.

Effects: Boosts the brain neurotransmitters epinephrine (adrenaline), norepinephrine (noradrenaline), and dopamine, though the mental stimulation only occurs if the brain has used up these neurotransmitters. Elevates mood and energy (it has been effective in treating patients with depression), improves reaction time, alertness, attention, and motivation. It may help protect the liver from damage due to carbon tetrachloride, and has been used to treat stress, PMS, cocaine abuse, hay fever, grass allergies, Parkinson's disease, and cases of uni-polar depression (i.e., unaccompanied by a manic phase) that do not respond to tryptophan.

Precautions: The fish or shellfish should be baked, broiled, grilled, steamed, or stewed, as fat and deep-frying destroys some of the beneficial effects. For best results, eat fish alone or with carbohydrate-rich foods (e.g., bread, potatoes).

Because it might increase blood pressure in a small percentage of susceptible individuals, those with high blood pressure should take it only under the guidance of a physician. Those taking MAO-inhibiting anti-depressants should not take tyrosine supplements, as they can have adverse effects on blood pressure, as well as other serious consequences. Tyrosine should not be taken by anyone with melanoma. It could also trigger headaches in those already susceptible.

Supplements should be taken with vitamins B-6 and C, as the brain needs these to turn the amino acid into norepinephrine. Supplements can create mild gastric problems if taken on an empty stomach. High doses can cause irritability, anxiety, and heart palpitations.

Dosage: The RDA has not been established. Three to four ounces of fish seems to be the optimal amount for most people; eating more will not result in any significant increase in effect. Leon Chaitow, N.D., D.O., recommends 100 mg per kilo of body weight per day; a dosage of 6 g/day in three divided doses for a two week period is recommended for the treatment of depression. Mark Mayell recommends that dosage not exceed 2 to 3 g/day (initial dosage should be 250 to 500 mg/day, working up to 750 mg twice a day until effects are noticed), that it be taken on an empty stomach, that it not be combined with other amino acids, and that it be taken with 25 mg/day of vitamin B-6 or B complex and 250 to 500 mg of vitamin C.

VALINE

AKA: L-valine.

Effects: Normalizes the nitrogen balance in the body and it is necessary for proper mental and neural functioning, and for muscle coordination.

One study funded by the National Institutes of Health has found that, in combination with leucine and isoleucine — two other branched-chain amino acids — Valine has shown promise as a treatment for amyotropic lateral sclerosis (ALS), or Lou Gehrig's disease. Subjects given these amino acids over the course of a year retained more of their muscle strength and ability to walk than those given a placebo, a result which may have been due in part to leucine and isoleucine's assistance in the breakdown of glutamate; valine was added because of a deficiency noted in the blood and cerebrospinal fluid of ALS patients. This combination also may prevent, and even reverse, liver damage resulting from alcoholism. Positive results have been recorded in the treatment of hepatic encephalopathy, chronic liver disease, and muscle atrophy in chronic heavy drinkers.

Deficiency symptoms include nervousness, disrupted sleep patterns and mental functioning, and a nitrogen imbalance in the body.

Precautions: An overdose can lead to feelings of "crawling skin" and hallucinations. Any physical or mental benefits of supplementation by healthy individuals is unproven.

Dosage: 1 g/day. According to Leon Chaitow, N.D., D.O., it should be taken with the following amino acids in these proportions: one part tryptophan, two parts valine, two parts methionine, and three parts phenylalanine.

CHAPTER 5

Lipids

Lipids are fats and fat soluble compounds, and this category can encompass a variety of essential nutrients, including the fat soluble vitamins, various steroid hormones, cholesterol, and the different dietary fats.

AL721

AKA: Egg lecithin.

An extract of egg yolk, AL721 is seven parts neutral lipids, two parts phosphatidylcholine, and one part phosphatidylethanolamine.

Effects: Lecithin from egg yolk is said to improve thinking, but reports of improved mental abilities specifically from AL721 are only anecdotal. It shows some promise in enhancing the immune system and in the treatment of herpes, AIDS, drug addiction, and alcohol dependency.

Precautions: It should not be taken by those suffering from manic-depression, because it may deepen the depressive phase.

Dosage: 2 to 10 g/day is considered a sufficient dose, though it should be taken with 1 g/day of vitamin B-5.

CHOLINE AND LECITHIN

Choline, classified as a B vitamin, is a precursor to acetylcholine, an important neurotransmitter that aids memory, learning, and mental alertness, and is necessary in maintaining cell membrane fluidity. It works with inositol to emulsify fats and cholesterol, and seems to have a synergistic effect with nootropic drugs. Choline can be manufactured by the body from folic acid, B-12, and methionine, and both choline and inositol are components of lecithin, a fat-like compound which destroys fats such as cholesterol. There are at least three different forms of choline—choline bitartrate, choline chloride, and phosphatidylcholine (or pure lecithin)—all of which may enhance memory, though phosphatidylcholine is a necessary component of every cell membrane in the body and is believed to have the best memory-boosting effect.

Food Sources: Very little free choline is found in foods, most of what we get being in the form of lecithin: beans, Brazil nuts, brewer's yeast, cabbage, cauliflower, cheese, dandelion flowers, egg yolks, fenugreek, fish, liver, meat, peanuts, peas, poppyseeds, seed oils, soybeans, green leafy vegetables, and wheat germ. Soybean oil is the best source, containing 2 percent lecithin and supplying both essential fatty acids (Omega-3 [9 percent] and Omega-6 [57 percent]), unlike most other oils, which only supply Omega-6.

Effects: Reportedly improves memory in healthy people. One study found that MIT students showed a greater ability to recall a list of words after taking 3 grams a day; in fact, an improved memory can usually result after only a few days of taking choline or lecithin. Though Alzheimer's patients suffer from a deficiency of acetylcholine in the brain, attempts to reverse the symptoms (loss of memory, judgment, and orientation, for example) with supplements of phosphatidylcholine or choline have proved disappointing. Both have been shown to be effective treatments for bipolar disorder (manic-depression) in those individuals who have shown little or no improvement with standard drugs such as lithium.

Both choline and phosphatidylcholine have the same effects, and both also emulsify cholesterol, lowering the blood cholesterol level, though choline needs inositol (another B-complex vitamin) to achieve this. Choline and inositol also maximize the efficiency of vitamin E. There is no definitive evidence that either choline or phosphatidylcholine protect against cardiovascular disease. They have been used to effectively treat tardive dyskinesia, but results have proven inconclusive in treating such other neurological disorders as Parkinson's disease, Huntington's disease, Tourette's syndrome, and Friedreich's ataxia. Some studies have shown that phosphatidylcholine is effective against viral hepatitis types A, B, and C, and chronic hepatitis, but only when it is accompanied by unsaturated fatty acids; phosphatidylcholine with unsaturated fatty acids may also play an anti-aging role by keeping cell membranes fluid, as a decrease in phosphatidylcholine and an increase in cholesterol as a consequence of aging makes these membranes more rigid. It is this same imbalance of the two that creates gallstones, and it is believed that supplementation may prevent such stones from forming, though this has yet to be proven.

Deficiency may lead to high cholesterol, high blood pressure, certain types of cardiac problems, skin problems such as psoriasis, low tolerance of fats in the diet, cirrhosis and fatty degeneration of the liver, hardening of the arteries, gastric ulcers, gall stones, liver disease, memory deficits, and Alzheimer's disease.

Precautions: Choline should not be taken by those who are manic-depressive, as it may worsen the depression (even those who aren't manic-depressive may experience depression if taking doses in the range of 20 grams a day), nor should it be taken by those with

Parkinson's disease, epilepsy, or those taking prescription anticholinergic drugs. Those with gastric ulcers or a history of ulcers should only take choline under a doctor's orders.

Certain forms of choline, such as choline bitartrate and choline chloride can cause a fishy body odor and diarrhea, especially if more than 16 grams a day are taken. The body odor and diarrhea are often the result of intestinal bacteria breaking down the choline into trimethylamine (though liver disease may also be a cause), and may be prevented by eating yogurt, eating a high-fiber diet, or drinking acidophilus milk. Other overdose symptoms include nausea, vomiting, and dizziness. Choline can also cause muscle tension, a stiff neck, headaches, restlessness, insomnia, and gastric cramps. Lecithin may not cause these, but it does have two significant drawbacks — the supplements sold in health food stores usually have lots of fat, and they can usually peroxidize (go rancid) quite easily. Peroxidized fats in lecithin can damage DNA, impair the immune system, and cause atherosclerosis, cancer, and abnormal blood clots.

Very high doses of choline over an extended period of time may produce a vitamin B-6 deficiency. There is no known toxicity level for choline.

Choline and lecithin can be destroyed by alcohol, estrogen, food processing, refined flour, refined sugar, sulfa drugs, and water. Consuming large amounts of caffeine (coffee, tea, soft drinks) can deplete the amount of inositol in the body.

Choline may interact with antidepressant drugs and morphine.

Dosage: Phosphatidylcholine is more beneficial when consumed in foods that have polyunsaturated fatty acids (e.g., soybeans and soybean products, cauliflower, cabbage) than in foods that are high in saturated fatty acids (e.g., egg yolk, meat, and other animal products). The intake of phosphatidylcholine by the average American is 3.1 g/day, or 300 mg of choline; this is higher than that consumed by Europeans, but may still be too low, according to some. The RDAs of both have not been established, and much research needs to be done in this area. Recommended dosage is 2.5 to 3 g/day in three to four divided doses; other B vitamins, including 1 gram of B-5, should be taken with any form of choline or lecithin to help convert them to acetylcholine. Sheldon Saul Hendler, M.D., Ph.D., states that up to 10 g/day of phosphatidylcholine or 1 g/day of choline can be taken without side effects. If taking lecithin, a supplement of chelated calcium should also be taken to keep a stable balance of phosphorus and calcium in the body. Dharma Singh Khalsa, M.D., also recommends taking DMAE with lecithin, despite the fact that it may be too stimulating for some people. Lecithin has a time-release effect, so it is only necessary to take it twice a day, though the dose may have to be larger, as most supplements only contain 10 to 20 percent phosphatidylcholine (look for supplements that contain at least 35 percent phosphatidylcholine).

DHA

AKA: Docosohexaenoic acid.

A polyunsaturated fat that is the main structural fatty acid in the brain's gray matter, it is mainly found in fish oils.

Food Sources (in descending order

of total beneficial fish oils): Herring, salmon, bluefish, tuna, cod, shrimp, flounder, swordfish.

Effects: An important component in the development of vision, and necessary for the transmission of messages via the nervous system throughout the body. It can also protect against cardiovascular disease, arthritis, and possibly cancer, and may prove to be useful in treating kidney disease.

Precautions: It lacks sufficient vitamin E to prevent it from rapidly peroxidizing, or going rancid. Supplements should be used only under a physician's guidance by those who have a tendency to hemorrhage or bleed easily, as it can reduce the ability of the blood to clot, or by diabetics, as it can increase blood sugar and decrease insulin secretion in the body. Taking very high doses could also result in hemorrhaging in normal individuals. The need for vitamin E may increase as a person's intake of DHA increases.

Dosage: Sheldon Saul Hendler, M.D., Ph.D., does not recommend taking supplements, except for those with hypertension, ischemic heart disease or any other condition that could lead to health-threatening clotting of the blood, rheumatoid arthritis or related inflammation, or psoriasis; in these cases, he recommends 2 to 4 g/day under a doctor's supervision. It is best utilized when combined with eicosopentaenoic acid (EPA), another fish oil fatty acid, and taken with adequate amounts of vitamin E and selenium.

FATS AND OILS

The largest number of fat cells in the body are found in the brain, where they make up 60 percent of the total brain mass. The body manufactures all the fats it needs, except for two— alpha-linolenic acid (also known as Omega-3 or Alena, short for *alpha-linolenic acid*), and linoleic acid (also known as Omega-6 or CLA, short for conjugated linoleic acid), which are called the essential fatty acids (EFAs). There are different types of Omega-3 fatty acids, including eicosapentaenoic acid or EPA (found in fish oil), gamma-linolenic acid (found in borage seed and primrose oil), docosahexaenoic acid (DHA), and docosapentaenoic acid (DPA).

Unfortunately, the most important EFA, Omega-3, is the one people are most deficient in, and this can lead to such chronic degenerative diseases as cancer, heart disease, high blood pressure, and strokes. Lack of it can also lead to decreased mental functioning. The reason for this lack is threefold: the introduction of white flour, which removes important vitamins, minerals, and fiber; the consumption of beef as the main source of protein; and the processing (or hydrogenation) of vegetable oils. The kinds of fats commonly ingested, from those in beef to hydrogenated oils, don't do much good and, in the case of hydrogenated fats and oils, can even be toxic to the brain. Hydrogenated fats are known to increase levels of cholesterol and triglycerides in the body, leading to heart disease, heart attacks, and stroke.

While hydrogenated fats (also known as trans fats or trans fatty acids) are harmful because they are processed, natural and unprocessed fats and oils can be harmful, too. In addition to being classified as essential or non-essential, they can be categorized according to their degree of saturation. There are three basic types: saturated, polyunsaturated, and monounsaturated. Saturated forms, such as butter and animal fats, can contribute to cancer, cholesterol buildup, heart disease, and other degenerative illnesses. These fats compete with and slow down those metabolic processes dealing with the essential fatty acids, depriving cells of nutrients and prohibiting the evacuation of toxins, eventually leading to cells that are malnourished and loaded with toxins; when this happens, the results are poor thinking, memory loss, cardiovascular problems, and an overall loss of health. Polyunsaturated forms such as safflower oil, soy oil, and sunflower oil oxidate and turn bad quickly, particularly when heated and exposed to air. Monounsaturated oils like high oleic safflower, high oleic sunflower, olive, peanut, and sesame oils are more stable and less likely to oxidize. In general, cold-climate oils are more beneficial than warm-climate oils.

Food Sources: Eel and cold-water fish such as herring, mackerel, salmon, sardines, trout, and tuna (albacore and bluefin) are good sources of Omega-3, as is linseed oil, flaxseed oil, soybeans, tofu, walnuts, eggs, red meat, and animal organs. Primrose oil is a good source of Omega-6.

Effects: Since damage to fats is central to biological aging, eating good fats is important to developing and maintaining the healthy brain. Four grams a day of Omega-3 reduce cholesterol and blood pressure, and as little as two servings of fish a week may protect against heart disease. Omega-3 can also protect against rheumatoid arthritis by suppressing the prostaglandins and leukotrienes in the body that produce the symptoms of this affliction. One study has shown that subjects given fish oil

with 50 percent docosahexaenoic acid — or about four times as much as is normally present — showed a significant decrease in aggression.

A deficiency of Omega-3 seems to be associated with behavior, learning, and health problems (e.g., neuropathy). Other symptoms include thirst, frequent urination, and dry skin. A deficiency of Omega-6 seems to be associated with colds and increased use of antibiotics. An imbalance of these two fatty acids is said by some to be associated with cancer, heart disease, diabetes, arthritis, and obesity.

Precautions: Determine intake of Omega-3 and Omega-6 and reduce fat intake, particularly saturated fats, as eating a lot of fish cannot counteract a high-fat diet. Remove all partially hydrogenated fats from the diet and use cooking oils only once. Never deep-fry (avoid eating at fast-food restaurants). Use oils such as olive (especially extra virgin olive oil, as it is the most natural type), canola, high oleic sunflower, and high oleic safflower when quick-frying, and butter when sautéing; use butter or monounsaturated oil for baking. For salad dressings, use only unfiltered, expeller-pressed vegetable oils, and then only sparingly. Don't cook with polyunsaturated oils; they should only be used in salads and other uncooked foods. Keep oil in the refrigerator after opening; don't heat oil until it smokes, as it is highly carcinogenic. If an oil is rancid or smells bad, don't use it. Fish from fast-food restaurants are no good, being white fish cooked in unhealthy fats and almost completely depleted of Omega-3. Be aware that cultured or pond-reared freshwater fish, such as much of the white fish sold in the U.S., may have very little Omega-3 (they may also be high in pesticides and such industrial chemicals as PCBs). Diets heavy in highly unsaturated Omega-3 oils should be supplemented with anti-oxidants (vitamin C, vitamin E, selenium, beta-carotene), as Omega-3 is easily destroyed by light, oxygen, and high temperature.

Diabetics should avoid taking fish oil capsules; they can raise blood sugar and lower insulin secretion, worsening their condition. Taking too much Omega-3 in capsule form may overstimulate the prostaglandins, harming the body. It can also prevent the normal clotting of blood. Fish oil capsules are high in cholesterol, and those that aren't may contribute to cell-destroying lipid peroxidation. Additionally, other substances in fish may contribute to Omega-3's beneficial effects and may not be present in fish oil capsules. Because they could cause excessive bleeding, fish oil supplements should be stopped about two weeks before surgery. Avoid cod liver oil, which has high concentrations of vitamins A and D, fat-soluble vitamins that can easily build up to toxic levels in the body.

The effects of Omega-3 in flaxseed is assumed to have the same effects as the Omega-3 in fish, even though research has been conducted almost exclusively on fish oil and the results extrapolated to flaxseed, and even though the aphpalinolenic acid in fish oil is already converted to eicosapentaenoic acid (EPA) and docosahexaenoic acid (DHA) while that in flaxseed oil has to be converted in the body. A significant number of people, especially when ill, have a limited capacity to biochemically convert the flaxseed oil. Still, flaxseed oil has one hundred times the level of lignans, or beneficial compounds, of other plant foods, and it has been used to treat lupus, high cholesterol and other cardiovascular diseases, allergic and inflammatory conditions (e.g., psoriasis, eczema), and autoimmune diseases (e.g., multiple sclerosis, rheumatoid arthritis, cancer).

Omega-3 oil supplement should meet the following requirements: it should be in a black plastic bottle so as to prevent exposure to light (brown glass is unacceptable, as it still allows certain wavelengths of light to enter), and the bottle should have both a pressing date and a four-month expiration date; it needs to be refrigerated at all times when not in use; and it should have some color to it, as clear and colorless oils have most likely been deodorized and bleached.

Dosage: 3 or 4 ounces of fish. When taking flaxseed oil, take one tablespoon twice a day, and with fish oil capsules, it is recommended that no more than 5 g/day be taken. Dr. Donald Rudin recommends one teaspoon of linseed oil (about 2 grams of Omega-3 fatty acids) as a minimum daily requirement to correct any nutritional deficiency. Those with serious degenerative diseases might need more, but should take higher doses only under the guidance of a qualified health professional.

LIPOTROPES

Lipotropes are substances attracted to fat, the four most important being choline, folic acid, methionine, and vitamin B-12.

Effects: They play an important role in the synthesis of phosphatidylcholine, prevent the accumulation of fat in the liver, and are necessary for DNA synthesis, maintaining immunity, and preventing cancer.

Cytidine diphosphate choline (CDP-choline) and S-adenosylmethionine (SAM) are the active forms of choline and methionine. CDP-choline is used in Japan and Italy to stimulate brain circulation following brain injury or brain surgery, and to treat Alzheimer's disease, severe depression, Parkinson's disease, and similar degenerative brain disorders. Though the exact mechanism by which it works is unknown, it is believed to increase the blood flow and the utilization of oxygen in the brain. One of the forms, SAM, is being investigated as a treatment for depression, fibromyalgia, and osteoarthritis.

Precautions: CDP-choline can cause agitation, dizziness, headaches, nausea, and loss of blood pressure. As yet, SAM has no known side effects.

PHOSPHATIDYLSERINE

AKA: LECI-PS, PS.

One of the four main phospholipids found in lecithin; the others are phosphatidylcholine (PC), phosphatidylethanolamine (PE), and phosphatidylinositol (PI). All are vital components of cell membranes. Phosphatidylserine has its highest concentration in the brain, where it plays a role in various nerve cell functions. It has proven superior to ginkgo biloba and other herbs in its benefits.

Food sources: Fish, rice, soy products, green leafy vegetables.

Effects: It improves brain functioning in all areas measured: the functioning of nerve cells, electrical activity in the brain, the ability to handle stress, daily hormone rhythms, memory, learning, concentration, vocabulary skills, mood, alertness, and sociability. It has been used effectively in the treatment of people both in the early stages of Alzheimer's and in severe cases.

Precautions: No known side effects.

Dosage: 100 to 200 mg/day to be taken with meals. It should not be taken too late in the evening. A PS "complex" may only be 20 percent pure PS, and so the dosage should be adjusted accordingly.

CHAPTER 6

Nucleic Acids

Nucleic acids are large molecules which contain genetic material.

OROTIC AND INOSINIC ACIDS

AKA (inosinic acid): Hypoxanthine riboside, inosine.

Effects: Orotic acid is a possible B vitamin and is a precursor of the pyrimidines, which help manufacture nucleotides and nucleosides. Both orotic and inosinic acids are converted by the body into DNA. A few Russian studies have shown that they may be helpful in treating hearts damaged by heart attacks, congestive heart failure, and cholesterol, but much more research needs to be done. Inosinic acid promotes the dilation of blood vessels — increasing blood flow and oxygen delivery in the body — and increases both RNA and DNA production. Athletes use inosinic acid to stimulate protein synthesis in muscle cells, presumably building muscle mass.

Precautions: According to W. Nathaniel Phillips, dosages higher than 2 grams a day degrade into uric acid, which can cause joint pain and kidney stones after prolonged use. Those with kidney disease or other kidney problems should avoid using this supplement.

Dosage: Phillips recommends 1.5 to 2 g/day an hour before workouts or training, but only for athletes whose training sessions are long and rigorous. Sheldon Saul Hendler, M.D., Ph.D., does not recommend supplementation.

RIBONUCLEIC ACID

AKA: Ampligen, Poly (A)/Poly (U), Poly (I,C), RNA.

Levels of RNA decrease starting at age 40, along with its resistance to misprogramming of the genetic code caused by the by-products of lipid peroxidation.

Food sources: Brewer's yeast, sardines.

Effects: Has improved memory in lab animals and protects against oxidizing chemicals contributing to aging, thereby slowing the deterioration seen in older people. It has increased the life span of lab rats by 20 percent, increased immunity to bacterial and fungal infections in humans, and may have anti-cancer properties.

Poly (A)/Poly (U) and Poly (I,C) are two synthetic polyribonucleotides that have shown promise as anti-cancer treatments, particularly in regard to breast cancer.

Precautions: It should not be taken by those with gout or high urate levels, as it produces large amounts of uric acid, the cause of gout (the uric acids forms crystals in the joints and kidneys, resulting in extreme pain and permanent damage to the body). Its acidity can also cause upset stomach, possibly prevented with the ingestion of baking soda with the supplements.

Yeast can be 6 to 10 percent RNA but does little good because the cell walls of the plant cannot be digested to any significant extent by the body. Any supplement with less than 12 percent RNA is also of limited value, as it, too, can have too little RNA to have any effect.

Dosage: No side effects have been reported for normal people given up to 80 g/day. Sheldon Saul Hendler, M.D., Ph.D., recommends taking up to 1.5 g/day, or about one tablespoon of brewer's yeast.

CHAPTER 7

Miscellaneous Nutrients

ACETYL-L-CARNITINE

AKA: ALC, Alcar, carnitine, Carnitor, D-carnitine, DL-carnitine, L-carnitine, levocarnitine, N-acetyl-l-carnitine, ProXeed, VitaCarn.

Though a nutrient, ALC belongs neither to the vitamin nor the amino acid category. It is chemically similar to carnitine but is more efficient. While it is synthesized by the liver from lysine and methionine, adequate amounts of vitamins C, B-3, and B-6, plus iron, lysine, and methionine are needed in the diet for this to occur, and men run a greater risk of deficiency than women. There are two forms of carnitine: L-carnitine and D-carnitine, the former being the biologically active form and the latter being the inactive form which may counteract L-carnitine's benefits.

Food Sources: Meat, milk and dairy products. The amount of carnitine in meat is in direct proportion to the redness of the meat.

Effects: Chemically related to choline, ALC has many of the same effects. It acts as an anti-oxidant; increases the levels of choline acetyltransferase in the brain; transports fats into the mitochondria, the part of the cell which creates energy; enhances communication between the brain's hemispheres; reduces triglyceride levels and removes ketones (fat waste products) from the blood; helps control hypoglycemia; alleviates angina attacks; and has been used in the treatment of diabetes, infertility, liver disease, and kidney disease. It may help fight cancer by boosting the effect of lymphocytes, white blood cells that serve the immune system. It also slows down the cell damage caused by age-related conditions and may accelerate the repair of damaged DNA in cells ravaged by free radicals. It may help protect the brain from the effects of aging by preventing the accumulation of lipofuscin in the brain. Studies have shown that doses of anywhere from 2000 to 3500 mg a day can slow the onset of Alzheimer's and mental deterioration, specifically memory, attention, language ability, alertness, motor activities, and spatial abilities, though it may take up to six months to begin to work. Long-chain acetylcarnitines (LCACs) work counter to ALC, preventing the transportation of fats to the mitochondria and suppressing membrane enzymes.

It works synergistically with phophatidylserine.

A deficiency can cause damage to heart tissue, muscle weakness, extreme confusion, angina, and male infertility.

Precautions: Those with kidney damage should use supplements with extreme caution.

It may cause gastrointestinal disorders and a change in body odor, which can be reduced or eliminated with lower dosages. Less frequent side effects include diarrhea, abdominal pain, nausea, and vomiting. Overdosing can produce severe muscle weakness, though some have experienced only mild diarrhea with doses as high as 26,000 mg a day.

"Vitamin B-T" supplements contain dextro-carnitine as well, which cancels out the effectiveness of levocarnitine. Valproic acid, used in the treatment of epileptic seizures and manic-depression, will reduce the effect of L-carnitine.

ProXeed, a citrus-flavored drink mix containing two types of L-carnitine, is marketed as a cure for low sperm count, though experts point out that there are many causes of male infertility which carnitine does not cure.

Dosage: 1 to 3 g/day in two divided doses. At present, there is no RDA. Supplements should contain only L-carnitine, as DL-carnitine will cause some individuals to develop a myasthenia-type syndrome. According to Sheldon Saul Hendler, M.D., Ph.D., there is no evidence that supplements will benefit those whose levels are already normal, neither will it build muscle or protect against diabetes, kidney disease, or liver disease. At present, it is available in Europe, but not the U.S., and it can be very expensive.

COENZYME Q10

AKA: CoQ10, Ubiquinone.

Classified as a nonvitamin nutrient, CoEnzyme Q10 can be supplied by dietary means or from the body's own resources. The body can usually manufacture it from amino acids L-tyrosine and L-methionine. It is found in high amounts in the human heart and liver, the two organs in the body which need the most energy.

Food Sources: Beef, peanuts, polyunsaturated oils, sardines, seafood, and spinach all have significant amounts, with white albacore tuna packed in cans with spring water having the highest amount. It is also found in chicken, mackerel, monounsaturated oils, walnuts, and whole grains.

Effects: Helps manufacture ATP (used by the brain for energy), protects the cell membranes from free-radical damage, prevents cholesterol from sticking to arterial walls, prevents damage to tissues caused by hypoxia, increases the life span in lab animals up to 56 percent, helps cure some forms of gum disease, and protects against peroxidation (a means by which oxygen and unsaturated fats combine to form free radicals). In this last respect, it acts much the same way as vitamin E, but is superior in that, unlike E, it is not destroyed in the process. Interestingly, CoEnzyme Q10 may protect against or reverse some of the symptoms of vitamin E deficiency. Other effects include weight loss, stimulation of the immune system, improvement of athletic performance, decreased blood pressure, a lower incidence of heart disease, and improved mental abilities.

Works synergistically with the coenzyme NADH.

Deficiencies of CoEnzyme Q10 have been associated with cardiovascular disease, diabetes, muscular dystrophy, periodontal disease, and those undergoing tube feeding on a liquid intravenous diet (total parenteral nutrition).

Precautions: Can sometimes be metabolized by the body to create certain compounds that have damaging effects similar to those caused by free radicals; adequate amounts of anti-oxidant vitamins (beta-carotene, C, and E) should be able to prevent this, however. CoEnzyme Q10 should be yellow or orange in color; if not, it may contain fillers. High doses could cause overstimulation.

Drug use, exposure to cold, illnesses, physical activity, and stress can all drain the body's supply of this nutrient. Exercise, however, can increase levels. Some cholesterol-lowering drugs such as Lescol, Lipitor, Mevacor, Pravachol, and Zocor can also deplete levels of CoEnzyme Q10 in the body, and it is advisable to take supplements to counteract this; Joe and Theresa Graedon, Ph.D., say experts recommend between 50 to 150 mg a day.

Dosage: Optimal doses have not yet been determined, but research indicates that a range of 10 to 90 mg/day is safe and effective. Ward Dean, M.D., recommend 60 to 180 mg/day. Most supplements are in the 30 to 50 mg range. It is generally agreed that the liquid form in the soft gelatin capsule is better absorbed than the capsule form. CoEnzyme Q10 should be taken with oily or fatty foods (e.g., fish oil), as it is oil-soluble.

CYTOCHROMES

AKA: Cytochrome-C.

Cytochromes are a component of ATP production.

Effects: Said to increase energy and endurance.

Precautions: There is no evidence that supplementation produces any benefits.

IDEBENONE

AKA: Avan.

An anti-oxidant that is very similar to CoEnzyme Q10.

Effects: The same benefits as CoEnzyme Q10, without the hazard of metabolizing into free radicals.

Precautions: The few studies that have been conducted show no evident toxic side effects.

Dosage: 100 mg/day.

LIPOIC ACID

AKA: 1,2-dithiolane-3-pentanoic acid, alpha-lipoic acid, Alpha Lipotene, LA, thiotic acid.

A coenzyme.

Food Sources: Broccoli, carrots, heart, liver, meat, potatoes, spinach, tomatoes, yams.

Effects: A potent anti-oxidant which can regenerate other anti-oxidants, such as vitamins C and E, and form another anti-oxidant, dihydrolipoate, in cells. It is said to improve long-term memory by protecting brain cell membranes from damage by free radicals, insure that the two main enzymes that convert food into energy function properly, enhance the synthesis of glutathione, and, unlike other anti-oxidants, can attack free radicals in both the watery and fatty parts of the body. It produces a mild feeling of relaxation and well-being, plus a mild visual enhancement. It may also enhance the immune system and prevent atherosclerosis, and may prove helpful in treating diabetes, cataracts, brain and nerve degeneration, cardiovascular and cerebrovascular diseases, high cholesterol, infections (e.g., HIV), and cancer.

Precautions: Daily doses above 50 mg may result in gastrointestinal problems such as nausea and upset stomach, allergic skin reaction, and overstimulation. Very high doses may produce an abnormally low blood sugar.

Dosage: The body manufactures sufficient amounts on its own, though certain medical conditions may cause deficiencies. Ray Sahelian, M.D., recommends 10 to 50 mg/day. Allan Sosin, M.D., and Beth Ley Jacobs, Ph.D., recommend 50 to 100 mg/day and say that there are no serious side effects even in the 300 to 600 mg/day range used to treat diabetics.

OCTACOSANOL

Food Sources: Alfalfa, wheat germ, wheat germ oil, whole grains.

Octacosanol is one of several long-chain alcohol molecules found in wheat germ oil.

Effects: It is said to lower blood cholesterol, increase energy storage in muscle tissue, improve stamina and endurance, sharpen reflexes, help the body adjust to high altitudes, improve oxygen utilization, keep the body metabolism balanced under stress, and is an excellent source of vitamin E. It takes about three weeks before the effects are noticed.

Precautions: There is no scientific evidence to support any of its claims.

Dosage: Earl Mindell, R.Ph., Ph.D., recommends 1000 to 6000 mg/day.

SAPONINS

AKA: Triterpene glycosides.

Saponins are steroid-like chemicals connected to sugar molecules that occur naturally in plants. Saponins are only one of a class of nutrients called phytochemicals which are found in all fruits and vegetables, as well as legumes and whole grains. There are several thousand different phytochemicals, including lycopenes (found in tomatoes), genistein (found in soybeans), and flavonoids (found in citrus fruits).

Food Sources: Asparagus, bean sprouts, chickpeas, ginseng, guarana, oats, potatoes, soybeans, tomatoes.

Effects: Saponins are believed to have anti-oxidant, anti-cancer, anti-inflammatory, and anti-viral properties. They may also bolster the immune system. They have been used to treat diabetes; liver ailments such as hepatitis, cardiovascular problems such as high blood pressure, high cholesterol, and blood clots; and mental and physical stress.

SUCCINATES

Succinates are metabolites necessary for energy production in cells.

Effects: Said to increase energy and endurance.

Precautions: There is no evidence that supplementation provides any benefits.

SUPEROXIDE DISMUTASE

AKA: Cell Guard, Cu/ZnSOD, LIPSOD, MnSOD, SOD.

It ranks fifth among proteins in terms of the amount in our bodies, after collagen, albumin, globulin, and hemoglobin.

Food Sources: Barley grass, broccoli, brussel sprouts, cabbage, green plants, wheat grass.

Effects: An extremely powerful anti-oxidant enzyme that works synergistically with catalase to counteract superoxide, the most common and hazardous free radical. The production of SOD in the body decreases as we age.

There are two forms of SOD: copper/zinc SOD (Cu/ZnSOD), which protects the cytoplasm of the cell; and manganese SOD (MnSOD), which protects the mitochondria, where the genetic information resides and cellular energy is produced.

Liposomal superoxide dismutase (LIPSOD) is SOD that has been encapsulated in a liposome "delivery vehicle." Both SOD and LIPSOD have been used in the treatment of rheumatoid arthritis, damage caused by radiation therapy and heart attacks, unresponsive anemia, and various auto-immune disorders such as scleroderma, Crohn's disease, Behcet's disease, Raynaud's syndrome, and Kawasaki disease. It shows promise in the treatment of multiple sclerosis, Alzheimer's disease, Peyronie's disease, and possibly AIDS.

Superoxide dismutase works synergistically with copper, zinc, and manganese.

Precautions: Stomach acid destroys SOD, so tablet supplements must be enteric coated so that they can be safely absorbed in the small intestine.

TELOMERASE

Called the "immortality enzyme" because it encourages cell division for an indefinite period of time, preventing the cells from dying of old age (normal human cells divide approximately 75 times over a person's life span before the telomere — the protective end of the chromosome — wears away and becomes too short to protect the chromosome, leading to the death of the cell).

Effects: It could extend life span and health indefinitely.

Precautions: There is some debate whether it could be a carcinogen, as it has been found in 90 percent of all cancer cells. Some say that telomerase by itself does not create cancer cells, while others counter that its ability to promote cell division could cause cancer cells to proliferate unchecked.

CHAPTER 8

Hormones

Hormones are organic compounds secreted by specific cells that control the functions of other cells receptive to those hormone molecules.

ADRENOCORTICOTROPIC HORMONE ANALOGS

AKA: ACTH.

Effects: A class of neuropeptides currently under study for their brain-boosting effects. Pearson and Shaw cite ACTH 4-10, a polypeptide composed of seven amino acids, as one that has been shown to enhance learning.

ANDROSTENEDIONE

AKA: A-Dione.

A natural hormone produced by the adrenal glands, production of which is believed to decline with age. Though DHEA can be converted to A-Dione, the latter appears to be much more power-ful, converting more rapidly to testosterone than DHEA. It received much publicity in 1998 when it was revealed that the St. Louis Cardinals' home run king, Mark McGwire, used it to enhance his athletic performance.

Effects: It is said to increase energy and restore sexual drive — particularly in older individuals — increase muscle and bone mass, and enhance mood in those with depression. It can be depleted by stress, alcohol, and obesity.

Precautions: Possible side effects include prostate cancer and enlargement, baldness, and breast cancer. High doses (above 10 mg) may cause irritability, aggressiveness, and anxiety. In women taking estrogen, it may boost the estrogen to dangerous levels. Little is known about this hormone, and much more research is needed to uncover any additional side effects. A recent study has found that it has no effect on testosterone levels in the blood or muscular strength in men.

Dosage: It may not be needed by those under age 45. For men, 10 to 50 mg in the morning may be sufficient for energy and mood enhancement; it should be taken no more than two or three times a week, as it may result in the body's reducing or halting its own testosterone production. The risks for younger men include infertility, gynecomastia (breast growth), and testicular atrophy. For women, a dose of 5 to 25 mg two days a week may be sufficient, as women appear more responsive to the hormone than men. The risks for younger women include fertility problems, menstrual irregularities, facial hair, acne, and abnormal bleeding. It should be taken only under the guidance of a physician, and those taking it should start out at a low dosage. Ray Sahelian, M.D., considers any dose over 10 mg to be too high.

CHOLECYSTOKININ-8

AKA: CCK-8.

A neuropeptide currently under study for its brain-boosting effects.

DHEA

AKA: Astenile, Deandros, dehydroepiandrosterone, dehydroepiandrosterone sulfate (DHEAS), dehydroisoandrosterone, Diandron, Prasterone, Psicosterone, trans-dehydroandrosterone.

A steroid manufactured in the adrenal gland that is similar to testosterone and is a precursor to all steroid hormones in the body, including testosterone and estrogen. It is found in the bloodstream in greater amounts than any other steroid, and exists in normal brain tissue in amounts six and one-half times greater than in other parts of the body. It is found at its highest levels in the body between ages 20 to 25; after that, its production declines steadily. Those with Alzheimer's have levels lower than healthy individuals of similar age. Individuals under 40 should have their levels checked first, as they may not need supplementation.

Food Sources: Mexican wild yam.

Effects: Improves physical and mental health, as well as memory and thinking, by keeping the level of cortisol low and by helping neurons grow new dendrites. Its advocates believe it useful for those struggling with obesity, depression, arthritis, diabetes, osteoporosis, hypertension, viral and bacterial infections, cancer, and heart disease. It may increase the regeneration of body tissue and accelerate healing by encouraging the growth of the protein collagen. Levels of this hormone in the body decrease with age (by as much as 95 percent), so taking it may protect brain cells against mental deterioration such as Alzheimer's and senility, may increase mental abilities in those with normal capabilities, and may even extend life (it has been shown to extend the life span of animals by as much as 50 percent and, in humans, the amount of DHEA in the body has been found to bear an inverse correlation with mortality levels).

It has been used to treat epilepsy, Parkinson's disease, angina, diabetes, ulcers, alcohol and drug withdrawal, pain, cardiac arrhythmias, PMS, menopause, osteoporosis, arthritis, heart disease, fatigue, memory loss, autoimmune diseases, sexual problems, cryptosporidium infection, and systemic lupus erythematosus (SLE). Additionally, DHEA has been administered to those battling such disorders as depression, compulsive eating, moodiness, violent behavior, chronic anger, irritability, fear, impulsiveness, hostility, insomnia, impatience, agitation, worry, anxiety, and pessimism. Its use against such a wide range of disorders may be attributable to its ability to normalize and promote electrical activity in the body and brain in several ways.

Serum DHEA levels can be increased by taking supplements of chromium, and decreased by stress. Non-supplementation methods of increasing DHEA are simple and basic: exercise regularly, avoid smoking, avoid alcohol, avoid synthetic steroid hormones, avoid stress, get plenty of sleep, maintain ideal body weight, and reduce the percentage of fat in the body.

It works synergistically with vitamin E.

According to author Michael Hutchinson, it has also shown some success in treating AIDS, though the drug company involved is keeping silent until it can develop a variant that is patentable.

Precautions: Men with prostate problems should not take DHEA. For others, it is recommended that it be taken only under the guidance of a physician, and then only after having tests to determine the levels in the body and whether the liver is functioning properly. Side effects include acne (regardless of a person's age), anxiety, a sense of tightness in the chest, night restlessness, hair loss, voice changes, fatigue, oily skin, high blood pressure, diabetes, strokes, irritability and mood changes, overstimulation, aggressiveness, headaches, insomnia, heart palpitations, and heart irregularities, some of which are irreversible. Women may experience a slight increase in body hair and a deepening of the voice at dosages greater than 25 mg a day, and DHEA may carry the same risks as testosterone, such as the promotion of the growth of prostate cancer in men and breast and uterine cancers in women. Though stress may cause the body to decrease its production of DHEA and increase its production of cortisol, taking a DHEA pill cannot repair the damage to the body caused by stress. High doses (above 10 mg) may cause irritability, aggressiveness, and anxiety. Because sufficient research has not yet been done, use is experimental, and nothing is known about long-term effects, though epileptics have been taking it for nearly half a century. In tests where lab rats were given doses equal to dozens of times that normally taken by people, it has caused liver damage leading to the formation of tumors. It is not known if this same effect occurs in humans, but further tests with rat have shown that vitamin E can offset this damage.

Some researchers state that there is insufficient evidence to conclude that it has any beneficial effect on aging or any diseases (most studies have been short-term and involved a dozen people or fewer); any reports of people feeling better physically or mentally (especially with regard to sexual drive) are purely anecdotal. Over-the-counter brands are unregulated by the FDA, and their ingredients and purity may be questionable. Oral DHEA may be at least partially destroyed by the liver, making supplementation questionable. It is also possible that the increased energy levels felt by those taking it may be only short-term.

Caffeine can lower DHEA levels and raise cortisol levels, increasing stress to the body and decreasing the individual's panic threshold. It may cause harmful interactions if used in conjunction with aspirin or blood thinners, stimulants (including herbal stimulants), and thyroid medications; it may also interact with such anti-depressants as Prozac and Zoloft. Those on estrogen replacement therapy may have to adjust their dosage of DHEA accordingly, because the estrogen may induce a deficiency of DHEA. Too much insulin can also lower levels of this hormone.

Dosage: For humans, the optimal dosage is as yet not known, though usage has ranged anywhere from 50 to 2000 mg/day. For general health, some recommend a more modest dose of 19 mg/day for women, 31 mg/day for men. Most supplements are 25 mg. Michael Hutchinson recommends 100 to 300 mg/day (in two or three divided doses) for life-extending and cognitive-enhancing purposes, about half the dose normally taken by epileptics. However, one expert, Dr. Ray Sahelian, recommends starting out at 5 to 10 mg/day, and increasing the dosage by 5 mg/day until reaching the optimum daily dosage (which may be as little as 25 mg/day for women, 40 mg/day for men). He also recommends that users take only DHEA or DHEAS and avoid any product sold as a precursor to DHEA. Stephen Cherniske, M.S., also cautions against using any supplement that contains additional ingredients such as ephedra or yohimbe.

ESTROGEN

One of the six steroid hormones in the body.

Food Sources: Alfalfa sprouts, chickpeas, flaxseed, rye, soybeans, yams. Certain herbs such as blue cohosh, dong quai, hops, and licorice have estrogen-like properties, but may not have the same effects.

Effects: Can improve the mood of post-menopausal women, protect against osteoporosis (bone loss), and maintain the health of the heart. It may also relieve or even prevent the symptoms of Alzheimer's disease in post-menopausal women, particularly those of attention and memory loss, apparently by encouraging the growth of brain cells and the connections between them. It may even protect women's brains from damage caused by strokes. In combination with cholesterol-lowering drugs, it can reduce inflammation and clotting of the blood, both of which could otherwise lead to heart attacks and strokes.

Men also produce estrogen, which is needed to keep sperm strong and fertile.

Precautions: It should not be taken by anyone who is allergic to any drugs containing estrogen, anyone with impaired liver function or unexplained vaginal bleeding, anyone who smokes, or anyone who has had blood clots, a stroke, or a heart attack. Those who have had cancer of the breast or reproductive organs, fibrocystic breast disease, fibroid tumors of the uterus or endometriosis, migraine headaches, epilepsy, porphyria, diabetes, high blood pressure, asthma, congestive heart failure, kidney disease, gallstones, or are over age 60 should consult a physician first. It may cause an increased sensitivity to sunlight and sunlamps and, in rare cases, a blood clot in the lung, brain, or leg. Recent research has shown that older women with cardiac conditions risk a much greater chance of heart attacks and blood clots in the first year of estrogen treatment but, oddly enough, these risks dropped dramatically after four years of treatment. Women on estrogen are also given the hormone progestin, as the latter prevents the cancer and uterine tumors in post-menopausal women that sometimes develop from estrogen therapy.

It may deplete the levels of vitamins B6, E, folic acid, and DHEA in the body. Common side effects include stomach cramps, appetite loss, nausea, diarrhea, swollen feet and ankles, weight changes, water retention, vomiting, tender swollen breasts, acne, loss of tolerance to contact lenses, and a change in menstruation. Less frequent side effects consist of rash, stomach or side pains, bloody skin blisters, breast lumps, depression, dizziness, migraine headaches, irritability, bleeding gums, menstrual irregularities, PMS, mild diarrhea, jaundice, growth of uterine fibroids, brown blotches on the skin, hair loss, vaginal discharge or bleeding, and changes in sex drive. Rare symptoms include stroke, the formation of blood clots, involuntary incontinence, loss of coordination, chest pains, leg pains, breathing difficulties, slurred speech, vision changes, hypercalcemia in breast cancer, and involuntary movements. Profuse bleeding could be life-threatening. Overdose symptoms include nausea, vomiting, fluid retention, breast enlargement and discomfort, and excessive vaginal bleeding.

The effects of estrogen can be lessened by hydantoin anticonvulsants, carbamazepine, phenobarbital, primidone, Phenytoin, Ethotoin, Mephenytoin, barbiturates, and rifampin; it can be enhanced by meprobamate, alcohol, and vitamin C. Estrogen can lessen the effects of oral anticoagulants, Bromocriptine, clofibrate, dextrothyroxine, guanfacine (antihypertensive effects only), insulin, tamoxifen, terazosin, thyroid hormones, and ursodiol. It can increase the toxicity of tricyclic antidepressants and Phenothiazine tranquilizers, increase the amount of Cyclosporine and adrenal corticosteroid drugs in the blood, increase the amount of calcium absorbed in the stomach, increase the chance of liver damage from other drugs, cause unpredictable changes in blood sugar when combined with oral antidiabetics, increase the chance of blood clots when combined with antifibrinolytic agents, and increase the risk of pancreatitis when combined with didanosine. Menstrual irregularities and bleeding between periods may occur when combined with marijuana, and blood clots leading to stroke or heart attack may result when combined with tobacco. It should not be taken with grapefruit juice, birth control pills, or hormone replacement drugs.

GABA

AKA: GABA Calm, GABA Plus, Gaba-tol, gamma aminobutyric acid.

A neurotransmitter and central nervous system depressant.

Effects: It metabolizes to produce GHB in the brain, reducing anxiety and inducing relaxation and sleep by regulating the firing of nerve cells and countering the excitatory effects of acetylcholine, noradrenaline, and other neurotransmitters.

Precautions: One Chinese study indicates that increased levels of GABA in the brain are not conducive to learning and memory.

It should not be combined with other drugs, especially alcohol and other depressants.

Dosage: Mark Mayell recommends 500 to 750 mg to reduce anxiety, and 750 to 1500 mg an hour before bedtime for insomnia. Its effects may be enhanced by taking it with 25 to 50 mg each of vitamin B-3 and B-6.

HUMAN GROWTH HORMONE

AKA: Growth hormone, HGH, Humatrope, somatotrophin (STH).

Manufactured in the pituitary gland, it appears to be the main hormone associated with aging. It begins to decline about 14 percent each decade starting at about age 20, bringing about sagging skin, pot bellies, loss of vitality, and other symptoms of old age. It is used as a treatment for adults with deficiencies resulting from pituitary disease, hypothalmic disease, surgery, radiation therapy, and injury.

Effects: Higher energy levels, elevated mood, improved memory, enhanced sleep, increased muscle mass (up to 8.8 percent after six months), enhanced sexual performance, regrowth of vital organs, restoration of immune function, stronger bones, lower blood pressure, faster healing of wounds, smoother skin, regrowth of hair, sharper vision, and a reduction in fat (14.4 percent after six months). It may also extend the human life span.

Precautions: It should only be taken under the guidance of a physician, as side effects are still not known. Taking HGH when it is not needed may train the pituitary gland to release less and less of it. Some research does not confirm its supposed benefits; side effects may include carpal tunnel syndrome, hypertension, and gigantism. The use of synthetic growth hormone has been associated with heart disease and the production of anti-growth hormone anti-bodies.

Human growth hormone may be expensive and difficult to obtain, and synthetic growth hormone has only 10 percent of the effectiveness of the natural form. Most animal growth hormone is virtually ineffective.

Dosage: Not yet established, but clinical trials have shown that a single daily dose of 25 mg raised the hormone to optimum levels for subjects aged 64 to 81. High levels can be maintained by aerobic exercise (especially if separated from eating and sleeping by at least two hours), maintaining ideal body weight, avoiding eating before exercise, eating foods that have a high arginine-to-lysine ratio (e.g., peanuts, nuts, seeds, whole grains, carob, raisins), taking tryptophan supplements (banned since 1989 because some improperly manufactured supplements caused harm to some users), maintaining stable blood sugar and insulin levels (even if it means snacking), and following a diet that is high in healthy proteins and low in fat, sugar (particularly sugar ingested just before bedtime), and starch. Supplements of L-glutamine, arginine, and ornithine may stimulate the body to make more HGH.

MELATONIN

AKA: N-acetyl-5-methoxytryptamine.

A master hormone secreted by the pineal gland that regulates a number of the body's functions and life cycles, including the onset of puberty; it is stimulated by darkness and suppressed by light. Production decreases with age when the pineal gland becomes worn out and calcified, which may explain why older people have insomnia. Some elderly people lose their ability to produce it altogether.

Food sources: Oats, sweet corn, rice, ginger, tomatoes, bananas, barley, Japanese radish. Tryptophan, which can be converted by the body into melatonin, is found principally in spirulina, soy products, cottage cheese, chicken liver, pumpkin seeds, turkey, and chicken.

Effects: Regulates the body's clock, so it can be effectively used to treat insomnia, jet lag, and depression. Unlike sleeping pills, it doesn't interfere with REM sleep (the dream state), and leave the individual feeling groggy upon wakening, and it resets the body's clock rather than just knocking the person out. It is known to produce vivid dreams. It also works as a powerful anti-oxidant (as much as 500 times more powerful than DMSO), and is now being tested as a possible anti-cancer drug (it may inhibit some types of cancers, particularly those that are hormone-related — e.g., breast cancer, prostate cancer — when taken in doses of 40 mg a day or more). It has also been shown to boost the immune system, lower cholesterol, shrink the prostate, and lower heart rate and blood pressure. Researchers are looking into it as a possible treatment or cure for such things as Alzheimer's, Parkinson's disease, AIDS, PMS, menopause, osteoporosis, Down's syndrome, and even as a birth control pill. Some suggest it may even delay the aging process, though it may not be able to reverse it (it has been shown to increase the longevity of lab rats an average of 20 percent), and it may ease some symptoms of autism, epilepsy and diabetes.

Taking adequate amounts of vitamin B-3 can free up more tryptophan to be converted to melatonin. Vitamin B-6 can stimulate the body to produce more melatonin, as the body uses it to convert tryptophan into serotonin, which can then be converted to melatonin. Taking calcium and magnesium at night may also benefit melatonin production.

Precautions: It should not be taken by women who are pregnant, nursing, or trying to get pregnant, as it interferes with sex hormones; healthy children, as they produce enough on their own; those with severe mental illness, as it could worsen the symptoms; those taking steroid drugs such as cortisone and dexamethasone, as it could reduce their effectiveness; and those with overactive immune system abnormalities, including lymphoma, leukemia, allergies, and auto-immune diseases such as arthritis, multiple sclerosis, and lupus, as it could worsen these conditions.

It appears to be non-toxic, though much research still needs to be done, and harmful side effects may yet be uncovered. Most studies have been done on rats, which do not produce their own melatonin. Side effects may include depression, diarrhea, headaches, insomnia, nightmares, grogginess or fuzzy thinking upon arising from sleep, and a reduced sex drive. Taking it at the wrong time could cause problems, such as falling asleep at the wheel of a car; taking too much (more than 0.3 mg) in efforts to fall asleep could result in a melatonin hangover the next day. Paradoxically, women who take it for birth control do not get sleepy; why this happens is not known. When taken counter to the body's normal circadian rhythm (e.g., by those working night shifts), it can have negative effects on memory and cognitive processing. Optimum dosage has not yet been determined, and long-term effects are still not known. There may be a risk of contamination from viruses in the natural form, made from animals, as opposed to the synthetic form; on the other hand, most synthetic forms are manufactured outside the U.S., leaving open the question of quality control. Apart from this, natural and synthetic forms are identical. Melatonin is only effective as a sedative if the pineal gland's production is low; otherwise, doses as high as 75 to 150 mg will have no effect. It should not be used to treat insomnia, as there are numerous causes that result in a loss of sleep, and melatonin may not be effective in countering them. One study has shown that it can worsen clinical depression in some cases, and in non-depression cases can cause fatigue, confusion, and sleepiness.

Some medications, especially hypertension medicines, can interfere or react with melatonin. The production of melatonin can also be inhibited by exposure to electromagnetic fields, lack of sunlight during waking hours, lack of darkness during sleep (caused even by such seemingly innocuous offenders as night lights), aspirin (which can cut production by 75 percent), alcohol, beta-blockers, calcium-channel blockers, sedatives (such as Prozac, Valium, and Xanax), steroids, fluvoxamine (Luvox), desipramine (Norpramin, Pertofrane), most MAO inhibitors, caffeine (including coffee, green tea, colas, and chocolate), tobacco, doses of B-12 above 3000 mcg, ibuprofen, sleeping pills, tranquilizers, and indomethacin (which can completely block the nighttime increase of melatonin). Smoking one joint of marijuana, on the other hand, can increase melatonin levels in the body 4000 percent.

The sale of melatonin is banned in Canada, France, and Britain.

Dosage: Levels produced by the body are measured in picograms (trillionths of a gram), averaging around 10 pg per milliliter of blood per day and 50 to 150 pg per milliliter at night. Melatonin output in the body can be improved by eating the foods mentioned above; getting enough niacin, B-6, calcium, and magnesium; meditation, prayer, and other relaxation techniques; and smoking marijuana. Sub-lingual supplements allow the melatonin to reach the brain quicker, but a time-release supplement at bedtime is probably best, as it most mimics natural conditions. Researchers recommend taking only 0.5 to 5 mg a day one-half to one hour before bedtime, though some studies have shown that as little as 0.1 mg (equal in amount to a few grains of salt) can enhance sleep. Most pills are 2.5 to 3 mg, which, according to Dr. Russel J. Reiter, professor of neuroendocrinology at the University of Texas Health Science Center in San Antonio, may be "overkill," though probably not harmful. Women taking up to 75 mg a day for birth control research have shown no apparent side effects. Reiter himself takes less than 1 mg/day, and Ray Sahelian, M.D., does not recommend its use more than once or twice a week. On the other hand, Crook and Adderly advise its use only for combating jet lag, and Alan Gaby, M.D., who publishes the newsletter *Nutrition and Healing*, states, "We do not at this time believe that melatonin should be a routine part of the average nutritional-supplement program." Reiter recommends an alternative program of 100 mg of B-3, 1000 mg of calcium, and 500 mg of magnesium at night, plus 25 to 50 mg of B-6 early in the morning, to assist the body's own production of melatonin.

NADH

AKA: Nicotinamide adenine dinucleotide.

Effects: Provides needed energy to brain cells for neurotransmitter production and information processing. Taking it may improve the performance of brain cells and stimulate them to produce the cognitive-enhancing neurotransmitters dopamine, noradrenaline, and serotonin. As a person ages, the level of NADH decreases.

NEUROPEPTIDE Y

A neuropeptide currently under study for its brain-boosting effects.

Effects: Stimulates the appetite. Studies with rats and mice indicate that overproduction of this substance in the brain may lead to sensitivity to the sedative effects of alcohol and, consequently, less consumption of alcohol.

Precautions: The above studies also indicate that a deficiency may lead to decreased sensitivity to alcohol and, possibly, greater alcohol consumption.

PREGNENOLONE

A hormone formed from cholesterol in various organs of the body, including the adrenal glands, liver, skin, the sexual organs, and the brain. The body can use it as it is, convert it into progesterone, or convert it into DHEA and then to over 150 steroid hormones, including androgens and estrogen. Levels in the body decline with age.

Effects: May improve mental ability, memory, visual and auditory perception, alertness, awareness, and mood by facilitating the transmission of impulses between neurons. It also relieves the symptoms of PMS in women and prevents arthritis (it was first developed in the 1930s as an arthritis medication). Animal experiments suggest that it can extend life span, resist cancer, and prevent obesity.

Precautions: Too high a dose can result in irritability, anxiety, headaches, insomnia, and aggressiveness.

Dosage: Ray Sahelian, M.D., recommends starting out with 10 mg/day, then increasing the dosage every few days until positive effects are felt, then cutting back to 2 to 5 mg/day with occasional periods of non-use, because it accumulates in the body. He also recommends that it be taken only under the guidance of a physician, and maintains that it is not needed by healthy people under 40. It is available in a variety of forms — pill, capsule, sublingual tablet, cream, micronized pill, liquid, and spray — with pill dosages in the 10 to 50 mg range.

SEROTONIN

Food Sources: Complex carbohydrates (whole grains), fruit (eaten in place of sugary snacks), and plenty of vegetables will help maintain stable serotonin levels, as will regular exercise. Though foods may contain some serotonin, very little of it is biologically available; however, the body can manufacture it from tryptophan or 5-HTP in foods and supplements.

Effects: Serotonin has some of the most important functions in the brain and body. It is important in regulating mood and behavior and, among other things, it can regulate platelets (which help blood coagulate), the ability of blood vessels to expand and contract, the ability of smooth muscles to contract (including abdominal muscles, which push food through the digestive system), and the effects of other neurotransmitters.

Precautions: It cannot pass through the blood/brain barrier. The ability of carbohydrates to raise serotonin may be negated by just 5 percent protein in a meal.

Disruption in serotonin levels can result in any number of psychological disorders, including mania, depression and suicide fixation, aggression, impulsiveness, obsessive-compulsive disorder, eating and sleeping disorders, and possibly schizophrenia and Alzheimer's disease. Serotonin imbalances may also contribute to the onset of headaches, migraines, and certain cardiovascular conditions such as Raynaud's disease and hypertension. Those with low serotonin levels tend to binge on fatty or sugary foods, though this type of bingeing does not necessarily indicate a serotonin deficiency.

7-KETO

The hormone 7-keto is metabolized from DHEA.

Effects: Believed to be identical to DHEA, but without the side effects from metabolization.

THYROID HORMONES

AKA: Cytomel, Dextrothyroxine, Eltroxin, Euthroid, Levoid, Levothroid, Levothyroxine, Levoxyl, Liotrix, Liothyronine, Proloid, Synthroid, Thyroglobulin, Thyroid, Thyrolar, Thyroxine.

Effects: A class of drugs that mimic the hormone produced in the thyroid gland. Subclinical hypothyroidism, or a slightly underfunctioning thyroid, can be one reason for poor concentration,

mental confusion, and memory disturbances. The condition is also characterized by such symptoms as cold hands and feet, menstrual problems, dry skin, thin hair, and low energy levels. It is little-known and often overlooked by doctors.

Precautions: Any thyroid drugs should be taken only under the guidance of a physician. Common symptoms include tremors, headaches, irritability, insomnia, changes in appetite, diarrhea, leg cramps, menstrual irregularities, fever, heat sensitivity, unusual swelling, weight loss, and nervousness. Less frequent symptoms include hives, rash, vomiting, chest pain, heartbeat irregularities, and shortness of breath. Overdose symptoms, which can be life-threatening, consist of a "hot" feeling, heart palpitations, nervousness, sweating, hand tremors, insomnia, rapid and irregular pulse, headaches, irritability, diarrhea, weight loss, muscle cramps, angina, and congestive heart failure.

Thyroid hormones should not be taken by anyone who has had a heart attack within the past six weeks or for any reason other than a thyroid deficiency. Those who have heart disease, high blood pressure, diabetes, Addison's disease, who have had adrenal gland deficiency, or who use epinephrine, ephedrine, or isoproterenol for asthma should consult a physician first.

Its effect can be inhibited by cholestyramine, colestipol, oral contraceptives, estrogens, and phenytoin, and enhanced by large continuous doses of aspirin. In combination, it can enhance the effects of amphetamines, oral anticoagulants, tricyclic antidepressants, oral antidiabetics or insulin, ephedrine, epinephrine, and methylphenidate, and diminish the effects of barbiturates, beta-adrenergic blocking agents, cortisone drugs, and digitalis medications. It can also interact with sympathomimetics, possibly causing a rapid or irregular heartbeat. Combining it with cocaine can result in excessive stimulation.

THYROTROPIN-RELEASING HORMONE

AKA: TRH.

A neuropeptide which, along with its analogs, is currently under study for its brain-boosting effects.

VASOPRESSIN

AKA: ADH, Adiuretin SD, antidiuretic hormone, arginine-vasopressin, argipressin, AVP, DAV Ritter, DDAVP, Desmopressin, Desmospray, Diapid, L-desamino-8-D-arginine, LVP, lypressin, lysine-vasopressin, Minirin, Postacton, rinder-pressin, Syntopressin.

A hormone and natural brain peptide secreted by the pituitary gland that has anti-diuretic properties. Vasopressin is released by experiences of great trauma or intense arousal (which may be one reason why such emotional moments have such a strong impression and can be remembered with vividness long afterwards); stimulant drugs such as amphetamines, cocaine, LSD, and Ritalin (metahylphenidate) also release large amounts, and habitual use of these drugs depletes the brain's supply of this hormone. Conversely, depressant drugs such as alcohol and marijuana suppress the secretion, which may be why users frequently do not remember events when drunk or stoned. Diapid is the synthetic version, and it is only available as a nasal spray, which is prescribed for diabetes insipidus and memory loss

resulting from aging, Alzheimer's, amnesia, Korsakoff's syndrome, and senile dementia.

Arginine-vasopressin (argipressin) and lysine-vasopressin (lypressin) are forms of vasopressin that have an additional amino acid; their effects are basically the same.

Effects: Increases theta wave activity in the brain which, in turn, increases attention span, concentration, memory, short- and long-term recall, recognition, retention, and creativity. It may prove helpful in retaining new information (e.g., a language or new field of study), as it helps imprint this information in the brain. It has been shown to restore memory lost as a result of aging, traumatically-induced amnesia (caused by physical injury to the brain), and possibly chemically and electrically-induced amnesia, as well. It can counteract the effects of the drugs mentioned above. It may even have anti-depressant qualities, and reports claim it intensifies orgasms.

Precautions: It may create symptoms of toxicity when taken alone; these may be alleviated when taken in combination with Aldosterone. It is recommended that those with cardiovascular problems (particularly hypertension and angina pectoris) should not use vasopressin, as it narrows the blood vessels. Some say that angina patients will experience heart pain; Pearson and Shaw discourage use in such cases. It should also be avoided by those with kidney disease and epilepsy. For others, it occasionally results in nasal congestion, runny nose, itching or irritation of nasal passages, nasal ulcerations, abdominal cramps, heartburn, nausea, headaches, and more frequent bowel movements. Vasopressin should be snorted into the upper nasal cavities, as inhaling it deep into the lungs may trigger spasms of the larynx and shortness of breath.

Excessive use of the drug should not be combined with excess water consumption, as it could lead to a rare condition called water intoxication.

Dosage: A total dose of 12 to 16 units/day from a nasal spray bottle (one whiff, or approximately 2 U.S.P. [United States Pharmacopeia] Posterior Pituitary Units, in each nostril three to four times a day) will improve memory, according to most studies. It works extremely fast, as it is absorbed into the mucous membranes of the nose and taken directly into the brain, and improvements may be noticed within seconds.

CHAPTER 9

Essential Oils

Aromatherapy, or the use of herbal oils as medicines, has been practiced for thousands of years. Essential oils, or concentrated liquids extracted from various parts of plants, are believed to help protect plants from certain diseases and pests, and are thought to have effects on the human mind and body as well. They can either be inhaled (by putting a drop or two in a bowl of steaming water), absorbed through the skin (by using three or four drops as a massage oil, or a 1-to-10 ratio of essential oil to a carrier oil such as sweet almond, olive, or sesame seed oil), or both (by putting 5 or 6 drops in warm bath water). Some shops or catalogs sell dispensers, lamps, vaporizers, or diffusers that provide a longer-lasting effect.

Smells can have a direct influence on the brain, affecting emotion and memory by stimulating the hypothalamus, hippocampus, and amygdala. Stud-ies have shown that pleasant aromas increase productivity in the workplace by as much as 25 percent, and learning by as much as 17 percent. Many oils work synergistically with each other.

Pure, undiluted oils are extremely concentrated and should never be inhaled directly from the bottle or applied to the skin, and they should not be taken internally (as little as a half teaspoon of pure oil can be fatal). Also, avoid getting essential oils in the eye, as they can be irritating (a cotton swab soaked in vegetable oil and applied to the eye should relieve discomfort). They can last a year or more if stored properly in a cool, dry, and dark place, and the bottle is opened only when dispensing oil (they can evaporate or oxidize quite readily in the open air); a small amount of vitamin E can help preserve the freshness. As for their benefits, little is known about the specifics with which they work: only a handful of studies have been done on aromas and aromatherapy, and most of the purported effects are based on anecdotal evidence or folklore. Even among practitioners, there may be some discrepancy about specific effects, so caution is advised.

They should not be used by those suffering from epilepsy or other seizure disorders, those whose blood pressure is abnormally high or abnormally low, those with asthma, or those being treated for cancer. Allergic reactions or photosensitivity are possible, especially with spice oils such as thyme, sage, and oregano, which can be irritating (patch-test an oil by dabbing a drop of it on the skin with a cotton swab, placing a bandage over it, and checking it 24 hours later for any adverse reactions). Many essential oils can cause such side effects as headaches, dizziness, and nausea, while some may contain compounds which could be carcinogenic if used regularly for an extended period of time. Oils should generally be reserved for treating specific conditions, and not be used on a daily basis, especially for more than two or three weeks at a time, as they can produce effects that are the opposite of what they normally provide.

Prices can vary depending on such factors as the origin of the plant, the method of extraction, and whether it was grown organically or not. Absolutes — which are essential oils that are viscous or semi-solid — are cheaper, but may contain trace amounts of toxic solvents used in the extraction process, and are not recommended for therapeutic use. Perfumes and fragrance oils sold by cosmetics companies are synthetic (the term "nature identical" is a tipoff), and are of little benefit in aromatherapy. Essential oils themselves can be rather expensive, as it may take a hundred pounds of plants or more to produce one ounce of oil.

ANGELICA

AKA: *Angelica archangelica.*

Effects: Said to relieve stress and anxiety, as well as reduce nausea and weakness during recovery from illness, break up congestion in the lungs, and relieve stomach cramps, arthritis pain, PMS, and menstrual pain.

Precautions: Avoid sunlight if applying directly to the skin, as it may cause dermatitis. The fresh oil is colorless, and turns yellow, then dark brown, with age; the dark brown oil should not be used.

BASIL

AKA: *Ocimum basilicum.*

There are over a hundred different varieties of basil.

Effects: Contains high amounts of cineole, a compound which increases blood flow to parts of the brain. Said to increase concentration, mental functioning, and memory, relieve nervousness and fatigue, and promote feelings of contentment, happiness, and sexuality. It has been used to treat various respiratory infections, including bronchitis and whooping cough.

Precautions: Contains estragol, which may cause adverse reactions in some people and — possibly — cancer in large doses (varieties low in estragol include *Ocimum Americanum, Ocimum canum,* and *Ocimum gratissimum*). Constant use of basil may dull the mind, rather than stimulate it.

BAY

AKA: Bay leaf, *Pimenta acris.*

Effects: Said to promote psychic

awareness. It can also relieve arthritis pain and the symptoms of respiratory ailments.

Precautions: It may be irritating if applied directly to the skin, especially in its pure state.

BENZOIN

AKA: *Styrax benzoin.*

It is more of a resin than an oil, and has to be melted by heat before being used.

Effects: Said to increases energy, as well as ease the symptoms of common respiratory problems (colds, flu, coughs, sore throat) and skin conditions such as eczema and psoriasis.

Precautions: It may cause allergic reactions in some people.

BERGAMOT

AKA: *Citrus aurantium bergamia.*

Effects: Said to relieve stress, anxiety, and depression, and contribute to a calm sleep. It is used in Europe to treat infections of the skin, respiratory tract, and urinary tract.

Works synergistically with angelica, cedar, chamomile, geranium, lavender, lemon, neroli, rose, and ylang-ylang.

Precautions: Avoid sunlight if applying directly to the skin or using in bath water.

CAMPHOR

AKA: *Camphora officinarum, Cinnamomum camphora, Laurus camphora.*

Effects: Said to increase energy.

Precautions: Should not be used by those with asthma or allergies. It is a very strong oil, and extra caution should be used to prevent using too much.

CARAWAY

AKA: *Carum carvi.*

Effects: Said to increase energy. It is used to treat various digestive problems, including colic, colitis, dyspepsia, flatulence.

CARDAMOM

AKA: Cardamon, *Elettaria cardamomum.*

Effects: Said to elevate mood and improve memory and concentration. it is used as a digestive aid, and to treat heartburn, flatulence, and diarrhea.

Precautions: Should always be used with a base oil, as it can cause the skin to become sensitive.

CEDAR

AKA: Cedarwood, *Cedrus atlantica, Cedrus deodora, Cedrus libani.*

Effects: Said to promote a sense of spirituality, improve the respiratory system, and be an aphrodisiac.

Works synergistically with bergamot, jasmine, juniper, neroli, and rose.

Precautions: Some brands may be adulterated with other essential oils, including juniper, which may cause problems arising from the compound thujone. Though several different trees produce essential oils which are marketed as cedarwood, some aromatherapists recommend that only *Cedrus atlantica* be used, as that has the most reliable therapeutic properties.

CELERY

AKA: Ache, *Apium graveolens,* smallage.

Effects: Said to relieve fatigue,

contribute to a restful sleep, and be an aphrodisiac.

CHAMOMILE

AKA: *Anthemis nobilis* or *Chamaemelum nobile* (Roman chamomile), *Matricaria chamomila* or *Matricaria recutita* (German chamomile).

Effects: Said to relieve stress and stress-related headaches, anxiety, and depression, and contribute to a restful sleep. Roman chamomile is used to treat stomach aches, indigestion, diarrhea, muscle spasms, and PMS; German chamomile is used to treat skin conditions such as acne and eczema, and cold sores.

CINNAMON

AKA: Cassia, *Cinnamomum cassia*, *Cinnamomum ceylanicum*, *Cinnamomum zeylanicum*.

Effects: Said to increase energy and promote awareness.

Precautions: It should not be used without the guidance of a trained aromatherapist, as it can be quite toxic. It may cause an allergic reaction in some people. It should always be diluted before being applied to the skin, as it can be irritating in its pure state, possibly causing blisters and burns.

CLARY SAGE

AKA: *Salvia sclarea.*

Effects: Said to relieve depression, stress, and fatigue; improve memory and creativity; induce intense and colorful dreams; produce euphoria (in some people); act as an aphrodisiac; and relieve headaches and the symptoms of PMS.

Works synergistically with bergamot, cypress, geranium, jasmine, lavender, and sandalwood. Drinking alcohol is said to intensify its effects.

Precautions: Should not be used by anyone who suffers from epilepsy. Despite the synergistic effect with alcohol, combining the two can lead to a dangerously heightened sense of drunkenness (and accompanying hangover) with extreme nightmares.

CORIANDER

AKA: *Coriandrum sativum.*

Effects: Said to improve memory. It has been used to aid digestion and reduce flatulence.

Precautions: Do not use the essential oil internally unless under the guidance of an expert aromatherapist, as the wrong dosage could prove fatal. One case on record relates that several workers who tried to clean up fifty quarts of coriander oil spilled from a large container were overcome by the fumes within a half hour, laughing and giggling at first, they became aggressive and belligerent. Before they could be rescued, two suffered from extreme nausea, and all suffered from extreme fatigue for the next few days.

EUCALYPTUS

AKA: *Eucalyptus citriodora, Eucalyptus globulus, Eucalyptus radiata.*

Effects: Contains cineole and eucalyptol, both of which stimulate the central nervous system. The oil has antiviral and antibiotic properties, and has been used to treat a variety of respiratory problems. It is a common ingredient in cold remedies.

Works synergistically with angelica, hyssop, lemon, pine, and thyme.

FENNEL

AKA: *Foeniculum vulgare.*

Effects: Said to relieve nervous tension and increase life span. It has been used to treat muscular aches and pains, digestive problems, nausea, and hangovers.

Works synergistically with detoxifying and cleansing oils such as juniper.

Precautions: It should not be used by those suffering from epilepsy; it should not be used indiscriminately because it is high in phenolic resin; and it should not be used as a diuretic without supervision, as it could cause kidney damage. Some aromatherapists are also concerned about the combination of principal constituents anethol and estragol, which could cause serious side effects, though none have been reported.

FRANKINCENSE

AKA: *Boswellia carteri, Boswellia thurifera,* olibanum.

Effects: Said to slow down and deepen breathing, and to promote calmness and feelings of spirituality. It has been used to treat sinus congestion, asthma, and even skin cancer.

Works synergistically with sandalwood.

Precautions: It should be used with caution by asthmatics, as the hot steam could have an adverse effect.

GERANIUM

AKA: *Pelargonium graveolens, Pelargonium odoratissimum.*

Effects: Said to reduce stress and depression, induce calmness, and increase energy. It has been used to treat various skin disorders, as well as athlete's foot and hemorrhoids.

Works synergistically with benzoin, bergamot, chamomile, clary sage, lemongrass, melissa, patchouli, and vetiver.

Precautions: Since it is quite expensive, cheaper brands may be adulterated with artificial esters, cedarwood, lemongrass, and turpentine.

GINGER

AKA: *Zingiber officinalis.*

Effects: Said to increase energy. It has been used to treat diarrhea, catarrh, and rheumatism.

Precautions: It could cause a rash or blisters if applied directly to the skin or added to bath water.

GRAPEFRUIT

AKA: *Citrus paradissi.*

Effects: Said to relieve anxiety, stress, and depression.

Works synergistically with lavender.

Precautions: Can increase chances of sunburn when applied to the skin.

JASMINE

AKA: *Jasminum grandiflorum* (royal jasmine, Spanish jasmine), *Jasminum officinale* (common jasmine).

Effects: Said to relieve insomnia and depression, and promote feelings of optimism, confidence, sexuality, and euphoria.

Precautions: Since so many flowers are needed to produce an ounce of essential oil, virtually all of the products on the market since the late 1980s are absolutes, which may contain trace amounts of toxic solvents. Jasmine absolute using the process of enfleurage — placing leaves in trays of carrier oil to extract the essential oil — is considered the safest, though some still consider it unsuitable for use.

JUNIPER

AKA: *Juniperus communis.*

Effects: Said to increase happiness, energy, and strength. It is also used for its detoxifying, diuretic, and antiseptic qualities, as well as maintaining concentration during prayer and meditation.

Precautions: Should not be used for kidney problems. The oil could be adulterated with turpentine.

LAVANDIN

AKA: *Lavandula delphinensis, Lavandula fragrans,* lavendin.

Lavandin is a hybrid of lavender and aspic.

Effects: Said to have a mild calming effect similar to lavender. It is used to treat muscular aches and pains, colds, catarrh, and sinusitis.

Precautions: It is often sold as lavender, even though it has a sweet fragrance and is not as potent.

LAVENDER

AKA: *Lavandula angustifolia, Lavandula officinalis, Lavandula vera.*

Effects: Said to relieve stress and anxiety, and contribute to a deeper, more restful sleep. It is used for a wide variety of disorders and medical problems.

Works synergistically with bergamot, chamomile, clary sage, geranium, marjoram, neroli, rose, rosemary, and ylang-ylang.

Precautions: Individuals with other allergies or asthma may suffer an allergic reaction to lavender. Because it is so expensive, it is often adulterated with other oils such as lavandin.

LEMON

AKA: *Citrus limon.*

Effects: Said to increase energy and concentration, elevate mood, and contribute to health and healing.

Works synergistically with cedar, eucalyptus, fennel, juniper, lavender, and pine.

Precautions: If applied to the skin in its pure state, it can cause an allergic reaction or irritation, or even a skin rash if exposed to sunlight or ultraviolet light. Never use oil that is cloudy or pale.

LEMONGRASS

AKA: *Cymbopogon citratus, Cymbopogon flexuosus,* melissa grass.

Effects: Said to relieve fatigue, induce calmness, and increase concentration.

Works synergistically with eucalyptus, geranium, juniper, lavender, lime, and pine.

Precautions: It may be irritating when applied to sensitive skin. It is used to adulterate melissa and, along with geranium and citronella, it is often used to imitate rose and verbena.

LIME

AKA: *Citrus limetta.*

Effects: Said to increase energy, relieve depression, and improve memory and concentration.

Works synergistically with bergamot, cedar, clary sage, lemongrass, and pine.

Precautions: If applied to the skin, it can cause a rash when exposed to sunlight.

MARJORAM

AKA: Knotted marjoram, *Origanum marjorana*, sweet marjoram.

Effects: Said to relieve stress and insomnia. It has been used to treat such conditions as anorexia, diarrhea, flatulence, high blood pressure, PMS, menopause, migraines, and muscular aches and pains.

Works synergistically with bergamot and lavender.

Precautions: It should not be used on young or sensitive people, as it could produce an effect opposite to the one intended. It is often confused with oregano, whose calming properties are not as great.

MELISSA

AKA: Balm, bee balm, lemon balm, *Melissa officinalis*, sweet balm.

Effects: Said to relieve nervous tension, irritability, anxiety, depression, and insomnia. It has been used to stimulate the appetite and treat cold sores, high blood pressure, shock, migraines, and asthma.

Works synergistically with geranium, lavender, myrtle, neroli, and rose.

Precautions: It is a very strong oil and should only be used under the guidance of an expert aromatherapist. It may cause irritation when applied to the skin. Some brands may be adulterated with the much less expensive and less effective citronella, lemon, or lemongrass.

MYRRH

AKA: *Commiphora myrrha*.

Effects: Used as an aid in meditation. It is also used to treat skin and mouth problems.

MYRTLE

AKA: *Myrtus communis*.

Effects: Said to cleanse the mind, spirit, and body, and to aid concentration during meditation.

Works synergistically with cypress, lavender, lemon, neroli, and pine.

NEROLI

AKA: *Citrus aurantium*, *Citrus aurantium bugardia*, *Citrus bigaradia*.

Effects: Said to relieve stress, anxiety, fatigue, depression, insomnia, and pain, and to increase feelings of love and euphoria.

Works synergistically with jasmine and rose.

Precautions: It may increase the chance of a sunburn if applied to the skin. It is often adulterated with petitgrain.

NUTMEG

AKA: *Myristica fragrans*.

Effects: Said to increase energy. It is sometimes used as a tonic for the heart and digestive system.

Precautions: It can cause narcosis, vomiting, hallucinations, or even death; even the spice can cause severe adverse reactions. If applied to the skin, it can cause rashes and allergies. Its use is not recommended.

ORANGE

AKA: *Citrus aurantium, Citrus aurantium sinensis.*

Effects: Said to reduce stress and depression, increase energy, and induce feelings of calm and happiness. It has been used to treat such gastrointestinal disorders as gas, indigestion, and constipation.

Works synergistically with cinnamon, clove, lavender, and nutmeg.

Precautions: When applied to the skin, it can increase susceptibility to damage by the sun. The oranges used must be natural and organic, as most are sprayed with ethylene to give them more color and coated with wax to seal in the moisture.

PALMAROSA

AKA: *Cymbopogon martini.*

Effects: Said to elevate mood and refresh the spirits. It has been used to relieve the muscle aches accompanying flus and fevers.

Precautions: It is often adulterated with cedarwood and turpentine.

PEPPER

AKA: Black pepper, *Piper nigrum.*

Effects: Said to promote alertness. It has been used to treat dermatitis, flu symptoms, rheumatism, catarrh, colds, and hay fever.

Precautions: Undiluted, the oil can be toxic and irritating to the skin. Overuse could damage the kidneys.

PEPPERMINT

AKA: *Mentha piperita.*

Effects: Contains large amounts of cineole, a compound which increases blood flow to parts of the brain. When rubbed into the forehead, it can relieve tension headaches. It stimulates the nervous system, improves circulation, and increases awareness, alertness, and concentration. It has been used to treat motion sickness, gas, stomach aches, nausea, vomiting, heartburn, diarrhea, migraines, hangovers, shingles (herpes zoster), and congested sinuses.

Precautions: It should not be used in bath water, as it can be irritating to the skin. It should not be used as a massage oil, as at least half of the essential oil is menthol, an alcohol that has a cooling effect on the skin. And it should not be used undiluted, at night (as it will prevent sleep), or in addition to homeopathic remedies.

PETITGRAIN

AKA: *Citrus aurantium bigaradia.*

Effects: Said to relieve nervous tension, fatigue, insomnia, and sadness. Its effects are very similar to neroli, only milder.

Precautions: When applied to the skin, it can increase susceptibility to sunburn. It may cause insomnia in some people.

ROSE

AKA: *Rosa centifolia* (cabbage rose, Provence rose), *Rosa damascena* (damask rose), *Rosa gallica.*

Effects: Said to relieve stress, anxiety, depression, and insomnia, and contribute to feelings of contentment and love. It has been used by herbalists to treat digestive problems.

Works synergistically with jasmine, lavender, neroli, and sandalwood.

Precautions: Since it is so expensive, cheaper brands may be adulterated with other oils such as *bois de rose*, gaiac, geranium, and palmarosa. Its medicinal properties have not withstood scientific scrutiny. It is also sold as an absolute, which may contain trace elements of toxic solvents.

ROSEMARY

AKA: *Rosmarinus officinalis.*

Effects: Has anti-oxidant properties, and contains high amounts of cineole, a compound which increases blood flow to parts of the brain and stimulates the central nervous system. It can also increase alertness and concentration, improve memory, relieve stress, and promote feelings of happiness and well-being. It is said to increase life span.

Precautions: It may be adulterated with aspic, sage, and turpentine.

SAGE

AKA: *Salvia officinalis.*

Effects: Said to relieve fatigue and depression, and improve memory.

Precautions: Contains compounds (such as thujone) which could cause severe adverse side effects and be carcinogenic if used for an extended period of time, even in small amounts. It should not be used by young or sensitive individuals, and some aromatherapists advise using clary sage instead.

SANDALWOOD

AKA: *Santalum album.*

Effects: Said to reduce stress, increase concentration during meditation, and act as an aphrodisiac. It has been used to treat eczema and other skin disorders, sore throats, and urinary tract infections.

Works synergistically with benzoin, frankincense, jasmine, lemon, rose, and verbena.

Precautions: The huge demand for this oil has led to the practice of cutting trees before they reach maturity, depleting a once abundant crop. It may be adulterated with castor, linseed, and palm oils.

STAR ANISE

AKA: Badian anise, Chinese anise, *Illicium verum.*

Effects: Said to promote awareness. It has no medicinal properties.

Precautions: It is not recommended for use as an oil.

TANGERINE

AKA: *Citrus reticulata.*

Effects: Said to relieve stress, anxiety, tension, depression, and insomnia.

Precautions: If applied to the skin, it could make it more susceptible to damage from the sun.

VANILLA

AKA: *Vanilla planifolia.*

Effects: Said to reduce stress, irritability, and tension.

Works synergistically with bergamot, lime, and rose.

VERBENA

AKA: *Aloysia citriodora*, lemon verbena, *Lippia citriodora*, *Verbena triphylla.*

It should not be confused with vervein, or *Verbena officinalis.*

Effects: Said to relieve depression and fatigue, and increase concentration. It is used as a digestive aid, an antiseptic, and to clear up such skin problems as acne.

Works synergistically with cedar, hyssop, jasmine, juniper, myrtle, neroli, and orange.

Precautions: The pure oil may irritate sensitive skin, and more than two or three drops in bathwater may sting or blister the skin. It is quite rare and expensive, so cheaper brands may be adulterated with lemongrass and citronella.

VETIVER

AKA: *Andropogon muricatus*, khas-khas, khus-khus, *Vetiveria zizanoides*, vetivert.

Effects: Said to reduce stress and nervous tension. It is used mainly in perfumes and soaps, and as a fixative in aftershaves and colognes.

Works synergistically with cardamom, frankincense, jasmine, neroli, orange, rose, sandalwood, verbena, and ylang-ylang.

Precautions: it is quite costly, so less expensive brands may be adulterated with cheaper oils or synthetics.

YARROW

AKA: *Achillea millefolium*.
Effects: Said to increase awareness.

It has been used to speed the healing of wounds, and to treat headaches, skin rashes, varicose veins, hemorrhoids, vaginal infections, and acne.

Works syngergistically with clary sage, cypress, melissa, and myrtle.

Precautions: Yarrow should only be used in its diluted state, as it is quite powerful. When applied to the skin, it can make it more susceptible to skin rash when exposed to sunlight or ultraviolet light.

YLANG YLANG

AKA: *Cananga odorata*.
Effects: It can slow down rapid breathing and rapid heartbeat. It is said to relieve stress, anxiety, depression, and the mood swings of PMS, and promote feelings of love and sexuality.

Works syngergistically with bergamot, clary sage, lavender, lemon, and neroli.

Precautions: Prolonged or excessive use may cause headaches or nausea. Due to the neglect of this plant as a cash crop, this oil is now hard to come by, and most of the oil now sold is either cocoa butter, coconut oil, or the inferior variant *Cananga macrophylla*, popularly known as cananga.

CHAPTER 10

Entheogens

Entheogens, popularly known as psychedelics or hallucinogenics, are among the most powerful and controversial substances known to man, and comprise approximately one-tenth of the 600,000-plus plant species identified so far. These and other mind-altering substances act by intensifying the user's mood and the situation he or she is in when taking the drug; as such, they have often been used in religious ceremonies and, more recently, in therapeutic situations. There may be many more psychoactive plants that have yet to be identified; there are certainly many in which the psychoactive ingredient has yet to be identified. A number of these plants are used by various indigenous peoples around the world in their ceremonies, yet they appear to have no psychoactive ingredient, and the often theatrical and bizarre behavior exhibited by those partaking of the so-called hallucinogen may be due more to social expectations and psychodrama than to any actual pharmacological ingredient. The quality of the experience may reflect the variety and potency of the plant, the method with which it is prepared, the setting or circumstances under which it is taken, and possibly the physiology of the individual taking it.

AGARA

AKA: *Galbulimima belgraveana.*

A timber tree native to Malaysia and Australia that is related to the magnolias.

Effects: Causes violent intoxication, followed by a deep sleep characterized by vivid dreams and visions. Papuans boil the leaves and bark with the leaves of ereriba to make a drink, or just chew the leaves and bark. Although 28 biologically active alkaloids have been identified, the psychoactive principle has yet to be identified.

AMANITA MUSHROOMS

AKA: *Amanita muscaria* (bolond gomba, fly agaric, Gluckspilz, ha ma chun, mukhomor, Narrenschwamm, tu ying hsin), *Amanita pantherina* (panther mushroom).

The amanita family of mushrooms can range from those that are harmless (and actually quite delicious) to those that are deadly poisonous; the above are the only two that are psychoactive. The name "fly agaric" is derived from the fact that flies will drop into a helpless stupor after sucking on its juices. It is also noteworthy that the mushroom is believed to have contributed to the frenzied behavior of the Norse Vikings known as Beserkers. The degree of psychoactivity is related to its color — yellow is the weakest, red is the strongest, and orange is in between — on where and when it is grown, and on what trees it grows near. It can be dried and smoked; eaten fresh, cooked, or dried; or it can be brewed in a tea. In reindeer-hunting communities in Siberia, only the shamans were allowed to eat the fly agaric mushrooms, but others found they could participate in the experience by drinking the shaman's urine; supposedly, the unpleasant side effects of nausea and vomiting were lessened in this manner. This is because the kidneys detoxify muscarine, a toxin found in the mushroom, but allow muscimole, the hallucinogen, to pass into the urine largely intact (reindeer, who aggressively seek out this mushroom, will likewise consume the fly agaric–filled waste, and travelers are advised not to urinate in their presence out of fear for the person's safety). Urine can be recycled four or five times in this manner.

In Japan, there is mention in ancient literature of the maitake, or "dancing mushroom," which caused those who ate it to laugh and dance giddily; it has been identified as either *Paneolus papilionaceus* or *Pholiota spectabilis*, though the former is also known as waraitake, or the "laughing mushroom," and was once used as a cheap high in the U.S. and allegedly by witches in Portugal. Another "dancing mushroom" is *Gymnopilus (Pholiota) spectabilis*.

Effects: A pleasant, dreamy intoxication — accompanied by vivid hallucinations and giddiness — that lasts four to eight hours. The main psychoactive ingredients include muscazon, ibotenic acid, muscimole, and bufotenine.

It may work synergistically with the juice of the bog bilberry (*Vacinium uliginosum*).

Precautions: There are often unpleasant physical symptoms. An overdose can produce twitching, trembling, minor convulsions, numbness of the limbs, delirium, paranoia, aggression, nausea, vomiting and even death. *Amanita pantherina* has been known to make people sick for up to twelve hours, though these side effects usually start and end quickly. Other varieties of amanita (*Amanita phalloides*, *Amanita verna*) and other similar-looking mushrooms can be lethal when ingested, so extreme care must be taken when picking them in the wild.

Any mushroom should probably be sauteed before eating because in its raw state, it may contain methyl-hydazines, compounds similar to rocket propellants (which are, of course, carcinogenic and potentially deadly). Mushrooms may also accumulate such toxins as arsenic and cesium, though not in dangerous levels; cooking will not remove or deactivate them.

The use of atropine by some medical professionals to treat the negative effects is counterproductive; it intensifies, rather than nullifies, them. Mushrooms should not be combined with alcohol, either.

Dosage: One medium-sized mushroom is taken initally, to determine tolerance, with 1 to 3 mushrooms per dose thereafter. They are thoroughly dried first, and under no circumstances are more than 3 mushrooms taken at any one time.

ANIMALS

While it is common knowledge that toad secretions can induce altered states, what is not well-known is that other animals have psychoactive properties, as well. Much of the information is sketchy and anecdotal, however.

Ants. Several Native American tribes of Southern California have ingested ants as a means of inducing visions and obtaining supernatural powers, though the particular species has not yet been identified.

Bees and wasps. Honey made from the nectar of the belladonna plant will retain some of the plant alkaloids' psychoactive effects. Multiple bee and wasp stings can induce euphoria and heighten the perception of colors and geometric forms.

Cobra. Indian holy men supposedly smoke the dried venom of the king cobra (Ophiophagus hannah) and the common cobra (Naja naja).

Fish. The puffer fish is supposedly one ingredient of the Haitian zombie drug. A species of Kyphosus (possibly Kyphosus fuseus or Kyphosus vaigiensis) of Norfolk Island in the Pacific, two species of mullet (Mugil cephalus and Neomyxus chaptalli), and two species of goatfish (Mulloidichthys samoensis and Upeneus arge) are known by some as "dream fish" or "nightmare fish." That the effects are genuine — as evinced by infants who have shown all the classic signs of nightmares after consuming it — and that it is not an allergic reaction — as non-toxic species produce no reactions in those who have also eaten the toxic ones — has been proved, though the exact psychoactive principle remains a mystery. While German anthropologist Christian Ratsch states that the fish may contain DMT, others are not so sure (Jonathan Ott asserts that the DMT would not be psychoactive if taken orally, and would not exist in sufficient quantities to produce the required effects if it were), though bacteria from decay and algae eaten by the fish are two possibilities that are also considered unlikely. Disagreements by various Pacific Islanders concerning the physical characteristics of the relevant fish and the specific parts of the fish purported to be psychoactive only add to the confusion. The surgeonfish (Acanthurus sandvicensis) and the rudder fish (Kyphosus cinerascens) are also rumored to be hallucinogenic.

Giraffe. A drink, called umm nyolokh, made from the liver and bone marrow of a giraffe, is said by the Humr people of the Sudan to induce hallucinations and vivid dreams. Richard Rudgely speculates that the bone marrow may harbor DMT.

Moth larva. It has been said that a "bamboo grub," called bicho de tacuara by the Malalis of Brazil and identified as the larva of the Myelobia smerintha moth, induces an opium-like sleep filled with vivid dreams.

Salamander. It is possible that medieval alchemists had been able to extract some form of psychoactive substance from the salamander. The secretions have been found to contain steroid alkaloids, one of which is a neurotoxin that can cause convulsions and death.

Scorpion. One researcher has reported that those stung by a scorpion experience hallucinations. An analysis of such poisons has yet to be conducted to determine if they have psychoactive properties.

Spanish fly. This notorious aphrodisiac, also known as cantharides, is actually the wings of the *Cantharis vesicatoria* beetle, though its use can cause toxicity in sufficient doses.

ARBOL DE LOS BRUJOS

AKA: *Latua pubiflora*, *Latua venenosa*, latue, latuy, *Lycioplesium pubiflorum*, sorcerers' tree.

Related to the nightshade family, it is the only known species of latua and is used by the medicine men of the Mapuche Indians in central Chile.

Effects: Causes hallucinations because of the alkaloids hyoscyamine and scopolamine.

Precautions: Also causes delirium and insanity, which may be permanent, depending on the dosage.

Dosage: The dosage is a closely guarded secret, though the medicine men can reputedly control the duration of the madness quite accurately.

ARCHONTOPHOENIX

Effects: The nuts of this New Britain palm are said to be psychoactive.

AYAHUASCA AND CAAPI

AKA: *Banisteriopsis caapi* (caapi, oco-yaje, yage, yaje, yaje-uco), *Banisteriopsis inebrians*, *Banisteriopsis martiniana*, *Banisteriopsis muricata* (mii, sacha ayahuasca), *Banisteriopsis quitensis*, bejuco de oro, cadana, dapa, *Diplopterys cabrerana* (*Banisteriopsis rusbyana*, chagropanga, chacruna), kahi, mihi, natema, pilde, pinde, tiger drug, yake.

Ayahuasca and caapi are two species (of approximately 100) of a South American liana, or jungle vine.

Effects: Causes a pleasurable intoxication and colorful visual hallucinations lasting six to twelve hours, reportedly without the subsequent hangover, followed by a deep sleep. It also increases visual acuity and sensory awareness, and acts as an aphrodisiac. It is said to endow the user with telepathic abilities, but there is no scientific evidence to support this claim. The main psychoactive ingredient is the alkaloid harmine.

There is another type of caapi made from the vine *Tetrapteris methystica*, popularly known as caapi-pinima (painted caapi). The drink, made from the bark by the Maku Indians on the Amazon in northwestern Brazil, has an odd yellowish color and tastes very bitter.

Precautions: The initial effects are nausea, dizziness, intense vomiting and diarrhea. An overdose can result in nightmarish visions, violent intoxication, recklessness, and subsequent feelings of sickness.

It is an MAO inhibitor, and so should not be combined with any substances contraindicated for this type of drug, as it could cause headaches, heart problems, and death. It should not be combined with avocados, ripe bananas, broad beans, aged cheeses, chicken liver, excess amounts of chocolate, cocoa, dill oil, canned figs, pickled herring, excess amounts of licorice, milk or milk products, nutmeg, parsley oil, sauerkraut, wild fennel oil, yeast extract; amphetamines, antihistamines, ephedrine, sedatives, tranquilizers; or alcohol, excess amounts of caffeine, mescaline, or narcotics.

Combinations of tropical plants containing DMT and beta-carbolines may produce similar effects to ayahuasca, and are occasionally passed off as such on the underground drug market. These are sometimes referred to by ethnobotanists as ayahuasca analogues or ayahuasca borealis.

Dosage: The bark can be made into a drink, the bark and stems can be chewed, or the plant can be made into a snuff. Various other plants are often added to the drink depending on the region, some of which, like *Diplopterys cabrerana* (a third species, called ocoyaje by Colombian and Ecuadorian Indians along the Amazon) and various species of *Psychotria*, may be psychoactive themselves. *Diplopterys cabrerana* contains DMT (N,N-dimethyltryptamine) as well, producing higher, clearer visions, as the yage inactivates the stomach enzyme that usually destroys DMT.

An average cup of the native decoction can contain 400 mg of psychoactive alkaloids. The fact that it is prepared with other plants could present additional problems.

William Burroughs describes his experiences with yage in *The Yage Letters*.

BAIBAI AND BUDZAMAR

AKA: Bebai, *Cycas circinalis*.

Effects: The pollen of this New Guinea plant is said to induce narcosis. Another member of the *Cycas* genus,

locally referred to as budzamar, is used by magicians on islands in the Torres Straits to enter an altered state.

BELLADONNA

AKA: Apples of Sodom, *Atropa belladonna*, banewort, beautiful lady, black cherry, deadly nightshade, death's herb, devil's herb, dwale, hound's berries, morrel, murderer's berry, naughty man's cherry, petty-morrel, poison black cherry, sorcerer's cherry, witches' berry.

A member of the potato family, it is used in various medications including sleep remedies, cold remedies, treatments for ulcers and stomach problems, and some asthma drugs.

Effects: Hallucinations, which may contain elements of ecstasy and eroticism. It contains the psychoactive alkaloids atropine, scopolamine, and hysoscyamine, along with traces of nicotine.

Precautions: Contains the dangerous alkaloid apoatropine. Side effects include dry mouth, hot skin, rash, blurred vision, fear, restlessness, confusion, vomiting, convulsions, learning impairment, permanent eye damage, permanent brain damage, and death from heart failure.

Dosage: Some people in Asia and the Middle East eat or smoke the dried, crushed leaves (30 to 200 mg) or the root (30 to 120 mg). Toxicity may vary from plant to plant and from person to person, but can be as little as one berry.

BETEL

AKA: *Areca catechu*, areca nut, betel nut, ping lang, supari.

A favorite stimulant for thousands of years, it is still one of the most widely used drugs in the world, as popular in Asia as tobacco is in the West.

Effects: The stimulant is the alkaloid arecoline, which increases energy, elevates mood, and acts as an aphrodisiac, though this last effect may just may be an indirect result of the first two. The arecoline that is swallowed can rid the body of some intestinal parasites.

Precautions: Constant use will stain the teeth, mouth, and gums a dark red or black. An overdose can weaken the sex drive and create other unwanted side effects. Ingesting too much arecoline, or betel that is not yet ripe, can result in a feeling of drunkenness, followed by dizziness, vomiting, diarrhea, and possibly convulsions.

Dosage: A slice of betel nut is mixed with part of a leaf from the Piper betel vine and a piece of lime, plus cloves, nutmeg, tamarind, turmeric, cardamom, and sometimes resins, then placed in the mouth and chewed or sucked on for hours.

BOOPHANE DISTICHA

Effects: The bulb of this South African plant is hallucinogenic, and is used by the Basuto people for its male initiation rite, and some Zimbabweans to communicate with the dead.

Precautions: The Basuto also use the bulb as an arrow poison and as a method of committing suicide.

BORRACHERA

AKA: *Lochroma fuchsioides*.

A member of the nightshade family that is native to the highlands of South America.

Effects: Supposedly made into a hallucinatory drink by the Sibundoy Valley Indians of southern Colombia. The psychoactive principle has yet to be identified.

BORRACHERO

AKA: *Ipomoea carnea*, matacabra ("goat killer").

Effects: A psychoactive plant with ergot alkaloids found in Ecuador.

CAFFEINE

Food sources: Bissy nut, chocolate, cocoa, coffee, gotu kola, guarana, mate, soft drinks, tea (excluding many herbal teas), some stimulant drugs sold by mail or over-the-counter, and many over-the-counter medications.

Effects: Caffeine is one of the most powerful legal stimulants; it gives a mental boost by releasing adrenaline and noradrenaline into the bloodstream. It interferes on a cellular level with the compound adenosine, in effect flatlining the body's state of arousal, allowing the body to shift into high gear. It may also affect dopamine, acetylcholine, and other neurotransmitters. All coffee, including decaffeinated, contains at least three compounds that act like opiates, or heroin, on the brain. It improves typing skills, mental alertness, energy, reaction time, concentration, and accuracy in performing tasks, and relieves fatigue, mainly by causing the release of norepinephrine in the brain. It improves physical endurance by stimulating the skeletal muscles, increases the production of stomach acid and urine, causes bowel movements, and dilates the bronchial tubes (making it easier to breathe). According to studies, it has no effect on memory or clarity of thought. In addition, the presence of polyphenols in coffee and tea may prevent cancer by inhibiting the conversion of highly carcinogenic nitrosamines in the body. A few cups of coffee a day can help prevent gallstones in men, and four to five cups a day can reduce colorectal cancer by 24 percent.

Precautions: It should not be taken by anyone who is allergic to stimulants, has heart disease or irregular heartbeats, who suffers from insomnia, anxiety, or panic disorders, or has a peptic ulcer of the stomach or duodenum. A physician should be consulted first if any of the following conditions are present: hypoglycemia, epilepsy, or high blood pressure. To discontinue use, gradually decrease the amount over a month or more, or headaches, irritability, and drowsiness may result.

Not all researchers are convinced of its mental benefits. Some studies show no improvement in recall or response time, and others show that high doses can impair a person's ability to work with numbers. And it may have a negative effect on a person's ability to quickly process ambiguous or confusing stimuli. Any improvements in mental functioning may peak at a certain dosage, then decline with increasing consumption. Overall, caffeine may benefit the performance of simple tasks but have no effect on more complex ones such as reading comprehension or advanced mathematics.

Though it is readily absorbed into the bloodstream, researchers still do not understand its full effects upon the human body. Caffeine can lead to a condition in coffee drinkers called coffee intoxication, in which more than four or five cups a day results in irritability, muscle twitches, rambling speech and thought, and trouble sleeping. It can also worsen existing health problems, and may contribute to birth defects, bladder and colon cancer, kidney disease, osteoporosis, hypertension, abnormal heart

rhythms, stomach ulcers, and heart disease, though more recent studies refute these findings. When combined with sugar, as in many cola drinks, it can be particularly addictive or habit-forming. It does not replenish a person's noradrenaline once it is used up, and either depletes or limits the absorption of many vitamins and minerals. Withdrawal symptoms can begin 12 to 36 hours after the last dose, and can include lethargy, irritability, severe throbbing headaches, anxiety, depression, fatigue, and possibly even nausea and vomiting; symptoms can last from one and one-half to seven days.

Other adverse effects include heart palpitations, high blood pressure, muscle twitches, rapid heartbeat, low blood sugar, nervousness, insomnia, increased urination, anxiety, indigestion, increased production of gastrointestinal acid, rectal itching, constipation, impaired concentration, a weakened immune system, bladder irritation and urinary problems (especially in women), and interference with DNA replication. It has been shown to trigger panic attacks in susceptible people — which it does by lowering the body's production of DHEA and increasing its production of cortisol — and interfere with the ability to sleep in most coffee drinkers. Decaffeinated coffee still contains some caffeine and can also cause these symptoms. More severe and infrequent symptoms include confusion, nausea, stomach ulcers, indigestion, and a burning feeling in the stomach. Overdose symptoms include excitement, insomnia, rapid heartbeat, confusion, fever, hallucinations, convulsions, and coma.

More than five cups a day can increase the heart attack risk to three times that of a non-coffee drinker. Long-term high-dose caffeine intake can promote calcium loss due to its diuretic effect, weakening bones. The lethal dosage has been estimated to be about 10 grams. If caffeine must be consumed, it should be derived from plant sources, as the synthetic form does not have the fat-burning properties the natural form does. As for the natural forms, kola nut and yerba mate are the best caffeine sources, guarana is adequate, and tea and coffee rank lowest. Boiled or percolated coffee can increase serum cholesterol levels and the risk of heart disease; drip coffee does not, as the paper filters absorb the harmful oils in the coffee grounds.

Food and drug interactions are also a cause for concern. Grapefruit juice can increase the level of caffeine and extend its effects by up to one-third. Certain antibiotics such as Cipro (ciprofloxacin) and Penetrex (enoxacin) can significantly intensify and prolong the effects of caffeine. Consuming it with other caffeine-containing drugs, central nervous system stimulants, or sympathomimetics can result in overstimulation; with Cimetidine (Tagamet), oral contraceptives, or Isoniazid, increased sensitivity to the effects of the caffeine (Tagamet can increase caffeine levels by as much as 70 percent); with sedatives, sleep inducers, or tranquilizers, increased sensitivity to the sedative or tranquilizer; with MAO inhibitors, dangerously high blood pressure; and with thyroid hormones, an increase in the thyroid effect. Combined with caffeinated beverages, caffeine is likely to be more stimulating. Taken with alcohol, caffeine can slow a person's reaction time and intensify the effects of alcohol; with cocaine, it can lead to convulsions or extreme nervousness; with marijuana, it can lead to an increased effect of both

substances along with a rapid heartbeat; and with tobacco, it can lead to an accelerated heartbeat and a decreased caffeine effect.

Some mail-order "look-alike" drugs that mimic amphetamines have reportedly triggered strokes and irregular heartbeats that ultimately led to death, but this may be blamed more on the stimulant phenylprolanolamine (PPA) than on the caffeine and ephedrine found in these drugs. Still, the health problems associated with ephedrine and caffeine have led the FDA to ban drugs and diet aids that contain these two ingredients.

Dosage: The majority of the research shows that healthy people can consume up to two cups of coffee (200 mg) a day without suffering any ill effects; more than 300 mg of caffeine a day, however, is not recommended. Green tea, in addition to containing about 100 mg of caffeine per serving, contains polyphenols, or strong antioxidant nutrients (which protect against arterial damage that can eventually result in heart attacks or stroke), making it preferable to black tea. Adding milk ties up some of the beneficial chemicals, rendering them useless.

CALAMUS

AKA: *Acorus calamus*, flag root, grass myrtle, myrtle flag, rat root, sweet calomel, sweet cinnamon, sweet flag, sweet grass, sweet myrtle, sweet root, sweet rush, vacha.

Effects: Stimulates, energizes, and in high enough doses, produces a psychedelic effect similar to LSD. It contains the substance asarone, which is similar to mescaline and amphetamines, but may not create the feeling of tension that amphetamines do. It is used by some to treat such ailments as asthma, bronchitis, diarrhea, fever, hangover, headache, and toothache. According to James A. Duke, Ph.D., the root can kill lice when ground into a powder and applied to the infected area.

Precautions: It may cause vomiting in high doses. The plant is very similar in appearance to the highly poisonous blue flag. The calamus leaves give off a sweet smell when scratched and the roots have a pleasing aroma and sharp taste; blue flag does not give off any smell, and the roots have a bitter, unpleasant taste. The various species native to India, Europe, and North America may each have very different pharmacological properties.

MAO inhibitors should not be taken less than a week before or a week after taking calamus.

Dosage: An initial dose should be a 2-inch length of root the thickness of a pencil, which can either be chewed or brewed in a tea. This will produce stimulation and euphoria. A 10-inch length is said to produce mild LSD-like hallucinations. It should be taken on an empty stomach to prevent vomiting. The root should not be stored for more than a few months, as it will lose potency.

CALEA

AKA: Bitter grass, *Calea zacatechichi*, leaf of God, Mexican calea, thlepela-kano, zacatechichi.

A member of the daisy family that grows from Mexico to Costa Rica and is used by the Chontal Indians of Oaxaca.

Effects: Calea may produce a sense of calm, drowsiness, a clarity of the senses, vivid dreams, and hallucinations lasting for a day or more. The psychoactive property has not been identified, though William Emboden and Jonathan Ott say there is none. It is also used to treat fever, nausea, and mild diarrhea.

Dosage: Two tablespoons of dried leaves brewed for five minutes in a pint of boiling water, which is then slowly sipped. The Indians are said to finish off with a few puffs of calea leaves rolled into a joint.

CALIFORNIA POPPY

AKA: *Eschscholtzia californica.*

Effects: A mild marijuana-like high that lasts for about a half hour. It is not related to the opium poppy, but apparently does contain several psychoactive alkaloids.

Dosage: One joint per day — smoking more does not seem to extend or intensify the high. The leaves and petals are dried and rolled into joints.

CANAVALIA MARITIMA

A legume that is supposedly used as a marijuana substitute.

Effects: Similar to marijuana; its psychoactive properties have not yet been isolated. The mature seeds of *Canavalia ensiformis*, or the jack bean, are roasted and used as a coffee substitute in the West Indies.

CARDAMINE CONCATENATA

Effects: A hallucinogen.

CAWE

AKA: Chawe, *Pachycereus pectenaboriginum.*

A giant cactus found in Mexico.

Effects: Contains phenethylamine alkaloids, but it is not known if they are psychoactive. The Tarahumara Indians crush the branches in water to make cawe, a ceremonial beverage. It is sometimes added to San Pedro.

CHIRIC-CASPI AND CHIRIC SANANGO

AKA: *Brunfelsia chiricaspi, Brunfelsia grandiflora, Brunfelsia tastevinii* (keya-hone).

This genus of 40 species of South American and West Indian shrubs belongs to the nightshade family.

Effects: Used by several South American Indian tribes to make a hallucinogenic drink that takes effect in about 15 minutes and has a duration of four to five hours. The psychoactive ingredient has not yet been isolated. The plants are also used to treat fevers, snakebite, and rheumatism.

CHOCOLATE

AKA: Chocolatl, *Theobrama cacao*.

Though it is an addictive psychoactive which some believe mimics the effects of marijuana, not much is known about its pharmacology and cognitive effects. Caffeine may account for some of its psychoactive properties, but some researchers state that most of its effects are attributable to theobromine, an alkaloid found in chocolate that is similar to caffeine but which does not have as strong an effect on the nervous system. Researcher Daniele Piomelli has found that chocolate contains anandamide, a natural chemical also found in the brain, which reacts the same way marijuana does; it also contains two other ingredients that inhibit the natural breakdown of anandamide. Still, researchers agree that the "high" produced by chocolate is extremely mild; in fact, researcher Christian Felder of the National Institute of Mental Health calculates that a 130-pound person would have to eat the equivalent of 25 pounds of chocolate in one sitting to get anything close to a marijuana high. Theobromine mainly affects the muscles, kidneys, and heart. In addition to providing proteins, vitamins, and minerals (calcium, iron, niacin, potassium, riboflavin, sodium, thiamine, and vitamin A, among others), it may also have a sexually stimulating effect caused by theobromine and the possible ingredient B-phenethylamine, the latter a biochemical manufactured by the brain of a person in love. Chocolate can neutralize the effects of sugar, reducing tooth decay.

A 1998 Harvard study by Dr. I-Min Lee of 7841 older men found that those who ate chocolate lived longer than those who didn't, with those eating just three chocolate bars a month living the longest. Some have questioned the results of this study, as eating more chocolate was not correlated with longer life, and three chocolate bars a month was too little for it to be perceived as having any significant effect. (Chocolate does contain anti-oxidants known as phenols, but this alone could not account for the increase in life expectancy, and there are no other known chemicals that could account for this effect.)

Chocolatl is a bitter Aztec drink made from the cacao beans and flavored with pepper, vanilla, and other spices.

Precautions: It is addictive, and has a high (40 to 60 percent) fat content. Chocolate and nuts should be avoided by those with herpes, as the high arginine content can aggravate the symptoms. It should not be taken by anyone with allergies, as it can worsen symptoms, or anyone with canker sores, as it can delay healing. Sensitivity to chocolate can trigger migraine headaches.

It can decrease the effectiveness of antihistamines, tranquilizers, sedatives, and relaxants, and can cause severe hypertension in anyone taking an MAO inhibitor or antidepressant.

It can deplete the body of inositol and the B vitamins, particularly B-1, and partially prevent the absorption of calcium. It also has significant levels of caffeine, which can place stress on the endocrine system and deplete the body's stores of potassium and zinc.

CIMORA

A hallucinogenic drink consumed by the Indian witch doctors in Peru and Ecuador, who use it to foretell the future and diagnose their patients. Of its several ingredients, the main psychoactive ones are datura and San Pedro.

CLEMATIS VIRGINIANA

Effects: Supposedly induces strange dreams and hallucinations.

Precautions: It may irritate the skin or, if ingested, cause a burning feeling in the mouth.

CLUB MOSS

AKA: *Lycopodium complanatum, Lycopodium selago*, wolf's foot.

Effects: *Lycopodium selago* can induce a mild hypnotic narcosis or a comatose state, depending on the dosage taken, yet *Lycopodium complanatum* can have a stimulating effect. In Peru, another species of club moss is often added to San Pedro.

Precautions: James A. Duke, Ph.D., has found that Chinese club moss (*Huperzia serrata*) and *Lycopodium* club mosses both contain the beneficial compound huperzine; however, for psychoactive effects, it appears each species is distinctly different from the others, and different parts of each plant are used.

Dosage: According to William Emboden, three stems of *Lycopodium selago* will induce a hypnotic narcosis.

COCA

AKA: *Erythroxylum coca.*

The psychoactive ingredient of the coca leaf is cocaine, only one of over a dozen compounds in the coca leaf which have a similar effect. There are several different varieties of coca, none of which is related to cocoa.

Effects: It has been used for centuries as a gentle stimulant by indigenous peoples of South America, who use it to treat altitude sickness and brew it into a tea called mate de coca. Coca usually contains less than 0.5 percent active cocaine — because of this, and because it enters the body through the mouth and stomach, rather than through the more direct routes of the lungs and bloodstream common to cocaine users, it is rarely addictive. It contains many vitamins, including thiamine, riboflavin, and vitamin C, along with many compounds that modify the cocaine, rendering it safer to the user; all this is lost when it is refined into cocaine. It helps the body dispose of toxic metabolites, including uric acid. It appears to keep the teeth and gums healthy, have a positive effect on respiration, and alleviate somewhat symptoms of altitude sickness. According to its users, it increases the life span. It has not yet been determined whether it improves any mental functions, though its stimulant effect gives one the feeling of being smarter and mentally sharper.

Dosage: The average Indian consumes about two ounces of dried leaves a day, or about 0.7 grains of cocaine.

COLEUS

AKA: *Coleus blumei, coleus pumilus.*

Effects: Despite the fact that the Mazatecs of Oaxaca, Mexico, use these mint plants in the same way they use the hallucinogenic hojas de la Pastora, no hallucinogenic agent has been isolated in either of them or in any of the 150 species of coleus. William Emboden states that researcher R. Gordon Wasson has reported mind-altering effects, but these have not been verified by others. However, Young *et al.* claim that only the fresh leaves exhibit psychoactive properties, and that it takes 50 to 70 to do the trick, which manifests itself as a "trippy, psilocybin-like state, colorful visual hallucinations and patterns, and telepathic and clairvoyant insights" for a duration of some two hours.

Precautions: Brief nausea a half-hour after consumption.

Dosage: Between 50 to 70 large fresh leaves; dried leaves will not do. They can be chewed, smoked, or steeped in lukewarm water for an hour and drunk as a tea.

COLORINES

AKA: *Erythrina flabelliformis.*

Effects: A feeling of drunkenness accompanied by hallucinations.

Precautions: The toxic dose is very small. Some species of *Erythrina* are

known to contain isoquinoline-type alkaloids, which produce effects similar to the arrow poison curare. Symptoms include vomiting, a pounding heart, and convulsions, and death may result. The appearance of the bean is very similar to mescal beans — they are often mixed together by herb merchants, and both may be called by the same common name, colorin — and piule seeds (the *Rhynchosia* species — Young *et al.* in fact confuses these two).

Dosage: One-quarter to one-half bean; any more could trigger the toxic effects mentioned above. Use is not recommended.

CULEBRA BORRACHERO

AKA: *Methysticodendron amesianum*, mitskway borrachera.

The only known species of its genus, it may be a distant, and extremely divergent, relative of datura.

Effects: Excitement, hallucinations, and delirium.

Precautions: It is extremely potent, with 80 percent of its alkaloids consisting of scopolamine. Use can result in delirium and coma.

DAMA DE NOITE

AKA: *Cestrum laevigatum.*

Effects: Sold in Brazil as a marijuana substitute. No psychoactive ingredient has yet been isolated, though a related species, *Cestrum parqui*, is said to have psychotropic properties.

DAMIANA

AKA: *Turnera diffusa.*

Effects: A mild marijuana-like high for about an hour. It is said to induce a restful sleep filled with sexually oriented dreams when taken an hour before going to bed, and said to act as an aphrodisiac when taken an hour before sex. The psychoactive ingredient is not known.

Said to work synergistically with a teaspoonful of dried saw palmetto berries.

Precautions: Overuse may cause liver damage.

Dosage: It can be smoked like marijuana or brewed as a tea. Combining the two can supposedly increase the high.

DARNEL

AKA: Borrachera, borachuela, cizana, ivraie ("inebriating"), *Lolium temulentum*, tares, taumellolch ("delirium grass").

Effects: An inebriant with narcotic properties, this common wild grass contains psychoactive alkaloids. Loline, the main alkaloid, has been found to be non-toxic in doses of up to 200 mg per kilogram of body weight when injected into mice.

DATURA AND BRUGMANSIA

AKA (Datura): Concombre zombi (zombi's cucumber), *Datura alba*, *Datura arborea*, *Datura aurea*, *Datura candida*, *Datura ceratocaula* (tornaloco), *Datura discolor*, *Datura dolichocarpa*, *Datura fastuosa*, *Datura ferox*, *Datura inoxia* (*Datura meteloides*, dekuba, toloache, toloatzin, wichri, wysocean), *Datura metel* (dhatura, dutra), *Datura sanguinea*, *Datura stramonium* (devil's apple, devil's trumpet, devil's weed, James Town Weed, jimson weed, loco weed, qui-qui-sa-waal, stinkweed, thorn apple, white man's plant, yerba del diablo), *Datura suave-*olens, *Datura versicolor*, *Datura volcanicola*, *Datura wrightii*, jouzmathel, man-t'o-lo, tolouaxihuitl.

AKA (Brugmansia): Borrachero, *Brugmansia arborea*, *Brugmansia aurea*, *Brugmansia candida*, *Brugmansia insignis*, *Brugmansia sanguinea*, *Brugmansia suaveolens*, *Brugmansia vulcanicola*, buyes, campanilla, chamico, floripondios, huacacachu, huanco, huanto, huantuc, huanduj, kinde borrachero, maicoa, maikoa, misha toro, munchiro borrachero, tanga, toa, toe, tonga, tree datura, yerba de huaca.

A member of the nightshade family, the many varieties are divided into the plant forms and the tree forms, the latter of which is native only to South America and now considered to be a distinct genus: *Brugmansia*. The task of classifying the numerous species is made even harder by the ability of the indigenous people to produce hybrid plants. Datura was just one of the psychoactive plants used by European witches, and — according to Wade Davis — is used as an antidote to the zombi drug in Haiti. Scopolamine, one of the main psychoactive alkaloids, was tested as a "truth serum" by both the Nazis and the U.S. during World War II to unsatisfactory results.

Effects: Deep sleep and hallucinations. The main psychoactive alkaloids are hyoscyamine and scopolamine; the minor ones are atropine, meteloidine, and norscopolamine. Used by many shamans to foresee the future, speak with the dead, and diagnose illnesses. It has also been used in initiation ceremonies, to treat a number of physical ailments, and *Datura fatuosa* was once used by Incan priests to sedate patients during surgery.

Precautions: The main alkaloid is scopolamine, which is highly toxic; it has proven to have a negative effect on serial learning in doses as low as 0.5 mg. Initial intoxication may be so violent that the user may have to be physically restrained. Other side effects include diarrhea, nausea, confusion, incoherence, dizziness, agitation, and loss of motor coordination. Overdose symptoms include convulsions, coma, intoxication lasting days (up to twenty days in some cases, according to Richard Rudgley), permanent damage to the eyes, heart, and brain, and death. The side effects of *Datura stramonium* include fever, chills, loss of coordination, a dry burning in the mouth, difficulty swallowing, hot dry skin, rash, dizziness, pressure in the head, vomiting, loss of memory, agitation, and a blurring and distortion of vision. Overdose symptoms include mental disorientation, panic, convulsions, and coma. Like Rohypnol, the "date rape drug," it was once used by criminals to incapacitate their victims.

Similar methods of incapacitating a person occur in Fiji, where datura is sometimes added to kava, and Africa, where it is added to beer or wine.

Carlos Castaneda's *The Teachings of Don Juan* and subseqent books dealing with datura make up a fictional framework on which hang numerous bits of information cribbed from some 200 esoteric works, much of it inconsistent and inaccurate. The film based on Wade Davis' *The Serpent and the Rainbow* bears only a passing resemblance to the book, reinforcing old stereotypes; and Davis' conclusions about the ingredients of the zombi drug itself have been attacked by some as reliant on too little evidence.

Dosage: It can be smoked, eaten, drunk as a tea, or taken as an enema. In Africa and Asia, it is often combined with cannabis or tobacco and smoked, and in Tanzania it is added to beer. *Datura suaveolens* is often added to ayahuasca.

The ground seeds are often added to maize beer and, in Mexico, the dried leaves of *Brugmansia* are added to tobacco to induce diagnostic visions for treating various diseases.

DESIGNER PSYCHEDELICS

Custom-made synthetic drugs made by chemists. They may have names like MMDA, TMA, PMA, 2CB, and 2CT2.

Precautions: They can vary widely in potency, duration of effect, and type of effect.

DILL

Effects: Oil of dill will produce hallucinations.

Precautions: The level needed to induce hallucinations is very close to the toxic level. Side effects include epileptic-like convulsions, kidney damage, and liver damage.

Dosage: 5 to 20 drops of oil taken orally.

DMT AND RELATED TRYPTAMINES

AKA (DMT): *Anadenanthera colubrina, Anadenanthera peregrina, Anadenanthera rigida,* angico, businessman's trip, cebil, cohoba, dimethyltryptamine, hisioma, huilca, niopo, N,N-dimethyltryptamine, one-hit grass, parica, *Piptadenia peregrina,* sebil, vilca, yopo, yupa.

AKA (AMT): Alpha-methyltryptamine, IT-290.

AKA (DAT): N,N-diallyltrypta-mine.

AKA (DBT): N,N-dibutyltrypta-mine.

AKA (DET): N,N-diethyltrypta-mine, T-9.

AKA (DHT): N,N-dihexyltrypta-mine.

AKA (DIT): N,N-diisopropyl-tryptamine.

AKA (DPT): N,N-dipropyltrypta-mine.

AKA (5-MeO-DMT): 5-methoxy-N,N-dimethyltryptamine.

AKA (5-MeO-MMT): 5-methoxy-N-monomethyltryptamine.

AKA (5-OH-DMT): Bufotenine, 5-hdroxy-N,N-dimethyltryptamine.

AKA (5-MeO-MIPT): 5-methoxy-N-methyl-N-isopropyltryptamine.

AKA (MMT): N-monomethyl-tryptamine, NMT.

Existing naturally in human cere-brospinal fluid, DMT and its precursor tryptamine are similar to certain hor-mones secreted by the pineal gland. Fur-thermore, receptors for DMT have been discovered in the brains of mammals, and it is the active hallucinogenic ingre-dient in several South American plants. Other related tryptamines are listed above. AMT was made famous by Ken Kesey and his Merry Pranksters, as chronicled in Tom Wolfe's *The Electric Kool-Aid Acid Test.*

Effects: Possibly unique among psychedelics, DMT cannot be taken orally, as stomach enzymes break it down before it can pass to the blood-stream. South American Indians use it in the form of snuff (and variously call it cebil, cohoba, huilca, niopo, sebil, vilca, or yopo), and it can also be smoked or injected intramuscularly. As a snuff, it can produce an immediate

high that can last thirty minutes; when smoked, it can produce an immediate high that can last one to ten minutes. The high is similar to that of LSD or mescaline, but shorter. Parica is a generic name for snuffs of all kinds.

The tryptamine AMT produces a stimulating effect similar to LSD and amphetamines.

The tryptamine DET produces a trip that is milder and longer-lasting than DMT.

A close relative to DMT, 5-MeO-DMT is produced both synthetically and in the venom glands of the Sonoran Desert toad of Arizona. However, the two types of 5-MeO-DMT produce vastly different experiences, the former resulting in a frightening "dissolution of reality" when smoked and the toad venom producing a much gentler expe-rience when dried and smoked. Con-trary to tabloid reports, only the Sono-ran Desert toad has venom that is psychoactive (other toad venoms are just toxic), though it can cause a serious case of poisoning if brought into contact with the eyes or mouth.

Precautions: Some characterize the odor of DMT as the smell of burning plastic, which may be due to the conta-minant skatole. The psychedelic trip may be accompanied by dizziness, rapid heart and respiratory rates, disorienta-tion, and confusion. If taken on a full stomach, DMT could cause nausea. An overdose could result in blood rushing to the head and rupturing weak capil-laries. Addiction is unknown, though tolerance is rapid, and like any psyche-delic, it can result in bad trips.

An MAO inhibitor, DMT may cause severe headaches, vomiting, dan-gerously high blood pressure, heart problems, and even death when combined with avocados, bananas, broad beans, caffeine, aged cheeses, chicken liver, chocolate, cocoa, dill oil, fennel oil, canned figs, pickled herring, licorice, milk or milk products, nutmeg, parsley oil, pineapple, sauerkraut, yeast extract, alcohol, amphetamines, antihistamines, atropine, ephedrine, insulin, mescaline, narcotics, ritalin, sedatives, or tranquilizers.

Jonathan Ott and others have concluded that 5-MeO-DMT has "little recreational value," essentially agreeing with a colleague who compared it to "having a large elephant sitting on one's head." It should be noted that, since most types of toad venom are toxic, licking toads can be dangerous, and getting the venom in the eyes or mouth can cause severe poisoning. The venom must be dried and smoked to inactivate the toxins.

Reportedly, 5-MeO-MIPT acts more like amphetamines, providing stimulation without the hallucinations.

The reported hallucinogenic effects of 5-OH-DMT are disputed by research, which also suggests that it creates cardiopulmonary distress and may be toxic even in doses as low as 10 mg when injected intravenously. A CIA experiment nearly killed three individuals with 2.5 to 5 mg of an intramuscular injection after they were premedicated with reserpine and chlorpromazine.

Dosage: Readily snorted, eaten, and injected, DMT (in a dose of 3.5 to 5 mg) can also be combined with marijuana, parsley, or tobacco and smoked; there are several methods used to prepare the seeds for consumption. Writer William Burroughs self-experimented with DMT in doses of around 65 mg; he accidentally overdosed at 100 mg, producing a traumatic experience that left

him leery of the drug afterward. Timothy Leary and Ralph Metzner reported no ill effects at doses of 1 mg/kg of body weight. The CIA experimented on prison inmates and mental patients, revealing that the snuff is inactive in doses up to 1 gram, and oral doses are inactive up to 350 mg, but intramuscular injections produced visual hallucinations with as little as 10 to 12.5 mg.

According to Jonathan Ott,

> DMT is not active orally. Single doses of up to a gram orally have no effect … . Similarly, rectal doses of up to 125 mg DMT in 15 ml water were "without any discernable effect" … The average intramuscular dose of the hydrochloride salt is 50 to 60 mg, producing an entheogenic effect commencing in 2 to 5 minutes, peaking in 15 minutes, with the experience lasting a total of 30 to 45 minutes. An effect of equal intensity is produced by 25 to 30 mg of DMT free base smoked, with the entire experience accelerated dramatically. The onset following smoking is almost immediate, attaining a peak in 2 to 3 minutes, with the entire effect lasting only 10 to 20 minutes…. Although DMT-containing plant snuffs are active, intranasal administrations of 5 to 20 mg of pure DMT was inactive…. Orally, in combination with MAO-inhibitors, DMT is active in the same dose range as by intramuscular injection. Tolerance to the entheogenic effects of DMT develop rapidly, but dissipates rapidly as well, and DMT and LSD show cross-

tolerance.... Allowing about four hours between doses has been reported to avoid tolerance.

The effective oral dose of AMT appears to be approximately 20 mg.

Unlike DMT, DET is active orally, but only at high doses; when smoked or injected, its potency is roughly equivalent to that of DMT (a dose of 50–60 mg takes effect in 15 minutes, peaks quickly, and lasts 2 to 3 hours).

The effects of DPT are nearly identical to those of DET, with one exception: above 100 mg, the duration of the effects is dependent upon the dosage.

Unless combined with MAO inhibitors at a 10 mg dose, 5-MeO-DMT is not active orally. When smoked, it is four times as potent as DMT. Experiments have found that smoking 6 to 10 mg of the free base can result in a high that begins within a minute, peaks after two, and lasts twenty. Parenteral injections of 5 to 10 mg were also found to produce results.

DONA ANA

AKA: *Coryphantha macromeris.*

A small spiny cactus found in southern Texas and northern Mexico.

Effects: Similar to mescaline, but about 1/5 as potent. The hallucinogenic trip begins after about an hour or two and lasts for about twelve hours.

Precautions: Nausea and vomiting may result if taken on a full stomach. An overdose can be dangerous.

It should not be combined with any MAO inhibitors.

Dosage: The spines are removed from 8 to 12 fresh cacti, after which the plant can be chewed thoroughly and

swallowed or consumed as a tea; this latter method involves boiling in water for an hour and straining before drinking.

EPENA

AKA: Akurjua, ebene, hakudufha, nyakwana, parica, *Virola calophylla, Virola calophylloidea, Virola carinata, Virola cuspidata, Virola divergens, Virola elongata, Virola loretensis, Virola melinonii, Virola multinervia, Virola pavonis, Virola peruviana, Virola rufula, Virola sebifera, Virola surinamensis, Virola theiodora, Virola venosa,* yakee, ya-to, yopo.

A tree found in the rain forests of Colombia and Brazil, it is a member of the nutmeg family.

Effects: The hallucinogenic effects take hold almost immediately and lasts about thirty minutes. The chief psychoactive ingredients are DMT and 5-MeO-DMT.

Precautions: Indigenous peoples of Colombia and Brazil usually mix it with water and take it as an enema to avoid the side effects associated with snorting.

Side effects include uncontrollable trembling for five minutes, followed by headaches and confusion for another ten minutes. It can also cause numbness of the limbs, facial twitching, loss of muscular control, nausea, and irritation of the mucus membranes, resulting in uncontrollable sneezing. Epena can exaggerate any existing pain, and taking it on a full stomach can cause nausea.

If combined with any other MAO inhibitors, headaches, vomiting, heart problems, and death may result.

Dosage: Though preparation varies from one area to another, generally the thick red resin is scraped from the inner bark, dried or boiled down to an amber-red crystalline state, then ground and sifted. The resultant snuff is then blown into the nostrils with a tube. Other regional plants may also be added to vary the effect. Some people eat the resin in the form of pellets, and there are reports that it is even smoked.

ERERIBA

AKA: *Homalomena belgraveana, Homalomena ereriba.*

Research on the *Homalomena* genus is limited, despite the identification of over 140 species from South America to Asia.

Effects: Said to be a narcotic, the leaves of which are combined with the leaves and bark of agara or *Galbulimima belgraveana*, though no psychoactive compounds have yet been isolated from it. Natives of New Guinea use *Homalomena cordata* for "rain magic" and *Homalomena versteegii* for "love magic."

Precautions: The Malaysians use *Homalomena rubescens* as a fish poison which they call ipoh.

GUARUMA

AKA: *Cecropia mexicana, Cecropia obtusifolia.*

Effects: A marijuana-like effect when smoked.

HAWAIIAN BABY WOOD ROSE

AKA: *Argyreia nervosa*, baby Hawaiian woodrose.

Despite its popular name, it is not a member of the rose family, but is a woody liana in the morning glory family.

Effects: Similar to that produced by morning glory seeds. It is said to take effect in an hour and can result in an LSD-like trip that lasts a few hours. It may be accompanied by a feeling of contentment that can linger for a few days. Contains the highest amount of lysergic acid amines of any of the morning glories (0.3 percent), as well as several other alkaloids.

In addition to *Argyreia nervosa*, a dozen other species of *Argyreia* contain lysergic acid amines (*acuta, aggregata, barnesii, capitata, hainanensis, obtusifolia, osyrensis, pseudorubicunda, speciosa, splendens*, and *wallichii*).

Precautions: The white fuzz on the seeds, containing strychnine, are removed (often with a toothbrush). Filtered, cold-water infusions of the ground seeds are said to prevent fewer hazards than ground seeds eaten whole. Extreme nausea might be the result of strychnine ingestion. According to William Emboden, side effects include a hangover characterized by blurred vision, vertigo, and physical inertia. High doses could result in death.

It should not be confused with the Hawaiian woodrose (*Ipomoea tuberosa*), which is not psychoactive.

Dosage: 4 to 8 seeds. Cleaned seeds are chewed and swallowed or ground into a powder and put in gelatin capsules.

HELIOTROPE

AKA: All-heal, English valerian, German valerian, great wild valerian, phu, setwall, turnsole, valerian, *Valeriana officinalis*, vandal root, Vermont valerian, wild valerian.

Effects: A fairly strong sedative and tranquilizer.

Precautions: The tea's aroma is intolerable to most people; its taste is slightly less objectionable. The tea is not drunk more than twice a day for more than two or three weeks at a time, as overuse could cause poisoning.

Dosage: Half an ounce of roots or rhizomes boiled in a covered pot for five minutes and drained, then consumed as a tea. It can also be boiled down to a viscous residue and, with a small amount of flour added, can be put into gelatin capsules.

HENBANE

AKA: Bang (bangue, bengi), black henbane, castilago, devil's eye, fetid nightshade, goat's joy, henbell, henquale, hog bean, Hyoscyamus, *Hyoscyamus niger*, insana, Iusquiamus, Jupiter's bean, poison tobacco, sakiru, sakrona, shakhrona, stinking nightshade, stinking Roger.

A member of the nightshade family, it was one ingredient in witches' brews in the Middle Ages.

Effects: Hallucinations involving all the senses, along with a feeling of drunkenness and sedation. Various ancient cultures have used it as an anesthetic, or to treat various disorders. It is chemically similar to datura, containing high amounts of hyoscyamine — similar to atropine, but twice as powerful — plus scopolamine and several other active alkaloids.

It has traditionally been used in combination with the fly agaric mushroom in Afghanistan, occasionally smoked with tobacco or marijuana in Kashmir and Pakistan, and added to alcoholic drinks by Indians in California and Mexico.

Precautions: Side effects include dry mouth with accompanying thirst, hot dry skin, fever, profuse sweating, dilated eyes, inability to focus the eyes on close objects, rapid heartbeat, dizziness, confusion, nausea, diarrhea, constipation, difficult urination, throbbing headache, problems with ejaculation, restlessness, disorientation, delirium, irrational behavior, blackout, and temporary amnesia. It is very dangerous.

Dosage: The seeds and dried leaves can be smoked, or the crushed root can be brewed into a tea.

HIERBA LOCA

AKA: Huedhued, *Pernettya furens*.
Effects: Intoxication and hallucinations.

Precautions: It can cause mental confusion, madness, and permanent insanity.

HIMANTANDRA BELGRAEVEANA

Effects: The Gimi people of New Guinea use the bark of this tree to induce trance states.

HOJAS DE LA PASTORA

AKA: Hojas de la Maria Pastora, Hojas de Maria Pastora, pipilzintzintli, *Salvia divinorum*, shka-Pastora, Ska Maria Pastora, Ska Pastora.

Effects: An effect similar to sacred mushrooms, but not as intense or as long (about two hours). No psychoactive component has yet been isolated.

Precautions: The extremely bitter taste can trigger vomiting. Some nausea may also occur.

Dosage: Though common doses are said to range between 20 and 80 pairs of leaves (approximately 50 to 200 grams), one researcher experienced hallucinations after only 3 pairs of leaves. The leaves can be nibbled and held in the mouth, or the plants can be ground up, soaked in water for an hour, then filtered for use as a drink. Recent experiments with smoking the leaves has shown that this can also produce a short-term trip, and that the leaves can retain their potency even when dry, despite a commonly held belief to the contrary.

HOPS

AKA: *Humulus lupulus.*

A member of the hemp family, it is used to add flavor to beer.

Effects: Contains THC, the psychoactive ingredient in marijuana. It acts as a sedative and, in higher amounts, can produce a mild marijuana-like high.

Precautions: It may amplify feelings of depression. Overuse can cause dizziness and symptoms of jaundice.

HYDRANGEA

AKA: *Hydrangea arborescens, hydrangea paniculata grandiflora*, seven barks, wild hydrangea.

Effects: A pleasant, marijuana-like high accompanied by a slight feeling of drunkenness.

Precautions: Contains a cyanide-like compound which can result in death.

Dosage: No more than one joint of leaves; smoking any more than that could result in severe toxicity.

IBOGA

AKA: Eboga, eboka, *Tabernanthe iboga.*

The only member of the dogbane family known to be used as a hallucinogen.

Effects: Hallucinations similar to LSD, but stronger; shamans who use it claim to contact the dead. It is also said to act as a stimulant and aphrodisiac, and to increase muscle strength and stamina. The psychoactive ingredient is ibogaine, which can also be made synthetically. At the turn of the last century, it was used briefly as an antidepressant, and at least one psychotherapist (C. Naranjo) has found it to be useful in inducing fantasies and childhood memories. Early research indicates it may be a treatment for opiate addiction, though Jonathan Ott calls this "a dubious proposition."

Precautions: In high doses, it can cause vomiting, loss of motor coordination, convulsions, paralysis, respiratory failure, and death.

Dosage: One gram of bark or roots can heighten feelings of sexuality and awareness — users claim that they can engage in sex for up to seventeen hours and remain awake during hunting for two full days. Doses of 3 grams or more are needed to induce hallucinations; unfortunately, this is also very close to the toxic dose, and indigenous peoples use this high a dose only on rare occasions. The roots can be chewed or swallowed, or the roots and bark can be boiled into a tea.

IOCHROMA

AKA: *Iochroma fuchsioides.*

Effects: Used by Kamsa Indian shamans of Colombia as an inebriant.

It may also be used as an additive to ayahuasca.

JUREMA

AKA: Ajuca, caatinga, jurema branca, *Mimosa hostilis (Mimosa jurema*), *Mimosa nigra*, *Mimosa pudica* (dormilona, duermidillo, espina dormilona, guaring, muigin, pinahuihuitztli), *Mimosa somnians*, *Mimosa tenuiflora* (tepescohuite), *Mimosa verrucosa*, vinho de jurema.

Effects: The roots of this shrub in eastern Brazil said to produce a "miraculous drink" called ajuca or vinho de jurema. This once popular hallucinogen is now rarely used. The main psychoactive ingredient appears to be DMT.

KAEMPFERIA

AKA: Galanga, gisol, *Kaempferia galanga*, maraba.

A member of the ginger family commonly used as a condiment in Asian cooking. This and related species are used in cough medicines, stomach and headache medications, and perfumes.

Effects: Used by people native to New Guinea as a condiment and to treat boils, burns, and wounds. It is rich in essential oils, but appears to have no psychoactive ingredients, despite its local reputation as a hallucinogen and dream enhancer.

KANNA

AKA: Channa, gauwgoed, kaugoed, *Mesembryanthemum expansum*, *Mesembryanthemum tortuosum*, *Sceletium expansum*, *Sceletium tortuosum*, *Sclerocarya caffra*, *Sclerocarya schweinfurthii*, umganu.

There is some confusion about which of the above plants the Hottentots used to achieve an altered state.

Effects: Said to induce euphoria, giddiness, and hallucinations. The two species of *Sceletium* are known to contain an alkaloid which induces sedation.

Precautions: Side effects include headache, listlessness, loss of appetite, and depression. An overdose can result in delirium and loss of consciousness.

Dosage: About 5 grams of the alkaloid will induce lethargy; it is not known how much more is needed to produce hallucinations. The roots, leaves, and trunk can be chewed or smoked.

KARA

AKA: Capparis.
Effects: The roots and leaves of this plant are said to have psychoactive properties.

KAWANG

AKA: *Castanopsis acuminatissima*.
Effects: The seeds of this tree, when steamed and eaten, are said to induce an altered state.

KETAMINE

AKA: Green, Ketaject, Ketalar, ketamine hydrochloride, special K, super K, vitamin K, Vetalar.

A close relative of PCP, it was first used as a surgical anesthetic in the Vietnam War. It is also used as an animal tranquilizer.

Effects: Produces a vivid 30- to 45-minute LSD-like experience characterized by a dream-like state with intense visual images. Its potency is about 5 to 10 percent that of PCP.

Precautions: Side effects may be similar to those of PCP: loss of the ability to talk or communicate, rigid muscles, confusion, agitation, and paranoia. Heavy users may experience prolonged speech and memory impairment, which may persist even after use is discontinued. An overdose can cause respiratory failure.

Dosage: About 50 mg. It can be taken as pills, snorted as a powder, injected as a liquid, or even smoked in a cigarette; taking it orally is said to result in a high that lasts longer and is less intense than with the other methods. Surgical doses of the injectable liquid range from 400 to 700 mg. Medical researcher John C. Lilly describes his experiments with ketamine in *The Scientist: A Novel Autobiography*.

KEULE

AKA: *Gomortega keule*, hualhual.

Found only in a small section of central Chile, it is the only known species of tree in the rare gomortegaceae family, which is related to the nutmeg family.

Effects: The fruit is said to induce intoxication, though it is unknown whether this involves hallucinations or whether there is even a psychoactive ingredient.

KHAT

AKA: *Catha edulis*, chat, kat, miraa, qat, quat, tchat, tschat.

Effects: An Ethiopian shrub that is said to produce bliss, clarity of thought, euphoria, excessive energy, and hallucinations because of its amphetamine-like alkaloids cathine, cathidine, cathinine, norpseudoephedrine, and ephedrine, among others. It also contains high levels of vitamin C.

Precautions: Though it is not believed to be physically addictive, regular users do develop a dependence. Instead of the effects mentioned above, users may experience dizziness, stomach pains, weariness, and depression. Overuse can cause tremors, loss of appetite, heart trouble, and loss of sex drive.

Dosage: The buds, leaves, and stems can be chewed (the leaves are even swallowed, though they lose their potency when they dry out), or they can be brewed into a tea.

KIERI

AKA: Hueipatl, kieli, *Solandra brevicalyx*, *Solandra guerrerensis*, tecomaxochitl.

Effects: Used by Indians in northern Mexico as "visionary inebriants." Studies have shown that it contains some psychoactive alkaloids.

KIKISIRA

AKA: Bubbia.

Effects: The bark of this tree causes a dream-like state when smoked with tobacco.

KOLA NUT

AKA: Bissy nut, caffeine nut, *Cola nitida*, cola nut, cola vera, guru nut.

Effects: Can stimulate the central nervous system and improve mood. It contains about 2 percent caffeine, or as much as coffee, along with theobromine.

Precautions: Overuse can cause insomnia, nervousness, and loss of sex drive. Studies with animals have shown that, while low doses may be stimulating, high doses can have a depressive effect.

Dosage: The nuts can be chewed, or brewed into a tea consisting of 1 teaspoon of nut to one cup of water. More than one or two cups a day may be dangerous. Cola drinks contain very little kola.

KORIBO

AKA: *Tanaecium nocturnum.*
Effects: Altered states.
Dosage: The leaves are roasted and pulverized and mixed with tobacco that is then used as a snuff. Tea made from the root-bark is also said to be psychoactive. Researchers have said that even smelling the plant can induce altered states but as yet no studies have been done to determine the psychoactive elements of this plant.

KRATOM

AKA: Gra-tom, kutum, mambog, *Mitragyna speciosa.*

A member of the coffee family that is sold as an opium substitute in southeast Asia. *Kratom* refers to the leaves, which can be smoked like a joint or chewed, and *mambog* refers to the thick syrup made from the leaves.
Effects: A state of euphoria not unlike a very mild effect from hallucinogenic mushrooms or LSD. The psychoactive ingredients include the indole alkaloid mitragynine and eight other alkaloids, which act on the central nervous system and the autonomic system. While the leaves produce a stimulating effect, mitragynine itself is a depressant, which suggests that the other alkaloids play an important role. Because it can mimic other hallucinogens unrelated to each other, it is considered by William Emboden to be "one of the most complex of the hallucinogens."
Precautions: Though it does not appear to be addictive, it is habit-forming. Prolonged use can result in emaciation,

a distended stomach, pallor, darkened lips, dried skin, numbness in the peripheral regions of the body, twitching, and unusual cardiac disorders.
Dosage: The leaves can be smoked, chewed, or prepared as an infusion.

KUBILGIM

AKA: *Diospyros species.*
Effects: A New Guinea plant said to induce altered states.

KWASHI

AKA: *Pancratium trianthum.*
Effects: Though nothing is known of its psychoactive properties, it is considered a hallucinogen by Botswana Bushman, who rub the bulb into incisions cut into the their heads to induce visions. Other species of *Pancratium* are known to contain psychoactive alkaloids, though some may cause death (especially among people with heart conditions) or paralysis of the central nervous system.
Precautions: Though it is not known what toxic effects, if any, kwashi may have, William Emboden considers it "perhaps one of the most unusual hallucinogens in terms of mode of use, and one of the most dangerous." More recently, Jonathan Ott questions whether this is, in fact, a true hallucinogen.

KYKEON

A drink composed of barley mixed with ergot, water, and the mildly psychoactive mint *Mentha pulegium* that was popular in ancient Greece and Rome.
Effects: Said to produce bliss and hallucinations.

Precautions: The ergot, eaten whole, can interfere with blood flow, and cause muscle spasms, numbness of the limbs, gangrene, and death. Jonathan Ott warns budding experimenters that "ergot has poisoned and killed countless human beings throughout history."

LAGOCHILIS INEBRIANS

There are 35 different species of this plant that grow from the Middle East to Central Asia.

Effects: Sedation and hallucinations. Russian pharmacologists have found it to have a number of medicinal uses, especially as a treatment for skin diseases, allergies, nervous problems, and glaucoma.

LETTUCE

AKA: *Lactuca sativa, Lactuca virosa.*

Effects: The seeds are said to be psychoactive, producing a high similar to opium, but milder. Why bananas (which have no psychoactive ingredients whatsoever) have gained such a reputation and lettuce has not is somewhat of a mystery. Jonathan Ott says trace amounts of morphine have been discovered in lettuce (lactucarium, or lettuce opium), but then, it is a trace constituent in human milk and cow's milk also, and is a natural product of brain chemistry.

Precautions: It is not addictive, though large doses are toxic.

Dosage: The wild lettuce plant (or the hearts and roots of iceberg lettuce) is liquefied in a blender until about a pint of liquid is produced. The liquid is then left in a bowl under heat lamps or the hot sun until it has evaporated, leaving only a sticky brownish-green residue. The residue is placed in an opium pipe and heated, with the pipe pointed downward so that the residue does not get in the stem. The resultant white smoke is held in the lungs for about half a minute.

LICHENS

Effects: Some varieties of Alaskan lichens are reported to be psychoactive, a belief that has yet to be substantiated.

LOBELIA

AKA: Asthma weed, bladderpod, cardinal flower, emetic herb, emetic weed, gag root, Indian tobacco, *Lobelia inflata, Lobelia cardinalis*, pukeweed, red lobelia, vomitroot, vomitwort, wild tobacco.

Effects: A mild marijuana-like high.

Precautions: Those susceptible to migraines will experience headaches when smoking lobelia. It has an acrid taste when smoked, and causes a prickly feeling in the mouth and throat when consumed as a tea. Casual users sometimes experience vomiting and nausea, even when taken on an empty stomach. More than 15 grams may trigger sudden vomiting, circulation problems, nerve damage, and other toxic reactions. The term "Indian tobacco" may refer to any number of unrelated plants.

Dosage: About 2 tablespoons of crushed leaves and stems in a pint of water, which is simmered and strained. For use in a gelatin capsule, a double dose is boiled down to a gummy residue and mixed with dried leaves. It can also be smoked as a joint.

LSD

AKA: Acetyllysergic acid diethylamide (ALD-52, N-acetyl-LSD, Orange Sunshine), Acid, Delysid (LSD-tartrate), LSD-25, lysergic acid diethylamide, Methyllysergic acid diethylamide (MLD-41).

A semi-synthetic drug first made in 1938 by Swiss chemist Albert Hofmann from the ergot fungus in rye, though he did not become aware of its extraordinary properties until accidentally ingesting some five years later. It is one of the most powerful drugs known, producing a high from as little as 25 micrograms. There are numerous derivatives and analogues of LSD, the effects of which may range from totally inactive to mildly psychoactive (ALD-52 and MLD-41 are two of the more psychoactive ones).

Effects: A trip usually begins 45 to 90 minutes after ingestion, and can last eight to twelve hours. It elevates serotonin levels in every area of the brain except the cerebrum and cerebellum.

Precautions: There can be bad trips, which are sometimes attributable to the general surroundings and atmosphere in which the drug is taken, contaminants (including other drugs) mixed in with the LSD, and the mental instability of the user. After-effects include sluggishness, depression, anxiety, and occasional long-lasting psychological problems. It also causes contractions of the uterus in pregnant women. It could lead to a condition called the serotonin syndrome, where serotonin levels in the body are too high, and which is characterized by restlessness, confusion, sweating, diarrhea, excessive salivation, high blood pressure, increased body temperature, rapid heart rate, tremors, and seizures.

There is no evidence that it causes flashbacks, is addictive, or causes damage to the chromosomes, the brain, or the body in general. The original chemical, lysergic acid, will produce many side effects but few of the psychoactive benefits that users seek.

It is an MAO inhibitor, and so dangerous when combined with substances contraindicated for this type of drug.

John G. Fuller's *The Day of St. Anthony's Fire* purports to be the story of an entire French town that succumbed to the effects of a naturally occurring LSD in the grain used to make the town's bread. This drug does not occur naturally; the townspeople's hallucinations and temporary madness were the effects of a mercury compound used as a fungicide, the grain having been accidentally ground into flour for bread instead of being planted as seed.

Dosage: Approximately 50 to 500 micrograms will result in altered consciousness, though it could just as well produce a bad trip. The effects peak at 500 micrograms, with the result that the trip will not be longer or more intense with greater dosage. Lethal dosage is unknown, as some individuals have taken as much as 1 to 2 grams and survived.

MACE

A spice produced from the outer covering of the nutmeg seed, or *Myristica fragrans*, that is sometimes used to flavor cakes.

Effects: A high that can range from mild pleasantness to unbridled delirium.

Precautions: The dose needed to get high is close to the toxic level, resulting in a strong hangover the next day.

MACONHA BRAVA

AKA: *Zornia latifolia.*

Effects: In Brazil, the leaves are smoked as a "marijuana substitute."

MANDRAKE

AKA: Apples of the fool, apples of the genie, devil's testicle, European mandrake, love apple, mandragon, mandragora, *Mandragora officinarum*, may apple, Satan's apple, Satan's testicles.

"Of all the sedating-tranquilizing-psychotropic plants known," writes William Emboden, "the mandrake ... has the most extensive and bizarre history.... This member of the nightshade family has been used as a painkiller, sedative, aphrodisiac, trance mediator, and poison." According to the ancient "doctrine of signatures," medicinal plants resembled that part of the human body for which it could affect a cure and, since mandrake resembled the human form, its powers were seen as all-encompassing.

Effects: Hallucinations.

Precautions: The dosage needed to produce hallucinations is also close to the toxic dose, which are caused by the potent compound scopolamine. Side effects include a burning thirst, dizziness, fever, dilated eyes, rapid heart rate, severe headache, nausea, diarrhea, constipation, difficult urination, problems with ejaculation, cramps, restlessness, disorientation, confusion, delirium, coma, amnesia, heart damage, insanity, and death.

Mandragora officinarum (European mandrake) is a very different plant from *Podophyllum peltatum*, or American mandrake. Both, however, are very poisonous.

MARIHUANILLA

AKA: *Leonurus sibiricus.*

Effects: Smoked as a marijuana substitute in Mexico. Though it contains alkaloids, it is not known whether they are psychoactive.

MARIJUANA

AKA: Bhang, cannabis, *Cannabis indica*, *Cannabis sativa*, charas, dope, ganja, grass, hashish, hasheesh, hemp, kif, majun, pot, sinsemilla, weed.

After considerable controversy about its genus and species, it is now believed to belong to its own genus, *Cannabaceae*, consisting of one to three species: *Cannabis sativa*, *Cannabis indica*, and *Cannabis ruderalis*. The molecular structure of its psychoactive properties are unique in the plant world.

Effects: Its effects, which can vary widely, are mainly attributable to tetrahydrocannabinol (THC), and mainly involve euphoria, a sense of well-being, intense concentration, perceptual distortions, and — though marijuana is not classified as a hallucinogen — visual and auditory hallucinations for one to three hours. According to Young *et al.*, "marijuana is the least debilitating of all common intoxicants and has never accounted for a substantiated drug death. It does not cause brain damage, sterility, impotence, insanity, or drug addiction. ... Socially and medically, alcohol and tobacco are considerably more dangerous." Pharmacologically, it has been used in various medical preparations since ancient times and, even today, some advocate its use for relieving the symptoms of glaucoma, asthma, stiff muscles resulting from brain injuries and multiple sclerosis, and the toxic effects resulting from chemo-therapy.

Precautions: A user may experience dry mouth, rapid pulse rate, high blood pressure, tremors, vertigo, loss of coordination, dry reddened eyes, dilated pupils, depression, moodiness, temporary amnesia (because of its suppression of the brain hormone vasopressin), an uncontrollable fear of death, and panic. A 1986 Italian study found that smoking one joint can increase melatonin levels in the body 4000 percent. It is not physically addictive, but could result in psychological dependence, and habitual use could require higher and higher doses to achieve the same effects.

Hash smoke, especially when combined with tobacco smoke, can result in bronchitis and other respiratory ailments.

Additional dangers include buying marijuana laced with other drugs or the herbicide paraquat, or dealing with assassin bugs that tend to inhabit crops. Some growers have been able to produce super-potent strains that contain 20 percent THC, or almost double that of naturally grown plants.

Dosage: The dried leaves can be smoked as a cigarette (joint, reefer), the dried tops of the female plant full of resin smoked with tobacco (ganja, kif). It can be made into a drink with water or milk (bhang), made into a candy (majun), the resin smoked or eaten with spices (charas) or baked into brownies (hash brownies). Since the resin is soluble in oil but not water, it has a longer-lasting (if slower) effect when eaten, but very little effect when consumed as a tea.

Hashish, or hash, is the processed resin from the cannabis plant, and contains about 8 to 14 times the THC of marijuana. Hash oil, which is produced by boiling marijuana or hashish in a solvent, contains about 15 to 30 times the THC.

MASHA-HARI

AKA: Bolek-hena, curia, *Justicia pectoralis* var. *stenophylla*.

Effects: No psychoactive property has yet been isolated from this plant. It is generally mixed with epena, the snuff of the virola tree, though there are Indians in the Brazilian and Venezuelan forests that reportedly use some species of this plant by itself.

Precautions: William Emboden reports that at least three shamans have died from using the snuff of this plant.

MDA

AKA: EA-1298; Methylenedioxy-amphetamine; 3,4-methylenedioxyamphetamine.

The oldest and best-known of the synthetic chemical variants of the amphetamine molecule.

Effects: A calm and relaxing feeling, with a sense of physical and mental well-being, lasting eight to twelve hours.

Precautions: Side effects include a rapid pulse, high blood pressure, dilated pupils, insomnia, and loss of appetite. After-effects include a feeling of sluggishness, lack of energy, and inability to concentrate. It can cause orgasm problems in men and women, and erection problems in men. An overdose can result in painful muscular tension, particularly around the face and jaw.

Tennis player H. Blauer was killed in 1953 when given an intravenous injection of 500 mg of MDA in an experiment funded by the Army Chemical Corps.

Dosage: 50 to 150 milligrams.

MDMA

AKA: Adam, E, Ecstasy, Experimental Agent 1475, MDM, Methylenedioxymethamphetamine, XTC.

Effects: Same as MDA, but lasting only half as long. An analogue of MDA, it is usually defined as a psychedelic amphetamine, and releases the neurotransmitters serotonin and dopamine in the body. It has been used in psychotherapy and counseling, as it can enhance empathy between people.

Precautions: Side effects include severe muscle tension, sweating, and blurred vision. There is no evidence to support the claim that it damages nerve cells in the brain, but high doses can cause bad reactions. It could lead to a condition called the serotonin syndrome, where serotonin levels in the body are too high, and which is characterized by restlessness, confusion, sweating, diarrhea, excessive salivation, high blood pressure, increased body temperature, rapid heart rate, tremors, and seizures. It can cause orgasm problems in men and women, and erection problems in men. It produces the same rundown feelings the next day as MDA does, leaving users more vulnerable to colds, herpes outbreaks, and other infections, a problem that increases with the age of the user. There have been reports of dependency problems, and it has been implicated in some deaths, including that of former Dallas Cowboy Mark Tuinei.

The MDMA sold on the street can often contain such additives as MDEA (a close relative of MDMA), ketamine, selegiline, caffeine, amphetamine, and other, potentially hazardous, substances.

It reacts adversely with alcohol or depressants.

MESCAL BEAN

AKA: Coralillo, frijolitos, red bean, *Sophora secundiflora*, Texas mountain laurel.

Effects: Said to induce hallucinations.

Precautions: None of its alkaloids are known hallucinogens. It contains the alkaloid cytisine, which is highly toxic and has resulted in many deaths. Side effects include over-excitement, headache, nausea, vomiting, sweating, salivation, diarrhea, sluggishness, heart palpitations, convulsions, unconsciousness, paralysis of the respiratory muscles, and death from asphyxiation.

The beans are often confused with colorines.

Dosage: No more than one-quarter to one-half bean, which is roasted, crushed, chewed, and swallowed. Even a fraction of a bean more could result in toxicity and death.

MESCALINE

AKA: Mescal buttons; 3,4,5-trimethoxyphenylethylamine.

Mescaline is chemically similar to the hormone epinephrine and the neurohormone norepinephrine. It is the main psychoactive alkaloid in peyote, San Pedro, and other hallucinogenic plants.

Effects: Hallucinations, which begin one to two hours after consumption, peak after two hours, and last for approximately twelve hours. It has been used in psychotherapy and as a treatment for opiate and alcohol addiction.

Precautions: Use by borderline schizophrenics may worsen their condition irreversibly.

Initial side effects include vomiting,

nausea, stomach disruption, followed by uncontrollable bursts of emotion that may mimic schizophrenia. Tremors, insomnia, and anorexia may also occur. It is not physically or psychologically addicting, though tolerance does develop rapidly.

Aldous Huxley, author of *Brave New World*, reported on his wondrous experiences with the drug in the equally-famous books *The Doors of Perception* and *Heaven and Hell*. Religious scholar R. C. Zaehner, in his books *Mysticism Sacred and Profane* and *Drugs, Mysticism and Make-Believe*, strongly disagrees with Huxley's positive assessment.

MEXICAN MARIGOLD

AKA: *Tagetes lucida*, tumutsali, xpuhuc, yahutli, yauhtli, ye-tumutsali, yia, yyahhitl, yyahitlm, yyahutli, yyauhtli.

Effects: A narcotic or mild psychedelic that is said to induce feelings of tranquility when smoked. Reports of the effects of this plant vary considerably, and much chemical analysis needs to be done to determine its psychoactive properties.

Precautions: No psychoactive compounds have yet been identified in this plant. One expert has claimed that it is "toxic."

MORNING GLORY

AKA: *Ipomoea purpurea*, *Ipomoea violacea* (badoh negro seeds, *Ipomoea tricolor*, tlitliltzin), Mexican morning glory, piule, *Turbina corymbosa* (coaxhuitl, Ipomoea sidaefolia, ololiuqui, Rivea corymbosa).

Contains a chemical called ergine (d-lysergic acid diethylamide), the closest substance to LSD found in nature. "Morning glory" actually refers to two distinct species which, due to the uncertainties regarding this family, have other botanical names (see above). Although other members of the morning glory family in other parts of the world have higher levels of psychoactive compounds, only in Mexico is it used as a hallucinogen.

Effects: Intoxication and hallucinations lasting four to fourteen hours.

Precautions: They should not be used by anyone with liver problems.

They are mildly toxic, producing nausea and vomiting, though taking it on an empty stomach may prevent the nausea (Jonathan Ott states that side effects may be due to the fact that users eat whole ground seeds rather than filtered, cold-water infusions of the ground seeds). Stomach cramps may also occur, though these may pass quickly, especially if the individual lies on his back and breathes deeply. Overdose symptoms may include psychotic reaction, shock, and heart failure. Not all varieties of morning-glory seeds are psychoactive (Flying Saucers, Heavenly Blue, Pearly Gates, and Wedding Bells are among those that are) and, of those that are, it may take a whole cupful to produce the desired effect. Commercially sold seeds may be coated with a poison to discourage use as a psychedelic, and may produce such symptoms as dizziness, diarrhea, nausea, vomiting, chills, and severe abdominal pain.

Dosage: 100 to 300 seeds (about 5 to 10 grams) to produce the same effects as 200 to 300 mcg of LSD. The hard seeds must be cracked or ground up to release the ergine, as they will produce no results when eaten whole. Young *et al.* state that only 15 of the crushed

Turbina corymbosa seeds in one-half cup of water will produce the desired effect.

MUSHROOMS AND PSILOCYBINE

AKA: Liberty caps, magic mushrooms, 'nti-si-tho, *Psilocybe cubensis*, sacred mushrooms, teonanacatl, tey-huintli.

Aside from the fly agaric mushrooms, there are four other genera that have hallucinogenic properties: *Conocybe*, *Panaeolus*, *Psilocybe*, and *Stropharia*. They are found all over the world, but only in Mexico are they used in rituals. The *Copelandia cyanescens* fungus that is cultivated in Bali is more potent than any of these mushrooms. The main psychoactive ingredients in all of these is psilocine and psilocybine, the latter of which can be manufactured synthetically.

Effects: Produces vivid hallucinations similar (though reportedly less intense) to LSD — beginning within a half hour and lasting three to six hours — muscular relaxation, and giddiness.

Precautions: Common side effects include nausea, pupil dilation, rapid pulse, high blood pressure, high body temperature, shivering, anxiety, numbness in the face, dizziness, difficulty concentrating, disorientation, paranoia, panic, and bad trips. Not everyone sees the "infinite clockwork," or the cosmic secrets of the mushroom. According to Mexican Mazatec healer Maria Sabina in de Rios' *Visionary Vine*, as "the mushroom is similar to your soul. It takes you where the soul wants to go. And not all souls are the same." Potency can vary widely, and they can be somewhat indigestible and mildly toxic if not cooked. An overdose (generally said to be in the 50 to 60 mushroom range) can result in severe poisoning. Prolonged excessive use is said to result in permanent insanity, premature aging, and senility. Mushrooms are usually sauteed before eating as, in their raw state, they may contain methyl-hydrazines, compounds similar to rocket propellants which are carcinogenic and potentially deadly. Mushrooms may also accumulate such toxins as arsenic and cesium, though not in dangerous levels; cooking will not remove or deactivate them.

They can easily be mistaken for other, poisonous mushrooms. Some dealers may sell ordinary mushrooms laced with LSD.

There is a myth that the mushrooms can be preserved in honey. Jonathan Ott was offered one such sample which, he said, was not only unlikely to contain any psilocybine but was a "disgusting, fermenting mess, crawling with bugs."

It is an MAO inhibitor, and so should not be combined with any substances contraindicated for this type of drug.

Readers should not be misled by popular books that contain misleading and erroneous information, notably Carlos Castaneda's *The Teachings of Don Juan* and subsequent sequels, John Sandford's *In Search of the Magic Mushroom*, John Allegro's *The Sacred Mushroom and the Cross*, or Andrija Puharich's *The Sacred Mushroom: Key to the Door of Eternity*.

Dosage: Psychedelic mushrooms can be eaten, smoked or snorted as a powder (it can be years before dried mushrooms lose their potency), or boiled and the liquid drunk with Kool-Aid or injected. 1 to 5 grams (dry weight), 10 to 15 grams of fresh mushrooms, or 5 to 15 mushrooms, depending on the size and species.

NIANDO

AKA: *Alchornea floribunda.*

Effects: Used as an aphrodisiac, stimulant, narcotic, and hallucinogen by some Africans.

NICOTINE

AKA: *Nicotiana attenuata, Nicotiana benthamiana, Nicotiana bigelovii, Nicotiana gossei, Nicotiana glauca, Nicotiana ingulba, Nicotiana megalosiphon, Nicotiana rustica, Nicotiana tabacum, Nicotiana trigonophylla, Nicotiana velutina.*

Of the over 500 compounds in tobacco, the alkaloid nicotine is the most powerful, and the only addictive one. In fact, it is one of the most addictive substances known — even more addicting than most hard drugs, such as heroin — and one of the most toxic drugs known.

Sources: Bell peppers, eggplant, tobacco, tomatoes.

Effects: It is believed to improve both short- and long-term memory, improve the ability to perform various tasks, reduce the risk of developing Parkinson's disease, help those with Alzheimer's focus better on tasks, prevent toxic chemicals from killing off brain cells, help schizophrenics function better, reduce feelings of hunger, increase tolerance to pain, and reduce stress. It may someday result in drugs that treat Alzheimer's and Parkinson's diseases, schizophrenia, and anxiety disorders. It was used by native peoples throughout the Americas to induce trance states and visions.

Precautions: Concentrated nicotine can enter the brain within seconds of smoking a cigarette, even faster than heroin injected into the arm. It is extremely addictive, and may contribute to Alzheimer's disease and other forms of dementia; it is known to stimulate, and then block, sensory receptors, preventing the neurotransmission of new information. Common side effects of smoking are believed to include persistent cough, shortness of breath, elevated heart rate, increased salivation, irritated and damaged lung tissue, increased bronchial secretions, constriction of blood vessels, increased blood pressure, slightly enlarged pupils, overstimulation of the central nervous system, tremors, stroke, heart damage, visual impairment, kidney dysfunction, reduced appetite, increased susceptibility to disease, cancer, emphysema, and death. Overdose symptoms may include delusions and hallucinations.

Common side effects of nicotine chewing gum include nausea, vomiting, and upset stomach. Less common side effects include dizziness, lightheadedness, irritability, headache, dry mouth, hoarseness, coughing, high blood pressure, heart palpitations, rapid and abnormal heartbeat, sneezing, sleeplessness, confusion, convulsions, depression, euphoria, numbness, tingling in the hands and feet, fainting, weakness, rash, and a buzzing or ringing in the ears. Overdose symptoms include excessive salivation, nausea, vomiting, diarrhea, abdominal pains, headache, cold sweats, dizziness, hearing and visual abnormalities, weakness, and confusion, followed by fainting, dangerously low blood pressure, a weak, rapid, and irregular pulse, convulsions, and paralysis of the breathing muscles leading to death.

The effects of nicotine can be increased when combined with sugar. Nicotine can alter the effects of any central nervous system drug. The cessation of nicotine intake — cigarettes in particular — may increase the effects of many drugs, including Acetaminophen, caffeine, Furosemide, Glutethimide, Imapramine, Insulin, Oxazepam, Pentazocine, Propoxyphene Hydrochloride, Propranolol, and Theophylline.

Dosage: The lethal dose is 50 mg, and just 60 to 120 mg (a drop or two) of pure nicotine can kill the average adult if applied to the skin; in fact, the nicotine in one cigar can kill at least two people, though most of it is destroyed by burning. Chewing tobacco and snuff is not believed to be as addicting, as the nicotine does not enter the brain directly, but goes through the bloodstream first.

NIGHTSHADE

AKA: *Solanum nigrum.*

According to legend, it has been used by witches in ancient Greece and medieval Europe, and in the Voodoo and Santeria religions. It should not be confused with deadly nightshade, or belladonna.

Effects: Hallucinations.

Precautions: Contains the alkaloid solanine — also present in green potatoes — which is somewhat toxic, and can cause headaches, fever, and hallucinations.

NUTMEG

AKA: Made shaunda, *Myristica fragrans.*

Called a pseudohallucinogen because its primary effect is delirium, one aspect of which is a form of hallucination. It contains the drug myristicin, which can be converted by the body into an amphetamine-like psychedelic.

Effects: The high can range from mild euphoria to full-blown delirium that lasts four to twelve hours.

Precautions: It should be avoided by anyone with liver problems.

Common side effects include severe nausea and diarrhea. Overdose symptoms (above 10 grams) include dizziness, a flushing of the skin, dry mouth and throat, rapid heartbeat, bloodshot eyes, constipation, difficulty urinating, agitation, and panic. The dose needed to get high is close to the toxic level, resulting in a strong hangover the next day, aching muscles, a washed-out feeling for a day or two, and possible liver failure.

Dosage: 5 to 20 grams, though one level teaspoon is said to produce euphoric effects.

OSTEOPHLOEUM

AKA: *Osteophloeum platyspermum* (*Osteophloeum platyphyllum*).

Effects: Though it was not known as a hallucinogen when Jonathan Ott's *Pharmacotheon* was published (1993), subsequent research has shown that it is used as a hallucinogen by the Quichua tribe of Ecuador.

Precautions: An overdose can be fatal.

Dosage: The tree sap is heated with pieces of bark, then drunk after it has cooled.

PAGAMEA MACROPHYLLA

Effects: The powdered leaves are used as a snuff and are reportedly psychoactive.

PANDANUS

Effects: The Wopkaimin people of New Guinea induce an altered state of consciousness, called the "Karuka madness," by eating the nuts of this plant. This altered state can last up to 12 hours, its primary manifestations being excitability, restlessness, and violent behavior. Another species of Pandanus on New Guinea has been found to contain DMT.

PARSLEY

AKA: Common parsley, garden parsley, *Petroselinum sativum*, *Petroselinum crispum*, rock parlsey.

Effects: The oil, when taken orally, can induce hallucinations.

Precautions: Side effects include epileptic-like convulsions and severe damage to the liver and kidneys.

Dosage: 5 to 20 drops.

PASSION FLOWER

AKA: Maypops, *Passiflora incarnata*, passion vine, purple passion flower.

Effects: A mild marijuana-like high when smoked; it even smells like marijuana. The tea produces feelings of tranquility and sedation. Contains the psychoactive alkaloids harmine and harmaline.

Precautions: The psychoactive alkaloids are MAO inhibitors, and when combined with other MAO inhibitors, vomiting and headaches will result.

Dosage: The dried leaves can be smoked or brewed as a tea (one-half ounce of leaves per pint of boiled water).

PCP

AKA: Angel dust, animal tranquilizer, hog, peace pill, encyclidine, Sernyl, t-tabs.

It has been used as a surgical and veterinary anesthetic (Sernyl and Sernylan respectively) but, unlike most anesthetics, it is not a depressant. Patients who received it during surgery remained aware, but "dissociated" from their bodies, and its use on people was discontinued when patients reported out-of-body experiences and disturbing visual hallucinations.

Effects: In low doses it can act as a stimulant, but in high doses it can act as a depressant. It produces a strong high with hallucinations (mainly out-of-body experiences and perceptual distortions normally associated with sensory deprivation) lasting one to six hours, though technically it is not a psychedelic. Medically, it has shown promise in protecting against brain damage resulting from stroke.

Precautions: If taken by those with any borderline psychosis, it has a greater chance of worsening the condition than any other drug, including LSD or mescaline.

Taking it may produce a dangerous and nasty delirium — according to Ronald K. Siegel, Ph.D., the chance of positive effects is 60 percent, while the chance of negative effects is 100 percent. Its association with violent behavior may be greatly exaggerated, however.

Common side effects at low doses (below 5 mg) include sedation, numbness of the extremities, high blood pressure, rapid heart rate, loss of muscular coordination, double or blurred vision, dizziness, nausea, vomiting, flushing of the skin, profuse sweating, apathy, depression, paranoia, despair, a preoccupation with death, and impairment of various mental functions (thinking, concentration, sensory input organization, learning, and memory). It may take at least a day before a person feels normal again.

Common side effects at moderate doses include decreased blood pressure, decreased respiration, decreased heart rate, nausea, vomiting, blurred vision, uncontrollable eye movements, shivering, increased salivation, repetitive movements, watery eyes, loss of balance, dizziness, and muscular rigidity. The psychological side effects are the same, except magnified.

Common side effects at high doses (above 10 mg) include agitation, convulsions, seizures, a coma that can last for up to 12 hours, schizophrenia-like delusions and mental confusion, and suicidal behavior. Speech and memory problems may persist for some time after use is discontinued.

Purity can range from high (white crystals) to low (moist and yellowish) and, on the street, it can often be passed off as mescaline or DMT. There are reportedly some 30 analogues of PCP available.

It reacts adversely with stimulants or depressants, though Valium is said to counteract its effects.

Dosage: It can be smoked, snorted, or taken orally, intravenously, vaginally, or rectally. It is dangerous at almost any level.

PEYOTE

AKA: *Lophophora diffusa* (*Anhalonium williamsii*), *Lophophora williamsii* (*Anhalonium lewinii*, *Echinocactus williamsii*, *Peyotl zacatecensis*), mescal buttons, peyotl.

Peyote is a small cactus with white tufts of hair and no spines; mescaline is its chief psychoactive alkaloid (its principal alkaloid is peyotline, which is not psychoactive), though it contains more than forty other drugs or compounds. Contrary to popular opinion, the white hairs do not contain strychnine (they are cellulose, or plant fiber). In fact, no hallucinogenic cactus contains strychnine.

Effects: It produces a complex high of spectacular hallucinations involving all senses that begins three hours after ingestion and lasts up to 12 hours. A peyote high is much different from a mescaline high. Users claim it has cured illnesses and alcoholism, and has been used to help cure personal problems.

Precautions: It has an extremely bitter taste that makes it hard to swallow and invariably induces vomiting and an hour or two of nausea. The vomiting and nausea can usually be minimized by fasting or taking Dramamine beforehand and remaining perfectly still during the visions.

Dosage: The usual dose is 6 to 12 dried buttons, which are moistened just before eating or, less commonly, chewed dry. Some Indians eat 4 to 30, or more. They can also be soaked in water (they dissolve quite readily) and the liquid consumed as a tea, or used as an enema.

PISHICOL

Effects: A psychoactive cactus: Research is needed to uncover its psychoactive components and effects.

PITURI

AKA: Bedgery, *Duboisia hopwoodii*, *Duboisia myoporoides*, pedgery, pitchery.

Effects: Used by Australian Aborigines to endure long journeys without suffering fatigue, hunger, or thirst. It contains the alkaloids nicotine, d-nornicotine (which is four times as toxic as nicotine) and, in the roots, hyoscyamine and scopolamine as well, the latter of which can cause excitement and hallucinations, even in small doses.

Precautions: Larger doses are fatal. The level of alkaloids varies widely from plant to plant.

Dosage: The leaves are roasted, moistened, and rolled into a "quid," which is then smoked. The leaves and stems are also said to be ground or chewed up, and then mixed with an alkaline plant to release the nicotine. Generally, only a tablespoon of leaves and stems are needed to achieve its effects.

PIULE

AKA: *Rhynchosia longiraceomosa, Rhynchosia phaseolides, Rhynchosia pyramidalis.*

Effects: It is a narcotic whose effects are similar to curare.

Precautions: The seeds differ from mescal beans and colorines only in the fact that they have a touch of black on the end. The term piule is also used to refer to morning-glory seeds, mushrooms, and other psychoactive plants.

PSYCHOTRIA

AKA: Batsikawa, kawa kui, matsi kawa, pishikawa, *Psychotria nitida, Psychotria viridis* (amirucapanga, chacruna, sami ruca).

A member of the coffee family that grows along the Amazon.

Effects: Contains the potent hallucinogen DMT. It is often added to ayahuasca. There are numerous species of *Psychotria*, some of which are as yet unidentified (e.g., batsikawa, matsi kawa) and some which may be devoid of psychoactive alkaloids.

PUCHURI

AKA: *Licaria puchury-major*, pixuri.

Effects: The seeds are used in Brazil as a sedative and tranquilizer, and have been found to contain safrole, eugenol, and methyleugenol, all of which are psychoactive.

PUERARIA PHASEOLOIDES

Effects: A plant in West Nakanai, New Britain near New Guinea, the leaves of which are reportedly psychoactive.

PUFFBALLS

AKA: Blind man's ball, *Bovista nigrescens, Calvatia utriformis*, devil's pepperpot, devil's snuffbox, dusty stars, fallen stars, fistball, fuzzball, pixie-puff, puckfist, *Lycoperdon marginatum* (gi-i-sa-wa), *Lycoperdon mixtecorum* (gi-i-wa), *Scleroderma citrina* (earth ball).

Effects: *Lycoperdon* is a Mexican fungi that produces auditory hallucinations; *Lycoperdon mixtecorum* is the more powerful of the two species. Eating half of a *Scleroderma* mushroom induces visual disturbances and a deep narcosis that lasts approximately two hours. Experiments by Jonathan Ott and others on eleven species of the *Lycoperdon* failed to discover any psychoactive effects or compounds.

Precautions: They smell like fecal matter.

RAPE DO INDIOS

AKA: *Maquira sclerophylla* (*Olmedioperebea sclerophylla*).

A member of the fig family found along the Brazilian Amazon.

Effects: The fruits of this plant were once prepared and used as a snuff by Indians in the Pariana region of Brazil. The exact method of preparation has apparently been lost over time, and, though no psychoactive property has yet been isolated from it, it has been found to have an amphetamine-like stimulation on the central nervous system of rats.

RHODODENDRON

AKA: *Rhododendron ponticum* (*Azalea pontica, Heraclea pontica, Rhododendron caucasicum*).

Effects: Was once used as a narcotic and hallucinogen by people in the northern Caucasus, who used it to induce prophetic dreams. This may be the same plant referred to by the Greek historian Herodotus, who stated that the burning smoke of the plant was as intoxicating as wine.

Precautions: The nectar may be toxic. Another Greek historian, Xenophon, relates how an entire army was poisoned from the honey of this plant.

ROSEMARY

AKA: *Ledum groenlandicum, Ledum hypoleucum, Ledum palustre* (marsh cistus, marsh tea, moth herb, narrow-leaved Labrador tea, swamp tea, wild rosemary).

Effects: The smoke from the burning leaves is said to be a narcotic. The Tungus people of Siberia preferred this over the fly-agaric mushroom, and another species is used by the Kwaikutl Indians of British Columbia as an inebriant.

Precautions: Believed to be at least partly responsible for the beserker frenzies of the Vikings. It is known that at least one species, *Ledum palustre*, produces a honey that is toxic (this plant can be used as a tea, though excessive use may cause toxicity).

SAFFRON

AKA: *Crocus sativus.*

Effects: Saffron oil, or safrol(e), can be processed to make the narcotic MDA.

Precautions: It contains a poison that can affect the central nervous system and damage the kidneys. It can be fatal at doses of 10 to 12 grams.

SAN PEDRO

AKA: Aguacolla, cardo, cuchuma, giganton, hermoso, huando, *Trichocereus pachanoi* (*Opuntia cylindrica*), *Trichocereus peruvianus.*

Effects: Contains the alkaloid mescaline, which is a hallucinogen. Though, like peyote, it is a cactus, the two are not related, and San Pedro produces a less stimulating, more tranquil high, reportedly without the nausea. The high, which begins in about an hour and lasts for about six hours, includes mental clarity, more intense auditory and visual perceptions, and brilliantly colored visions. Some medicine men use it for folk healing and divination, and it is probably used in the hallucinogenic drink cimora.

Precautions: It is usually consumed over a 45-minute period to avoid sudden overstimulation. Nausea, chills, anxiety, and feelings of terror may occur. It is not addictive, but psychological dependence may occur with habitual use.

Dosage: The lining of the inner skin wall can be chewed, or boiled in water for at least two hours and strained to make a drink.

Sassafras

AKA: Ague tree, cinnamon wood, gumbo, mitten tree, *Sassafras albidum*, *Sassifras variiflium*, saxifrax.

Effects: There is one report of a "visionary experience" after an ingestion of 10 ml of Brazilian oil of sassafras.

Precautions: The oil of any herb in any dose can be toxic.

Scirpus

AKA: Bakana, bakanoa, bakanawa.

Effects: A deep sleep accompanied by vivid hallucinations and bright colors. Said to induce psychic visions.

Scopolamine

AKA: Hyoscine.

An alkaloid found in belladonna, datura, henbane, and mandrake. In the early 1900s, it was used as an analgesic for childbirth until it was found to cause an abnormally high infant mortality rate. It was tested as a truth serum by the Germans and U.S. in World War II, both of whom found it unreliable. Nevertheless, the Soviets, according to William Burroughs, experimented with it and found that, even though the subject may have been willing to give up secrets, he oftentimes could not remember them. It is still used in some sleeping medications, and cold and allergy remedies, and can also be used to treat asthma, gastrointestinal spasms, and motion sickness.

Effects: Hallucinations.

Precautions: Common side effects include dry mouth, abnormal thirst, hot dry skin, fever, dilated eyes, inability to focus vision, rapid heart rate, constipation, difficult urination, difficult ejaculation, restlessness, disorientation, delirium, and amnesia. It has been found to impair serial learning at doses of 0.5 mg. In high doses it can cause poisoning. The roots of plants contain the lowest amount of scopolamine, the seeds the highest.

Dosage: The roots, seeds, leaves, and flowers can be smoked, eaten, brewed into a tea, or ground up and rubbed on the skin with fat.

Scopolia

AKA: *Scopolia carniolica*.

Effects: Hallucinations. Contains the psychoactive alkaloids scopolamine and hyoscyamine.

Scotch broom

AKA: Broom, *Cytisus canariensis*, *Cytisus scoparius* (Scotch broom), *Genista canariensis* (Canary Island broom), *Spartium junceum* (Spanish broom).

Effects: Intoxication, relaxation, euphoria, intellectual clarity, and a heightened sense of color for about two hours. It may also produce intense hypnagogic imagery (hypnagogia is the half-awake, half asleep state that can occur just before or after sleep), but not hallucinations. In Europe, it has been used as an ingredient in aphrodisiac drinks. It is used by the Yacqui medicine men of northern Mexico as a supposed hallucinogen, even though its cytisine alkaloid has not been proven to have psychoactive properties.

Precautions: Cytisine is known to be toxic (it is related to nicotine), and to cause overexcitement, a heavy drunken feeling, headaches, nausea, a severe strain on the heart, convulsions, unconsciousness, and death through respiratory failure when it is eaten, though no adverse side effects have been reported when the plant is properly prepared and smoked. Spanish broom contains the toxic alkaloid spartenine.

Dosage: Up to one joint of dried leaves is said to produce a relaxed feeling with no subsequent depression; several joints may produce the effects mentioned above. The blossoms of the plant are aged for about 10 days in a sealed jar until they are dry and moldy, then ground up and rolled into a joint. All 3 varieties (*Cytisus* and *Genista*) have about the same potency.

SENECIOS

AKA: Peyote, *Senecio canicida, Senecio cardiophyllus, Senecio cervarifolia, Senecio grayanus, Senecio hartwegii* (peyote de Tepic), *Senecio praecox, Senecio toluccanus.*

Effects: A peyote-like high.

Precautions: It is extremely dangerous, as it contains several chemicals that are toxic to the liver.

SHANIN

AKA: *Petunia violacea.*

A species of petunia, it is a member of the nightshade family and a close relative to tobacco.

Effects: Hallucinations, the main aspect of which appears to be the sensation of flight. The main psychoactive ingredient appears to be an as-yet-unidentified alkaloid.

SHANSHI

AKA: *Coriaria thymifolia*, pinan.

A shrub in the Ecuadorian Andes that is toxic to animals.

Effects: Intoxication and hallucinations — including the sensation of flight — which are due to some as-yet-unidentified glycoside.

Precautions: There are cases on record of poisonings from related species *Coriaria arborea* and *Coriaria ruscifolia*.

SINICUICHI

AKA: *Heimia salicifolia*, herva da vida, sinicuiche, sinicuitl.

Heimia myrtifolia and *heimia syphilitica* are geographical variants.

Effects: Hallucinations, including the following effects: giddiness, a darkening and shrinking of the surroundings, drowsiness or euphoria, and deafness or auditory hallucinations.

Precautions: Side effects, which include hypothermia, are reported to be rare, but excessive use is said to be harmful. Its supposed hallucinogenic effects are disputed by research. Sinicuichi can also refer to other, unrelated plants.

Dosage: The slightly wilted leaves are crushed and soaked in water, and the juice is placed in the sun to ferment.

STP AND RELATED DRUGS

AKA: DOM; serenity tranquility peace; 2,5-dimethoxy-4-methylamphetamine.

AKA (DOB): 2,5-dimethoxy-4-bromoamphetamine.

AKA (DOI): 2,5-dimethoxy-4-iodoamphetamine.

The synthetic drug DOM has a chemical structure similar to mescaline; DOB and DOI are related synthetic phenethylamines.

Effects: STP produces a strong intoxicating and stimulating state — similar to that induced by LSD or mescaline — which can last eight to twenty-four hours, though it does not elicit the euphoria associated with mescaline. Reports of STP trips lasting several days may be apocryphal, though DOI produces a trip that lasts up to 30 hours, and DOB may produce similar results.

Precautions: Side effects of STP include rapid heart rate, high blood pressure, loss of appetite, tremors, sweating, and pupil dilation. An overdose can lead to a bad trip.

DOB produces extremely long-lasting effects, and it has caused one death due to an individual's mistaking it for MDA and taking a massive dose.

Dosage: 1 to 5 mg of STP; doses of 20 mg can cause long-lasting effects which may lead to panic reactions. It can be taken orally or injected. DOB is active at doses of 1 to 3 mg, and DOI is active at doses of 1.5 to 3 mg.

SYRIAN RUE

AKA: African rue, harmal, harmel, harmul, hurmur, *Peganum harmala*, rue, spand, spend, techepak, wild rue.

Native to India, Mongolia, Manchuria, the Middle East, and Spain, it is unrelated to American or European rue.

Effects: Contains the hallucinogenic alkaloids harmine and harmaline,

among others, though it does not appear to play a part in any religious or ceremonial rituals. The seeds are commonly used as a spice, and the oil, sold in Egypt as zit-el-harmel, is reputed to be an aphrodisiac. Doses of 20 to 25 mg are mildly stimulating, but can result in drowsiness and dreaminess for an hour or two; doses of 300 to 750 mg may cause hallucinations.

Precautions: The alkaloids are MAO inhibitors and if mixed with any other drug or food contraindicated for this substance, may result in headaches, heart troubles, and death may result.

Dosage: Starting dose should be ⅓ ounce of seeds (or 250 mg) — no more — chewed thoroughly and swallowed. If dosage is increased, it should not exceed 1 ounce of seeds.

TAGLLI

AKA: *Pernettya parvifolia*.

Effects: Said to induce hallucinations, though it contains andromedotoxin and arbutin as its active ingredients, neither of which is hallucinogenic.

Precautions: It is toxic and may adversely affect the motor nerves.

TAIQUE

AKA: Borrachero de paramo, chapico, *Desfontainia hookeri*, *Desfontainia spinos*, michai blanco, trautrau.

Effects: Used as a folk medicine and narcotic in southern Chile. It is not known whether it induces hallucinations or contains any further psychoactive properties.

Precautions: It is related to a family

of South American plants from which arrow poisons are made.

TAKINI

AKA: *Helicostylis pedunculata, Helicostylis tomentosa.*

Effects: The fumes of the latex from this tree is said to be psychoactive. Some Indians of South America use it along with tobacco in shamanistic rituals.

TOAD

AKA: *Bufo alvarius, Bufo marinus,* Colorado River toad, Sonoran Desert toad.

Effects: The Sonoran Desert toad of Arizona produces large amounts of 5-MeO-DMT in its venom glands — which can induce a gentle high when dried or smoked — along with small amounts of the narcotic bufotenine, an alkaloid that is also found in some mushrooms and plants and which produces an LSD-like high. The effects, which include auditory and visual hallucinations, take hold in about five minutes and lasts for approximately an hour.

Precautions: Jonathan Ott and others have concluded that 5-MeO-DMT has "little recreational value," essentially agreeing with a colleague who compared it to "having a large elephant sitting on one's head." It should be noted that, since most types of toad venom are toxic, licking toads can be dangerous, causing seizures and resulting in hospitalization, and getting the venom in the eyes or mouth can cause severe poisoning. The venom must be dried and smoked to inactivate the toxins.

Wade Davis has reported that *Bufo marinus* was one ingredient of the Haitian zombi potion.

Interestingly, though 5-MeO-DMT is legal, bufotenine is not.

Dosage: Unless combined with MAO inhibitors at a 10 mg dose, 5-MeO-DMT is not active when taken orally. When smoked, it is four times as potent as DMT — experiments have found that smoking 6 to 10 mg of the free base can result in a high that begins within a minute, peaks after two, and lasts twenty. Parenteral injections of 5 to 10 mg were also found to produce results. The venom can remain potent for two years.

TSICTA

AKA: *Tabernaemontana sananho.*

Effects: Bark extracts of this Ecuadorian tree are used by hunters to sharpen the senses; there is good evidence to suggest that it contains psychoactive alkaloids.

Precautions: Some initial unpleasant effects.

TUPA

AKA: *Lobelia tupa,* tabaco del diablo.

Effects: The dried leaves are smoked by the Mapuche Indians of Chile as a narcotic, and by some North American Indians as an ingredient in love magic. None of the chemicals known to exist in tupa are hallucinogenic, though they may have a nicotine-like effect.

TURKESTAN MINT

AKA: *Lagochilus inebrians.*

Effects: Used as a folk medicine and intoxicant by various peoples of

Turkestan. The full extent of its effect is not yet known.

Precautions: It has a very bitter taste.

Dosage: The leaves and stems are boiled in water to make a tea.

2C-B

AKA: 2,5-dimethoxy-4-bromo-phenethylamine.

A designer psychedelic which is DOB without the side-chain methyl group.

Effects: Enhances all the senses without distorting them.

Dosage: It is active in the range of 12 to 24 mg. It is sometimes combined with MDMA.

UVA-URSI

AKA: *Arctostaphylos uva-ursi*, bearberry, kinnikinik, kinnikinnick.

Effects: An intoxication similar to opium. The dried leaves are used as a tobacco substitute.

Precautions: The term kinnikinnick can also refer to other plants and to mixtures of these plants.

VEPRIS AMPODY

Effects: One of the richest sources of DMT (up to 0.22 percent).

WATER LILY

AKA: *Nymphaea ampla, nymphaea caerulea.*

Effects: Hallucinations and narcosis.

Precautions: While it may be useful in treating schizophrenia in low doses, it can induce psychosis in higher doses.

WILD DAGGA

AKA: *Leonotis leonurus.*

A South African member of the mint species.

Effects: Used as an inebriant by the Hottentots.

WILD FENNEL

Effects: The oil, when taken orally, can induce hallucinations.

Precautions: Side effects include epileptic-like convulsions and severe damage to the liver and kidneys.

Dosage: 5 to 20 drops.

YUN-SHIH

AKA: *Caesalpinia sepiaria.*

Effects: A Chinese vine said to induce visions and "communication with spirits."

CHAPTER 11

Medical Drugs

ALENDRONATE

AKA: Alendronate sodium, Fosamax.

A drug used for the treatment of osteoporosis.

Effects: There are two anecdotal cases of patients who have had improved memory and mental functioning after taking it. As yet, this has not been supported by clinical evidence.

Precautions: It elicits adverse effects in those who have severe kidney disease or an allergy to Alendronate; it can also worsen such gastrointestinal disorders as swallowing difficulties, ulcers, and stomach irritations.

Common side effects include abdominal or stomach discomfort, nausea, breathing problems, constipation, gas, diarrhea, and ulcers. Less common side effects include difficulty in swallowing, muscle pain, and headache. Rare side effects include taste perception changes and vomiting. Overdose symptoms include upset stomach, heartburn, throat irritation, ulcer, and low levels of calcium and phosphate in the blood.

The absorption of Alendronate can be interfered with by antacids, calcium supplements, and other oral medications, which should not be taken within thirty minutes of Alendronate. Stomach or intestinal problems can result when mixed with aspirin, nonsteroidal anti-inflammatory drugs, or other anti-inflammatory drugs. Food or drink (including mineral water) should not be consumed for at least thirty minutes after taking Alendronate.

ASPIRIN

AKA: Alka-Seltzer with Aspirin, Arthritis Pain Formula, A.S.A., Ascriptin A/D, Ascriptin Extra Strength, Aspergum, Bayer, Bayer 8-Hour, Bufferin, Bufferin Arthritis Strength, Bufferin Extra Strength, Cama Arthritis Pain Reliever, Ecotrin, Ecotrin Maximum Strength, Empirin, Maximum Bayer, Measurin, Norwich Extra-Strength, ZORprin.

Effects: According to the authors of *The Pill Book*, "aspirin may be the closest thing we have to a wonder drug" and "is the standard against which all other drugs are compared for pain relief and for reduction of inflammation." It has proven effective against multi-infarct dementia (MID), a form of senility in which small blood clots form in the brain, which is believed to comprise about 20 percent of all cases of senile dementia. Some suggest that aspirin may be helpful in preventing Alzheimer's, though studies have yet to be done to confirm this. Aspirin can also help prevent migraines, heart attacks and strokes.

When combined with cholesterol-lowering drugs known as statins, aspirin may lower the risk of colon cancer, though more research needs to be done.

Precautions: It should not be used by those who have liver damage, who are allergic to aspirin or tartrazine (a common food coloring), who have peptic ulcers or a bleeding disorder, or who have a history of nasal polyps, asthma, or rhinitis. Buffered effervescent tablets and sodium salicylate should not be used by those who need to restrict sodium in their diet. Those with gout should consult a physician first. Use should be discontinued if dizziness, hearing loss, or ringing or buzzing in the ears develops.

Aspirin can significantly reduce blood coagulation, and so should not be taken at least a week before — and probably some time after — surgery, including dental surgery. It can also reduce the body's production of melatonin by 75 percent, and render urine tests for blood sugar inaccurate.

Common side effects include nausea, upset stomach, heartburn, loss of appetite, vomiting, and bloody stools. Other possible side effects include hives, rashes, liver damage, fever, thirst, difficulty sleeping, vision difficulties, and increased formation of stomach ulcers and stomach bleeding. Rare side effects include intense headaches, convulsions, excessive drowsiness, a flushing of the skin, a ringing in the ears, loss of hearing, excessive vomiting, facial swelling, vision problems, black or bloody stools, severe stomach pains or cramps.

Excessive doses of 2000 mg or more per day can lower blood sugar, which may cause problems for diabetics, and even a few aspirin can cause the body to excrete vitamin C at up to three times the normal rate. A mild overdose produces symptoms which include deep and rapid breathing, nausea, vomiting, dizziness, a ringing or buzzing in the ears, flushing, sweating, thirst, headache, drowsiness, diarrhea, and rapid heartbeat. A severe overdose produces symptoms which include fever, excitement, confusion, convulsions, hallucinations, liver or kidney failure, coma, and bleeding. The lethal dosage is 30 to 90 regular-strength tablets and 20 to 40 maximum-strength tablets.

Any product containing aspirin that gives off a strong vinegar odor should be discarded immediately, as the aspirin has started to deteriorate and is no longer effective.

The effects of aspirin can be decreased when combined with antacids, Phenobarbitol, Propranolol, and Rauwolfia alkaloids, while aspirin toxicity may occur when combined with Bumetanide, Ethacrynic acid, Furosemide, Para-aminosalicylic acid, Salicylates, and large doses of vitamin C. Aspirin can decrease the effects of Acebutolol, Allopurinol, Angiotensin-converting enzyme (ACE) inhibitors, beta-blocking drugs, Carteolol, Furosemide, Minoxidil, Oxprenelol, Probenecid, Sotalol, Spironolactone, Sulfinpyrazone, and Terazosin. It can increase the effects of Cortisone, Dextrothyroxine (in large, continuous doses), Methotrexate, and Valproic acid. The effects of both drugs are enhanced when aspirin is combined with other anti-coagulants, penicillin, or Ticlopidine. The possibility of stomach ulcers and/or bleeding increases when it is taken with adrenal corticosteroids, anticoagulants, cortisone drugs, Diclofenac, Indomethacin, Ketoprofen, nonsteroidal anti-inflammatory drugs (NSAIDS), or Phenylbutazone. Aspirin can result in low blood sugar when combined with oral anti-diabetic medication, a greater susceptibility to kidney damage when combined with gold compounds, an increased risk of bleeding when combined with Levamisole, a sudden drop in blood pressure when combined with Nitroglycerin tablets, and sodium and fluid retention when combined with Terazosin. It can also interfere with the effects of some diuretics when taken by those with severe liver disease. Terfenadine can mask some symptoms of aspirin overdose, and doses of tetracyclines and aspirin are taken at least an hour apart to avoid any interactions.

When combined with alcohol, it can aggravate any stomach irritation and bleeding caused by aspirin, and increase the risk of aspirin-related ulcers. Combined with marijuana, it may slow the body's recovery from injury or illness; experts strongly recommend that this combination be avoided. Aspirin should be taken with food, milk, or water to reduce the risk of upset stomach or bleeding.

Dosage: One tablet a day. If taken on a regular basis, caution must be exercised, as aspirin can accumulate in the body over time, making overdosage much more likely.

BENACTYZINE

An anti-cholinergic drug used in Europe.

Effects: According to Pearson and Shaw, it can block phobic memories and projections.

BROMOCRIPTINE

AKA: CB-154, Parlodel, 2-bromo-alpha-ergokryptine.

An ergot derivative like LSD and Hydergine, bromocriptine is prescribed for the treatment of certain symptoms of Parkinson's disease such as muscle rigidity, tremors, and problems with walking. It is also used for the treatment of infertility (both male and female), acromegaly, and some pituitary tumors.

Effects: It is an anti-oxidant and anti-depressant, and may play roles in enhancing memory, extending life span, reducing fat, and boosting immunity. It activates dopamine in the brain and, as a side effect, increases the libido.

Precautions: It should not be taken by those allergic to bromocriptine or Ergotamine, who have taken an MAO inhibitor in the previous two weeks, or who have narrow-angle type glaucoma. A physician should be consulted first if an individual has diabetes, epilepsy, high blood pressure, heart or lung disease, liver or kidney disease, a peptic ulcer, or who is going to have surgery within the next two months (including dental surgery) requiring general or spinal anesthesia. For those over 60, adverse side effects may be more frequent and severe.

Common side effects include mood swings, body spasms, diarrhea, nausea, dry mouth, and body odor. Less common side effects include dizziness, fainting, headache, insomnia, nightmares, rash, itching, vomiting, irregular heartbeat, flushing of the face, blurred vision, muscle twitches, dark or discolored urine, difficulty in urinating, muscle cramps, loss of appetite, abdominal discomfort, nasal congestion, tingling and numbness of the hands and feet, constipation, and tiredness. Rare side effects include high blood pressure, hallucinations, psychosis, anemia, impotence, and hair loss. Life-threatening or overdose symptoms include muscle twitches, spastic blinking, nausea, vomiting, diarrhea, irregular and rapid pulse, weakness, fainting, confusion, agitation, hallucinations, and coma. There is evidence that bromocriptine may be addictive.

The effects of bromocriptine may be diminished by oral contraceptives, estrogens, Haloperidol, Methyldopa, Papaverine, Phenothiazines, Progestins, vitamin B-6, and Rauwolfia alkaloids; they may be enhanced by other anti-Parkinson drugs. The effects of both drugs can be enhanced when combined with Guanfacine. When combined with levodopa, bromocriptine may weaken the anti-Parkinson effect. It can decrease the blood pressure when taken with antihypertensives, and dangerously increase blood pressure when taken with other ergot alkaloids or MAO inhibitors.

It can lead to a decreased tolerance for alcohol. When taken with cocaine, the effects of bromocriptine may be decreased. Tobacco will interfere with the drug's absorption; marijuana and bromocriptine may result in fatigue, lethargy, and fainting.

CYCLOSPORINE

AKA: Neoral, Sandimmune.

An immune-suppressing drug used to prevent transplanted organs from being rejected.

Effects: It has been found to cause neurons to grow new fibers that connect to other brain cells, which could possibly overcome brain damage caused by strokes, Alzheimer's disease, and Parkinson's disease.

Precautions: Cyclosporine should be prescribed only by doctors who have had experience in immunosuppressive therapy and organ transplantation, and it should always be used in conjunction with adrenal corticosteroid drugs. It should not be taken by anyone with chicken pox or herpes zoster. Individuals who have liver problems, infections, or kidney disease may find that cyclosporine aggravates their conditions. Continued use may cause reduced kidney function and hypertension.

Common side effects include kidney toxicity, gum inflammation and growth, bloody urine, jaundice, tremors, and increased hair growth. Less common side effects include fever, chills, sore throat, shortness of breath, frequent urination, headaches, leg cramps, brittle hair or fingernails, convulsions, diarrhea, nausea, vomiting, reduction of white blood cells, sinus inflammation, male breasts that are painful or swollen, drug allergy, conjunctivitis, fluid retention, a ringing or buzzing in the ears, hearing loss, high blood sugar, and muscle pains. Rare side effects include confusion, irregular heartbeat, numbness or tingling in the hands and feet, nervousness, facial flushing, severe abdominal pain, weakness, acne, heart attack, itching, anxiety, depression, lethargy, mouth sores, swallowing difficulties, intestinal bleeding, constipation, pancreas inflammation, night sweats, chest pain, joint pains, visual disturbances, and weight loss. Use of cyclosporine becomes life-threatening if the symptoms include wheezing and shortness of breath, seizures, and convulsions. The effects of overdosing are irregular heartbeat, seizures, and coma.

The oral solution is mixed in a glass (paper, plastic, and styrofoam cups should be avoided); it can be mixed with apple juice and orange juice, but grapefruit juice can affect the breakdown of the drug, and milk may render it unpalatable. It is consumed immediately after mixing, and more juice should be poured into the glass and drunk to insure that the complete dose has been taken. Taking it with food may help prevent an upset stomach. Allopurinol, androgens, Bromocriptine, Cimetidine, Clarithromycin, Danazol, Diltiazem, potassium-sparing diuretics, Erythromycin, estrogens, Fluconazole, Itraconazole, Methylprednisolone, Metoclopramide, Micardipine, and Verapamil enhance the effect of cyclosporine; anticonvulsants, Carbamazepine, Nafcillin, Phenobarbital, Phenytoin, Octreotide, Ticlopidine, Rifampin, and possibly Rifabutin diminish the effect. Cyclosporine can cause problems with the body's ability to remove Digoxin, Lovastatin, and Prednisolone, so the dosage of any of these drugs must be reduced when

it is taken. Cyclosporine produces adverse effects when combined with a number of drugs: Itraconazole or Nimodipine increase its toxicity; immuno-suppressants may increase the risk of infection; Amphotericin B, Azapropazon, Cimetidine, Diclofenac, Gentamicin, Ketoconazole, Melphalan, Ranitidine, Tacrolimus, Tiopronin, Tobramycin, Trimethoprim-Sulfamethoxazole, or medicines toxic to the kidneys (e.g., NSAIDS, sulfonamides, and those using gold, such as arthritis medications) may cause kidney damage; potassium-sparing diuretics, Enalapril, Lisinopril, potassium supplements, salt substitutes, or high potassium/low sodium foods can increase blood potassium; Lovastatin may cause heart and kidney damage; Vancomycin may cause hearing loss or kidney damage; and virus vaccines may cause adverse reactions to the vaccines. Other common substances that could cause toxic reactions include alcohol, cocaine, marijuana, and tobacco.

DONEPEZIL

AKA: Aricept.

Effects: Increases the availability of acetylcholine in the brain, improving memory in Alzheimer's patients for a short period of time.

FK506

AKA: Prograf, Tacrolimus.

An immune-suppressing drug used to prevent transplanted organs from being rejected.

Effects: It has been found to cause neurons to grow new fibers that connect to other brain cells, which could possibly overcome brain damage caused by strokes, Alzheimer's disease, and Parkinson's disease.

Precautions: It should not be taken by transplant patients who are sensitive or allergic to FK506. The elderly may be given a lower dosage to compensate for loss of kidney function.

It may cause kidney damage in liver patients, especially in high doses, and mildly elevate blood potassium. It may also cause tremors, headaches, changes in muscle function, seizures, changes in mental state and sense perception, or other nervous-system problems. It may increase the chance of developing a lymphoma or other malignancy; a viral infection related to Epstein-Barr may also occur. A mild to moderate elevation in blood pressure may indicate kidney damage.

Common side effects include headaches, tremors, sleeplessness, tingling in the hands and feet, diarrhea, nausea, constipation, loss of appetite, vomiting, dental infections (in the absence of good oral hygiene, or where careless or excessive brushing and flossing causes bleeding), liver or kidney abnormalities, high blood pressure, urinary infection, decreased frequency of urination, anemia, increased white blood cells count, reduced blood-platelet count, changes in blood potassium level, reduced blood magnesium, high blood sugar, lung problems (including fluid in the lungs), breathing difficulties, itching, rash, abdominal pains, pain, fever, weakness, back pains, buildup of abdominal fluid, and fluid retention.

Less common side effects include dream abnormalities, anxiety, confusion, depression, dizziness, instability, hallucinations, poor coordination, muscle spasms, psychosis, tiredness, strange thoughts, visual disturbances (including double vision), a ringing or buzzing in the ears, upset stomach, a yellow discoloration in the skin or whites of the eyes, swallowing troubles, stomach gas, stomach bleeding, fungus infection of the mouth, bloody urine, chest pain, rapid heartbeat, low blood pressure, diabetes, black-and-blue marks on the skin, aching in the muscles and joints, leg cramps, muscle weakness, asthma, bronchitis, coughing, sore throat, pneumonia, a stuffy and runny nose, sinus irritation, voice changes, sweating, skin rashes, and herpes infections.

An overdose will result in increased side effects.

Excessive suppression of the immune system can occur when it is taken with other immunosuppressants. Additional kidney damage may occur when taken with other drugs that cause kidney problems, such as aminoglycoside antibiotics, Amphotericin B, Cisplatin, and—when taken within 24 hours of each other—Cyclosporine. Blood levels of FK506 (and attendant side effects) can increase when taken with antifungal drugs, Bromocriptine, calcium channel blockers, Cimetidine, Clarithromycin, Danazol, Diltiazem, Erythromycin, Methylprednisolone, and Metoclopramine; blood levels of FK506 can be decreased by Carbamazepine, Phenobarbitol, Phenytoin, Rifampin, Rifampicin. Vaccination efficacy may be reduced by FK506, and live vaccines such as BCG, measles, mumps, oral polio, rubella, TY 21 typhoid, and yellow fever should be avoided. The drug should be taken one hour before or two hours after meals to avoid absorption be food.

Dosage: For its use in transplant surgery, the usual dose is 0.075 to 0.15

mg per pound of body weight a day in 2 divided doses, often adjusted to the lowest effective level to reduce side effects.

INTERFERON BETA

AKA: Betaseron, Interferon beta-1b.

A preliminary study has shown that interferon beta can counteract the memory loss that often occurs with multiple sclerosis.

Precautions: Nothing is known about the effects it might have on those without MS. Those taking Interferon beta may experience flu-like symptoms (fever, chills, muscle aches, sweating), mood swings, excessive sleep, severe depression, and suicidal tendencies.

Common side effects include some form of pain at the site of injection, sinusitis, migraine headaches, fever, weakness, chills, muscle aches, abdominal pain, flu-like symptoms, menstruation that is painful or irregular, constipation, vomiting, liver inflammation, sweating, and a reduction in white blood cells. Less common side effects include swelling, pelvic pain, cysts, suicidal tendencies, thyroid goiter, heart palpitations, high blood pressure, rapid heartbeat, bleeding, laryngitis, breathing difficulties, stiffness, tiredness, speech problems, convulsions, uncontrolled movements, hair loss, visual disturbances, pink eye, feelings of a need to urinate, cystitis, breast pain, and cystic breast disease. Rare side effects encompass symptoms occurring almost everywhere on the body.

Overdose symptoms are not known, but may be more severe manifestations of the above side effects.

There are no known food or drug interactions.

Dosage: A subcutaneous injection of 8 million units every other day.

L-DOPA

AKA: Larodopa, levodopa, Lopar, L-3,4 dihydroxyphenylalanine.

A precursor of the neurotransmitter dopamine, L-dopa is an amino acid found naturally in the body, even though it is classified as a prescription drug. It is metabolized from tyrosine, which in turn is converted from phenylalanine. It is used to treat Parkinson's disease, restless leg syndrome, and the pain resulting from herpes zoster (shingles).

Food Sources: Velvet beans.

Effects: It may reverse or even prevent the deterioration of the body generally associated with aging by fully restoring the hypothalamus' ability to maintain the body's biochemical homeostasis; it may increase energy without the addiction and depressive aftermath associated with amphetamines; it can aid in weight loss by suppressing the appetite and stimulating the release of growth hormone; it is a powerful anti-oxidant; and it may act as a sexual aid by increasing the levels of the neurotransmitters norepinephrine and dopamine in the brain, stimulating the release of growth hormone, decreasing the levels of prolactin, and reducing the levels of serotonin.

Taking vitamin C may maintain the levels of norepinephrine and dopamine in the body, while taking one or more of such anti-oxidants as vitamins B-1, B-5, B-6, and E, the minerals selenium and zinc, and the drug Hydergine may prevent free-radical damage caused by dopamine byproducts. It is sometimes administered with Carbidopa, which allows it to cross the blood/brain barrier much more easily and allows the dosage to be reduced by as much as 75 percent, reducing side effects considerably.

Precautions: It should not be taken by those who are allergic to L-dopa or Carbidopa, have taken an MAO inhibitor in the previous two weeks, have narrow-angle type glaucoma, have a history of stomach ulcers, or who have malignant melanoma or suspicious skin lesions. The hazards of L-dopa may be increased for those with diabetes, epilepsy, high blood pressure, heart or lung disease, a history of heart attacks, glaucoma, asthma, kidney disease, liver disease, hormone disease, peptic ulcer, or who have had surgery within the last two months (including dental surgery) that required general or spinal anesthesia. It should be used with extreme caution by those with a history of psychosis, and adverse reactions may be more frequent and severe in those over age 60.

Common side effects include muscle spasms, loss of appetite, nausea, vomiting, stomach pain, dry mouth, drooling, eating problems arising from a loss of muscle control, tiredness, hand tremors, headache, dizziness, numbness, weakness or feelings of faintness, confusion, insomnia, teeth grinding, nightmares, euphoria, hallucinations, delusions, agitation, anxiety, an overall feeling of illness, mood changes, diarrhea, depression and suicidal feelings, and body odor. Less common side effects include heart palpitations or irregularities, dizziness when standing up, paranoia, some loss of mental abilities, difficulty in urinating, muscle twitches, a burning feeling on the tongue, bitter taste, constipation, unusual breathing patterns, blurred or double vision, hot flashes, changes in weight, dark urine,

heavy perspiration, itchy skin, eyelid spasms, a flushing in the face, and tiredness. Rare side effects include stomach bleeding, ulcer, high blood pressure, convulsions, blood changes (including anemia), feelings of stimulation, hiccups, hair loss, hoarseness, the shrinking of male genitals, fluid retention, increased libido, and pain in the upper abdomen. Overdose symptoms include muscle twitches, eyelid spasms, nausea, vomiting, diarrhea, rapid or irregular pulse, weakness, fainting, confusion, agitation, hallucinations, and coma.

It could cause a condition called the serotonin syndrome, in which serotonin levels in the body are too high, and which is characterized by restlessness, confusion, sweating, diarrhea, excessive salivation, high blood pressure, increased body temperature, rapid heart rate, tremors, and seizures.

The effects of L-dopa can be increased by antacids, Selegiline, or other anti-Parkinsonian drugs, and decreased by anticholinergic drugs, tricyclic anti-depressants, anti-convulsants, antihypertensives, benzodiazepine-type tranquilizers and sedatives, Haloperidol, Methionine, Methyldopa, Molindone, Papaverine, phenothiazine antipsychotic medications, Phenytoin, Pyridoxine (vitamin B-6), or Rauwolfia alkaloids. When combined with Albuterol, it can increase the risk of heartbeat irregularities; with tricyclic antidepressants or anti-hypertensives, it can lead to lowered blood pressure and weakness or faintness when standing up; with Guanfacine, it can lead to increased effects of both drugs; with MAO inhibitors, it can lead to dangerously high blood pressure (individuals should cease taking MAO inhibitors two weeks before starting L-Dopa); with Metoclopramide, it can lead to a higher absorption of L-dopa in the blood and a diminishing in the latter drug's effects on the stomach.

Pyridoxine (vitamin B-6) or a high protein diet can decrease the effects of L-dopa; B-6 and L-dopa may have to be taken one-half to four hours apart to prevent this. While B-6 can increase dopamine levels in the blood, it can decrease dopamine levels in the brain, and some take Sinemet (a combination of L-dopa and Carbidopa) to keep brain dopamine levels high. When combined with cocaine, it can lead to a greater risk of heartbeat irregularity, and when combined with marijuana, it can lead to fatigue, lethargy, and fainting. It should be taken with food to avoid upset stomach.

Dosage: For Parkinson's patients, 0.5 to 8 grams/day according to a person's individual needs. For life-extension and cognitive enhancement purposes, it is generally suggested that 125 to 500 mg/day be taken, or 35 to 125 mg/day in combination with Carbidopa. Taking it just before sleep is probably the best strategy for stimulating the release of growth hormone.

METHYLPHENIDATE

AKA: PMS-Methylphenidate, Ritalin.

A central nervous system stimulant used to treat attention deficit disorder in children, narcolepsy and mild depression in the elderly, plus other psychological, educational, and social disorders.

Effects: According to Durk Pearson and Sandy Shaw, it has been shown to improve learning, memory, and information processing by releasing norepinephrine in the brain.

Precautions: Continued or excessive use can lead to dependence or addiction, and possibly severe psychotic episodes. It should be used with caution by those with glaucoma or other visual problems, high blood pressure, epilepsy or seizures, or those who are generally tense, agitated, or allergic to the drug. It is a stimulant that can mask symptoms of fatigue, and so should be used with caution by those driving or using hazardous equipment. Since it is a stimulant that causes the release of norepinephrine, feelings of depression and a severely compromised immune system could occur between the time the neurotransmitter is metabolized and the body is able to make more.

Common side effects in adults include nervousness and insomnia (which are usually controlled by reducing or eliminating the afternoon or evening dose), dizziness, headache, appetite loss, skin rash, itching, fever, joint pains, nausea, abnormal heart rhythms, drowsiness, changes in blood pressure or pulse, chest and stomach pains, psychotic episodes, some hair loss, and uncontrolled body movements. Rare side effects include blurred vision, sore throat, convulsions, and extreme tiredness.

Overdose symptoms include vomiting, agitation, tremors, convulsions, coma, euphoria, confusion, hallucinations, delirium, sweating, flushing, headache, high fever, abnormal heart rate, high blood pressure, and dryness in the nose and mouth.

Methylphenidate can reduce the effectiveness of antihypertensives, Guanadrel, Guanethidine, Minoxidil, and Terazosin, whereas its effectiveness can be reduced by anti-depressants and Cisapride. The effects of both drugs can be diminished if combined with Acebutolol, Nitrates, or Oxprenolol.

Dextrothyroxine can greatly enhance the effects of Methylphenidate, as will MAO inhibitors, the latter also elevating blood pressure to dangerous levels. Methylphenidate can reduce the rate at which the following drugs are broken down in the body, resulting in higher levels in the bloodstream: anticholinergics, anticonvulsants, central nervous system stimulants, anticoagulants, antidepressants, Phenylbutazone, and Oxyphenbutazone. When combined with Pimozide, it can hide the cause of tics. Combining with caffeine drinks and foods containing tyramine can raise blood pressure; with alcohol can result in drowsiness; and with cocaine, can raise blood pressure and increase the risk of heartbeat irregularities. It is best taken 30 to 45 minutes before meals.

Dosage: For the treatment of various disorders in adults, 20 to 30 mg/day in two to three divided doses, though dosage is always adjusted according to the individual.

NIMODIPINE

AKA: Nimotop, Periplum.

Effects: Prevents the constriction of blood vessels, which increases the flow of blood in the brain and decreases the chance of oxygen deprivation to the brain cells. It accumulates in the highest concentrations in the brain and spinal fluid, and is usually prescribed for strokes and migraine headaches. In fact, it is the only calcium-channel blocker known to improve neurological function after a stroke; however, it is probably the only calcium-channel blocker not used for angina or high blood pressure. It may also increase acetylcholine levels.

One study has found that 90 mg in three divided doses over a 12-week period had a significantly positive effect on memory, depression, and general mood, though further research has been unable to replicate these results (it is still not fully known how the drug works). It is considered a possible treatment for Alzheimer's, dementia, age-related degenerative diseases, epilepsy, and ethanol intoxication, and may have some anti-stress and anti-aging properties.

Precautions: It should not be taken by those who are sensitive or allergic to it, or who have very low blood pressure. Nimodipine may pose risks to those who have kidney or liver disease, high blood pressure, and heart disease (excluding coronary artery disease). Those over 60 may find that side effects may be more frequent or severe.

Side effects are generally mild. Common side effects include tiredness, flushing of the skin, diarrhea, low blood pressure, headache, and swelling of the feet, ankles, and abdomen. Less common side effects include itching, acne, rash, anemia, bleeding or bruising, unusual blood clotting, stomach bleeding, a heartbeat that is abnormally slow or fast, high blood pressure, heart failure, wheezing, coughing, shortness of breath, dizziness, a numbness or tingling in the hands or feet, a swelling of the arms and legs, muscle cramps, difficulty urinating, nausea, constipation, depression, memory loss, psychosis, paranoia, hallucinations. Rare side effects include temporary blindness, increased angina, fainting, chest pain, fever, liver inflammation or jaundice, joint pain and swelling, hair loss, vivid dreams, headaches, vomiting, and sexual difficulties.

Overdose symptoms include nausea, weakness, dizziness, drowsiness, confusion, slurred speech, a heartbeat that is abnormally fast or slow, changes in blood pressure, loss of consciousness, and cardiac arrest.

The effects (and possible toxicity) of Nimodipine can be enhanced by antiarrhythmics, Betaxolol eye drops, Cimetidine, Levobutanol eye drops, Timolol eye drops, and decreased by calcium (large doses), Phenytoin, Rifampin, and vitamin D (large doses). Nimodipine can increase the effects (and possible toxicity) of oral anti-coagulants, hydantoin anticonvulsants, Carbamazepine, Cyclosporine, Digoxin (large doses), Quinidine, and Theophylline, and weaken the effects of Lithium. The effects and possible toxicity of both drugs can be increased when combined with antiarrhythmics and Nicardipine. When combined with Angiotensin-converting enzyme (ACE) inhibitors, it can lead to high levels of potassium in the blood; with antihypertensives, it can lead to changes in blood pressure; aspirin, can cause bleeding; with beta-adrenergic blocking agents, it may result in an irregular heartbeat and a worsening of congestive heart failure; with Disopyramide, it may cause the heartbeat to be dangerously fast, slow, or irregular; with diuretics, it may cause a dangerous drop in blood pressure; and with Tocainide, it may increase the risk of adverse reactions from either drug.

Nimodipine can lead to dangerously low blood pressure when combined with alcohol, a possible irregular heartbeat when combined with cocaine and marijuana, and a possible rapid heartbeat when combined with tobacco. Experts advise that all such interactions be avoided. Nimodipine is taken at least one hour before or two hours after meals. It can be taken with food or drink if stomach upset occurs, though grapefruit juice should be avoided.

Dosage: For migraine headaches, the usual dosage is 120 mg/day in three divided doses; for cognitive enhancement, the recommended dosage is 60 mg in two divided doses.

PEMOLINE

AKA: Cylert, magnesium pemoline.

An amphetamine derivative and central nervous system stimulant prescribed for attention deficit disorders in children and daytime sleepiness.

Effects: Increases the level of norepinephrine in the synapses of the brain, creating greater nerve stimulation and possible improvements in learning, memory, and concentration.

Precautions: Releases vasopressin in the body, which could result in a depletion and feelings of depression. It should not be taken by those allergic or sensitive to it, and for those who do take it, regular liver function tests are recommended.

Common side effects include loss of appetite, depression, drowsiness, dizziness, hallucinations, headache, irritability, nausea, rash, insomnia, and stomachache. Rare symptoms include hypersensitivity to the drug, wandering eye, weight loss, seizures, jaundice, and involuntary movements of the lips, face, tongue, and limbs.

Overdose symptoms include agitation, hallucinations, rapid heartbeat, restlessness, involuntary muscle movements, fever, confusion, convulsions, and coma.

Taking it on an empty stomach may cause stomach upset, and taking it too late in the day may result in troubled sleep.

Dosage: For therapeutic uses, 37.5 to 75 mg/day, not to exceed 112.5 mg/day; for brain-boosting effects, 18.75 to 75 mg/day is said to provide 6 to 12 hours of mental stimulation accompanied by physical relaxation.

PENICILLAMINE

AKA: Cuprimine, Depen.

A drug modified from an amino acid in penicillin; it is prescribed to treat rheumatoid arthritis, prevent kidney stones, and treat heavy metal poisoning.

Effects: Removes heavy metals from the body.

Precautions: It should not be taken by those who are allergic or who have severe anemia. Penicillamine may be dangerous for those who suffer from kidney disease or who are allergic to any penicillin antibiotics. Those over 60 should exercise caution, as it could damage blood cells and kidneys.

Common side effects include rash, itchy skin, swollen lymph glands, loss of appetite, nausea, diarrhea, vomiting, and loss of taste. Less common side effects include sore throat, fever, increased incidence of bruising, swollen legs or feet, urine that is bloody or cloudy, an increase in weight, fatigue, weakness, and joint pain. Rare side effects include general pain, vision problems, tinnitus, mouth sores (including ulcers and white spots), breathing difficulties, coughing up blood, jaundice, abdominal pains, blisters, and peeling skin. Life-threatening and overdose symptoms include ulcers, sores, convulsions, coughing up blood, and coma. Prolonged use can damage the liver, kidneys, and blood cells. According to John Mann, additional side effects include loss of the skin's tensile strength (an effect that may be prevented by adequate nutrition) and a loss of zinc and vitamin B-6 (possibly prevented by supplementation of 100 mg/day of each).

Combining Penacillamine with gold compounds or immunosuppressants can damage the kidneys and blood cells; with iron supplements, it can lessen the effect of penicillamine (they should be taken at least two hours apart); and with vitamin B-6, it can increase the need for this vitamin. The effects of penicillamine can be enhanced when combined with alcohol, cocaine, or marijuana, and diminished when combined with food.

Dosage: John Mann recommends 250 mg/day to start, increasing to 1000 to 2000 mg/day in four divided doses.

RAPAMYCIN

An immune-suppressing drug used to prevent transplanted organs from being rejected.

Effects: It has been found to cause neurons to grow new fibers that connect to other brain cells, which could possibly overcome damage caused by strokes, Alzheimer's disease, and Parkinson's disease.

RISPERIDONE

AKA: Risperdal.

A drug used in the treatment of schizophrenia and psychotic disorders.

Effects: It is believed to improve short-term memory by about 20 percent in patients taking the drug.

Precautions: Its memory-enhancing effects on non-schizophrenics are still unknown. It should not be taken by those who are allergic to it. It may be dangerous for individuals with liver or kidney disease, allergies to other medications, or a history of seizures. A small percentage of Caucasians and Asians are poor metabolizers of the drug because of a lack of inadequate liver enzyme to break it down, taking five days for a steady dose to reach the blood instead of the usual one. Side effects may be more pronounced in the elderly, and it may lead to photosensitivity in some people. Those taking it should refrain from driving or piloting any craft, or working in high places.

Common side effects include trouble with swallowing or speaking, profuse sweating, stiffness or spasms in the muscles of the neck and back, stiffness or weakness in the limbs, anxiety, hand tremors, pale skin, unnatural tiredness, nervousness, irritability, difficulty in walking or balancing, stomach pain, gas, insomnia, dizziness or lightheadedness when moving from a prone or sitting position to a standing position, coughing, stuffy nose, nausea, vomiting, headaches, constipation, and drowsiness. Less common side effects include chest pain, fainting, breathing problems, vision changes, joint pain, fever, lowered sex drive, impotence, rash or other skin problems, sore throat, increased saliva in the mouth, and toothache. Rare side effects consist of such involuntary actions as smacking the lips, puffing out the cheeks, moving the tongue, and uncontrolled movements of the head, neck, arms, and legs. Life-threatening symptoms are known as the neuroleptic malignant syndrome (NMS), and include high fever, muscle rigidity, mental changes, pulse or blood pressure irregularities, sweating, and abnormal heart rhythms. This last symptom is known as *torsade de pointes*, and is life-threatening. Overdose symptoms are

merely more extreme manifestations of expected side effects.

Risperidone can increase levels of the hormone prolactin, possibly leading to tumors of the pituitary gland, breast, and pancreas, though no documented cases have been noted.

The effects of Risperidone are enhanced when taken with Clozapine; Clozapine can also diminish the effects of the drug, as can Carbamazepine. It can strengthen the effects of anti-hypertensives, deepen the sedative effect of other central nervous system depressants, and cause various problems when combined with levodopa. It also has an intensified sedative effect when combined with alcohol. What effects it has when combined with cocaine or marijuana are not known.

SELEGILINE

AKA: Deprenyl, Eldepryl, Jumex, Jumexal, Juprenil, L-deprenyl, Movergan, Procythol, SD Deprenyl, selegiline hydrochloride.

A standard prescription drug used in the treatment of Parkinson's disease in combination with levodopa and Carbidopa, and mental depression when taken by itself. The molecular structure is similar to phenylethylamine (PEA), which exists in both plants and animals (and is the so-called "love chemical" in chocolate), and also resembles such compounds as amphetamine, norepinephrine, dopamine, phenylalanine, tyrosine, L-dopa, and tyramine.

Effects: It can help slow the progress of Alzheimer's to a moderate degree by protecting the brain cells from the damaging effects of oxygen. It also benefits memory, attention, and reaction times in those with Parkinson's, and may also increase concentration, alertness, and mental stamina. In doses of 15 to 60 mg a day, it has relieved depression in 50 percent of those who suffered severely from this illness; one study has shown that it may work synergistically with vitamin B-6 and phenylalanine in this regard (5 mg of selegiline, 100 mg of vitamin B-6, and 1 to 6 grams of phenylalanine). It has increased the life span of rats by an average of 30 percent, and, more significantly, many of them lived beyond the maximum life expectancy for that species. Anecdotal evidence indicates it may be an aphrodisiac.

Precautions: While some studies show dramatic improvements in those with Alzheimer's, others have shown no significant increase for several types of memory tasks.

It should not be taken by anyone allergic to selegiline. It may be dangerous for those with a history of peptic ulcers, profound dementia, severe psychosis, tardive dyskinesia, excessive tremors, or a previous bad reaction to selegiline. Those over 60 may be able to get by on smaller doses for a shorter period of time, as side effects may be more pronounced and more frequent. Driving or piloting any craft, operating any heavy machinery, or working in high places should not be undertaken while under the effects of the drug.

Common side effects include increased sensitivity to ultra-violet rays from the sun, mood changes, unusual or uncontrolled body movements, hallucinations, headaches, lip smacking, difficult urination, abdominal pain, dizziness, dry mouth, insomnia, and mild nausea. Less common side effects include chest pain, irregular heartbeat, wheezing, swollen feet, speech difficulties, bloody or black stools, constipation, anxiety, tiredness, eyelid spasms, unpleasant tastes, blurred vision, leg pain, ringing in the ears, chills, skin rash, a burning on the lips or in the mouth, drowsiness, frequent and decreased urination. Rare side effects include weight loss, heartburn, jaw clenching or teeth gnashing, impaired memory, and uncontrolled body movements. Life-threatening symptoms include severe chest pain, enlarged pupils, irregular heartbeat, severe nausea and vomiting, and a stiff neck. Overdose symptoms (which can occur in doses of more than 10 mg/day) include high (and possibly fatal) blood pressure, difficulty in opening the mouth, muscle spasms in the neck and heel, sweating, fast and irregular heartbeat, hyperactive reflexes, cold or clammy skin, chest pain, agitation, fainting, seizures, coma, vivid dreams, nightmares, insomnia, restlessness, weakness, drowsiness, flushing of the skin, convulsions, incoherence, confusion, severe headache, high fever, heart attack, shock, excitement, overstimulation, irritability, anxiety, and muscle spasms in the face.

It should not be taken with any foods that contain the enzyme tyramine — avocados, bananas, figs, and raisins; cheese; beer (including non-alcoholic beer), wine, and liquors; yeast extracts, bean pods, bean curd, fava beans, miso soup, or soy sauce; pickled or smoked fish, meat, or poultry; fermented sausage (summer sausage, salami, pepperoni); bologna; liver; overripe fruit — chocolate, or caffeine, as it could result in severe toxicity or death. Mark Mayell, however, insists that, since it only inhibits MAO-B and not MAO-A, it avoids this dangerous interaction. It should not be taken with any over-the-counter medications such as cough and cold medications, laxatives, antacids, diet pills, nose drops, or vitamins without consulting a physician first.

There is an increased risk of mental instability and, possibly, death when combined with fluoxetine (there should be at least a five-week span between the time one drug is stopped and the other is taken). When taken with levodopa, there is a greater risk of side effects. With Meperidine (Demerol) and other MAO inhibitors, there could be a severe drop in blood pressure — as well as potentially fatal reactions — and with narcotics, there could be a toxic interaction that may result in seizures, coma, or death. With Sertraline, an increased depressive effect may result. With Sinemet (a combination of Carbidiopa and levodopa), there could be an increase in levodopa's side effects. It should not be combined with Milacemide, opiates, yohimbe, or yohimbine. The effects when combined with Sumatriptan are unknown. Combined with marijuana or tobacco, it could result in a rapid heart rate and, with cocaine, a rapid heart rate and high blood pressure.

Dosage: Smart drug users prefer the liquid form to the pill because it is easier to calibrate into smaller doses and is more readily absorbed into the body. For Parkinson's, the usual dose is 5 mg with breakfast and lunch, which may be enough to produce feelings of well-being and increased energy in the average person. Dr. Jozsef Knoll, who developed selegiline, recommends 10 to 15 mg/ week for the average healthy person age 45 and over. Even less may be effective, especially if taken with vitamin B-6 and phenylalanine. Ward Dean, M.D., *et al.*, state that some individuals have taken up to 60 mg for three weeks with no significant side effects. Discovery Experimental and Development, one manufacturer of selegiline, recommends the following dosages:

Age	Dosage
30–35	1 mg twice a week
35–40	1 mg every other day
40–45	1 mg/day
45–50	2 mg/day
50–55	3 mg/day
55–60	4 mg/day
60–65	5 mg/day
65–70	6 mg/day
70–75	8 mg/day
75–80	9 mg/day
80+	10 mg/day

CHAPTER 12

Nootropics

Nootropics is a term used by proponents of smart drugs to describe medical drugs and nutritional supplements that have a positive effect on brain function.

AMPAKINE

Effects: A drug developed from ampakines, a class of biochemicals, has been found to enhance communication between brain cells. Subjects have been shown to have enhanced performance on memory tests, and it may show promise in helping those with such disorders as Alzheimer's disease and schizophrenia, in which the high-speed electrical signals that link the brain's complex neural circuits are failing.

ANIRACETAM

AKA: Draganon, Ro 13-5057, Sarpul. Chemically similar to piracetam, but is about ten times stronger and treats more symptoms. How it works is still unknown.

Effects: Has been shown to protect the brains of lab animals.

Precautions: Toxicity and side effects seem minimal, but it has not been adequately tested on humans as yet.

Dosage: The most effective cognitive-enhancing dose is 1000 mg/day, though this is based only on one study.

BD

AKA: Enliven, GHRE, NRG3, 1,4 butanediol, Revitalize Plus, Serenity, Somatopro, Thunder Nectar, Weight Belt Cleaner.

Effects: Increases energy and promotes sleep. When taken orally, it is converted by the body into GHB.

Precautions: Products containing BD have been associated with over 120 cases of adverse side effects, including three deaths. Side effects include dangerously low heart rate and breathing, vomiting, seizures, unconsciousness, and coma.

BEMEGRIDE

Effects: May increase learning ability and slow the advance of senility.

Precautions: Causes convulsions.

CENTROPHENOXINE

AKA: Brenal, Cellative, Clocete, 4-chlorophenoxyacetic acid 2-dimethylaminoethyl ester, Helfergen, Lucidril, meclofenoxate, Marucotol, Methoxynal, Proserout.

It is very similar structurally to the important neurotransmitter acetylcholine. In the bloodstream, it breaks down into DMAE and supplies the same basic building blocks as DMAE for manufacturing acetylcholine and speeding nerve transmissions across synapses.

Effects: It is believed to improve memory, increase mental alertness, improve mood, increase learning ability, protect against aging (has been shown to increase the life span of lab animals 30 percent), remove lipofuscin deposits (it may be better than DMAE in this respect, though some say that this is just speculative), repair synapses, attack free radicals, protect animal brains from the effects of hypoxia (in this respect, it may be useful to those who could suffer loss of oxygen to the tissues, such as some victims of angina, atherosclerotic dementia, intermittent claudication [severe pain in the calves when walking due to restricted blood flow in the legs], and stroke), and increases the rate of synthesis of RNA and the manufacture of new proteins. Despite this, it probably has no effect on Alzheimer's. In Europe, it has been used to treat reading problems, dysfunctions in speech and motor skills, and various age-related mental problems.

Precautions: Centrophenoxine may be dangerous to those who suffer from severe hypertension (high blood pressure), convulsions or involuntary musculoskeletal movements, hyperexcitability, insomnia, tremors, motion sickness, paradoxical drowsiness, and depression. Toxicity is uncommon in therapeutic doses; side effects are also rare, but include depression, dizziness, headaches, hyperexcitability, insomnia (especially if taken later in the day), motion sickness, sleepiness, and tremors.

Dosage: Some say 1000 to 3000 mg/day, though others say that such doses are unnecessarily high, and that 80 mg/kg of body weight (the dosage most often used in clinical trials) is sufficient. It takes effect very fast.

DIAZADAMANTOL

Effects: May increase learning ability and slow the advance of senility.

Precautions: Causes convulsions.

DMSO

AKA: Dimethyl sulfoxide, RIMSO-50.

Legally, it is only prescribed for interstitial cystitis and bladder inflammation, and is not recommended for any other use, though many use it to treat arthritis and sports injuries. It appears to be an all-purpose solvent, and has been used as a degreaser, paint thinner, and anti-freeze.

Effects: It works, not by lubricating joints or by deadening pain, but by scavenging free radicals. It has been shown to increase circulation; protect against the effects of radiation and freezing; reduce keloids, scars, and the effects of burns; help protect against fungus, bacteria, and viruses; be a beneficial supplement to cancer therapy; stimulate immunity; stimulate wound healing; and useful in treating such eye problems as cataracts, macular degeneration, and glaucoma, among others.

It has been found to reduce the severity of paraplegia in cats subjected to crushing spinal cord injuries, and the San Francisco General Hospital Brain Trauma and Edema Center has used it to treat brain injuries. Anecdotal evidence indicates it may provide benefits to those with Down's syndrome, learning disabilities, and senile dementia, as well as those with other forms of brain damage and dysfunction. Because it has so many benefits, proponents tout it as the wonder drug of the 21st century.

Precautions: It may be dangerous for those with a bladder malignancy, kidney or liver problems, diabetes, or who is allergic to DMSO. Those with fair skin use no more than a 50 percent concentration, as they are more sensitive to DMSO.

Concentrations of 40 percent or more may prolong bleeding, and concentrations greater than 50 percent are not applied to the face and neck, as they are more sensitive to DMSO than the rest of the body. It should be dabbed on, not rubbed in, and any excess wiped off after half an hour; toxicity may occur if it is inhaled, as it evaporates slowly. It may exacerbate the effects of some allergens. Injections should only be administered by a physician.

It is difficult to perform double-blind studies on DMSO; it imparts to the breath and skin an immediate garlic odor.

A common side effect is a harmless garlic taste that can persist for up to three days. Less common side effects are vision problems (these have occurred quite frequently in lab animals, but are undocumented in humans), and possibly nausea, headaches, and skin rash, along with redness, itching, burning, discomfort, or blistering on the areas where it has been applied. Rare side effects include nasal congestion, itching, hives, and facial swelling. One life-threatening symptom is breathing difficulties. No overdose symptoms are known, though W. Nathaniel Phillips reports that concentrations greater than 70 percent can cause the skin problems, along with headaches, nausea, diarrhea, a burning sensation when urinating, photophobia (light intolerance), and disturbances in color vision.

When combined with any other bladder medication, the effects of both drugs may be intensified. As it can carry other substances directly into the blood, DMSO should not be applied to the skin where skin medications, cosmetics, lotions, bath oils, or soaps have already been applied.

Most of the industrial grade, or solvent grade, solutions contain acetone, which is readily carried into the blood by DMSO, and which can cause liver damage and death. According to Pearson and Shaw, much of the DMSO sold over the counter or by mail order contains unwanted impurities such as dimethylsulfone, dimethylsufide, nitrogen oxides, and benzene. In addition, after it has scavenged the hydroxyl radicals from the body, it converts to a sulfoxide free radical. While this new free radical is less damaging than the one removed and can be counteracted with the various vitamin, mineral, and amino acid anti-oxidants, impurities can be carried directly into the bloodstream.

Dosage: The typical oral dose is 1 to 2 teaspoons a day, mixed with tomato or grape juice to mask its foul taste. The effects appear to be cumulative, so that the dosage can be reduced over a period of time.

The drug appears crystal clear and has a very distinct sulfur or garlic odor; a cloudy or discolored appearance indicates impurities. It is not used for more than 30 days at a time, with a 30-day interval between periods of use. It is dabbed on, never rubbed in, and it is always stored in its pure state, with the bottle securely capped to prevent the absorption of moisture which might deteriorate the solution. The amount needed is mixed at the time of application.

DOET

A substitute phenylalanine.

Effects: Said to greatly increase the creativity in people who are already creative, it contributes nothing to people who are not so inclined.

ETIRACETAM

A nootropic drug similar to piracetam.

FIPEXIDE

AKA: Attentil, BP 662, Vigilor.

Effects: Can enhance dopamine to a certain degree. In one study, forty older people with advanced cognitive disorders improved their scores on a number of various tests after taking it. It may improve learning, but not recall; improved learning may be attributed to the higher levels of dopamine, which can improve motor coordination, strengthen

the immune system, and promote a sense of well-being, thus providing a better atmosphere for learning to take place.

Precautions: No side effects, toxicity, or contraindications known, though more research is needed.

Dosage: Studies to date have used 600 mg/day in three divided doses.

GEROVITAL

AKA: Gerovital H3, GH-3.

Gerovital is a chemical mixture of procaine hydrochloride, potassium metabisulfate, disodium phosphate, and benzoic acid. In the body, procaine breaks down into the B vitamin paraminobenzoic acid (PABA) and diethylaminoethanol (DEAE), a chemical relative to DMAE that is, in turn, converted into choline by the cells. While the work of Dr. Ana Aslan has made it a very famous and popular anti-aging drug, it is also very controversial — its promoters claim that it can cure over 200 diseases and ailments associated with premature aging.

Effects: May improve memory by promoting better utilization of oxygen in the brain. It is an anti-depressant as a result of it's being an MAO inhibitor.

The Gerovital product PABA helps in forming blood cells, metabolizing protein, and performing the various functions of the skin. It also aids the intestinal bacteria in producing the vitamins folic acid, pantothenic acid, biotin, and vitamin K. Symptoms of deficiency include constipation, depression, digestive disorders, fatigue, gray hair, headaches, infertility, and irritability. By itself, it is not very effective, but produces good results when taken with procaine hydrochloride.

Composed of choline and acetylcholine, the Gerovital product DEAE is an anti-depressant.

Precautions: Other researchers have been unable to duplicate discoverer Ana Aslan's positive results; some claim it is because they used straight procaine rather than GH-3, but there is much evidence to suggest that they are virtually identical. Additionally, Dr. Aslan's research has been attacked for not being well-designed and controlled, and critics assert that most of the improvements are merely the result of its anti-depressant properties. A review of the scientific literature seems to back these criticisms. Dr. Stuart Berger states that PABA is not a vitamin, but a sunblock, and that it can severely deplete the body's white blood cells, and create adverse fatty changes in the heart, liver, and kidneys if taken internally in significant amounts. According to *Prevention* magazine and Dr. Ronald Klatz, the "active ingredient" is evidently the anesthetic novacaine, which begins to break down as soon as it enters the blood. Side effects, though not common, are life-threatening: allergic reactions, a sudden drop in blood pressure, respiratory problems, and convulsions.

Because it is a weak MAO inhibitor, it does not elicit the side effects normally associated with these types of substances. There are rare allergic reactions, but otherwise no adverse effects have been reported, mainly because PABA and DEAE are quickly excreted by the body.

Use of GH-3 and related formulations is avoided by anyone on MAO inhibitors, sulfa drugs, sulphonamide drugs, or combinations like cotrimoxazole.

Dosage: One tablet/day for 25 days, followed by a 5 day period of abstinence.

GHB

AKA: Alcover, 4-hydroxybutyrate, gamma hydrate, gamma-hydroxybutyrate, gamma-hydroxybutyrate sodium, Gamma OH, Liquid Ecstasy, Liquid X, sodium oxybate, sodium oxybutyrate, Somatomax PM.

A natural component of every cell in the body, GHB is found in the greatest concentrations in the kidneys, heart, skeletal muscles, brown fat, hypothalamus, and basal ganglia. It is a precursor to the neurotransmitter GABA, and may be a neurotransmitter itself. Unlke GABA, it can cross the blood/brain barrier. It rapidly metabolizes to carbon dioxide and water.

Food Sources: Meat.

Effects: It produces a mild high, with feelings of bliss, placidity, euphoria, and sensuality. It stimulates the release of growth hormone in the body and, unlike drugs with a similar effect, GHB also increases levels of prolactin. Other physiological effects include a slight elevation of blood sugar, a significant decrease in cholesterol, a mild slowing of the heart, a slight lowering of body temperature, and a stimulation of the release of acetylcholine in the brain (which may improve memory and cognition, though this is, as yet, unproven). Sleep induced by GHB tends to be slightly deeper and somewhat shorter than sleep attained without the use of drugs; unlike other remedies for insomnia, it often does not produce grogginess upon waking.

It may be useful in treating alcoholism, anxiety, and sleep disorders. Anecdotal evidence indicates it may reduce fat and help build lean muscle tissue, possibly because of its effect on growth hormone. Some speculate it may have aphrodisiac and life-extension properties.

Precautions: It should not be used by anyone suffering from epilepsy, convulsions, slowed heartbeat arising from conduction problems, Cushing's syndrome, severe cardiovascular disease, severe hypertension, hyperprolactinemia, or any kind of severe illness.

Before it was banned by the FDA in 1990, it had been studied for 25 years, with the result that it has shown extremely low toxicity. Of 10 known cases of individuals who have suffered side effects, the dosages taken were not known; four of those cases involved combining it with alcohol, two involved individuals with a history of epilepsy or grand mal seizures, and two involved combining it with tranquilizers or such central nervous system depressants as Vicodin and diphenhydramine hydrochloride. Bodybuilders who had taken GHB switched to GABA after the ban. It remains a popular "rave" drug, with many deaths attributed to it, though how many of these are due to impurities, misidentification, and combining with other drugs is unknown.

Common side effects include abrupt sedation, loss of coordination, sleepwalking, unarousability, and decreased inhibition in those taking 2 to 6 teaspoons (approximately 5 to 15 grams) twice nightly over a period of several years. Mild side effects include a numbness of the legs, headache, lethargy, dizziness, a tightness in the chest, extreme ebullience, intense drowsiness, breathing difficulties, and uncontrollable muscle twitches. Severe side effects include confusion, nausea, diarrhea, incontinence, temporary amnesia, sleepwalking, uncontrollable shaking, vomiting, seizures, and brief (one to two hours) non-toxic coma. Complete recovery from even the most severe side effects, however, appears to occur within a few hours and with no apparent long-term side effects. In a 1992 report, epidemiologist Ming-Yan Chin and Richard A. Kreutzer, M.D., both working for the California Department of Health Services, concluded, "there are no documented reports of long-term [adverse] effects. Nor is there any evidence for physiological addiction." Others report that there has been one documented case of addiction, though there is no evidence of withdrawal symptoms.

Because it may deplete levels of potassium in the body, GHB is often administered with a potassium supplement in which the elemental form is equal to 10 percent of the weight of the GHB consumed. It is not combined with central nervous system depressants such as benzodiazepines (e.g., Valium, Xanax), phenothiazines (e.g., Thorazine, Stellazine), various painkillers (e.g., opiates, barbiturates), alcohol, or over-the-counter allergy and sleep remedies. Food can dissipate or delay its effects, and caffeine can block its dopamine-related effects.

Dosage: In various studies doses of 6 to 8 g/day for eight to ten days, 20 to 30 g/day for a week, and 2.5 g/day for several years produced no adverse side effects. The initial dosage is small — an eighth to a fourth of a gram — and dissolved in water, increasing gradually to the desired dose (one level teaspoon equals approximately 2.5 grams). The dosage is adjusted according to body weight, though Ward Dean, M.D., *et al.*, published the following general dose-related expectations: less than 1 gram gives rise to mild relaxation, reduced anxiety, and increased sociability; 1 to 2 grams, strong relaxation; 2 to 4 grams, sleep of three to four hours; 4 to 8 grams — very deep sleep of three to four hours; 10 to 30+ grams, a prolonged, very deep sleep of up to 24 hours. It is taken on an empty stomach (preferably three to four hours after the last meal) to avoid nausea, vomiting, and a delayed onset of effects. About three-quarters to one and a half grams produces a high, while 2.5 grams induces sleep.

Illicit GHB invariably contains dangerous — even toxic — impurities. Pure GHB powder has a salty/licorice taste, turns from a chalky texture to a greasy one when rubbed between the fingers, will fully dissolve in water, and will easily absorb water and turn liquid overnight.

GRISEOLIC ACID

Derivatives are known metabolic brain-enhancers.

HYDERGINE

AKA: Circanol, Deapril-ST, dihydroergotoxine, ergoloid mesylates, ergot alkaloids dihydrogenated, Hydroloid, Niloric.

Hydergine is one of a class of drugs called ergoloid mesylates, which are a combination of three substances produced by the ergot fungus. It was discovered by Albert Hofmann, the chemist who discovered a more famous ergot derivative, LSD-25. The exact method by which it works is unknown, as ergot — a deadly poisonous dark purple or black fungus which thrives on wet grains such as rye — generally causes hallucinations,

convulsions, gangrene, and death. Similar in chemistry to LSD, but non-hallucinogenic, it is — paradoxically — one of the easiest smart drugs to obtain. It is also one of the most widely researched and prescribed. It is generally prescribed to slow age-related memory loss and impaired concentration. In Europe, it is used routinely on accident victims — those suffering from shock, hemorrhage, strokes, heart attacks, drowning, electrocution, and drug overdose can sometimes be revived by intravenous injection — and on hospital patients just before standard surgeries (it gives doctors more time to handle any medical emergencies should they arise in the course of the operation).

Effects: Has been claimed to be an "all-purpose brain booster," as it improves blood flow to the brain, improves the oxygen supply to the brain, increases brain cell metabolism, protects the brain from hypoxia, decreases the development of age pigment (lipofuscin) in the brain, protects brain cells from free-radical damage, keeps a proper balance of several major neurotransmitters in the brain, normalizes systolic blood pressure, and decreases cholesterol levels. It is believed to improve memory, learning, intelligence, and recall. It may also increase the levels of some transmitters in the brain and may promote the growth of some dendrite nerve fibers. Some obscure French studies done in Africa may indicate it is an effective treatment for sickle-cell anemia.

Works synergistically with piracetam.

Precautions: It is not taken by individuals who are allergic to ergot or any of its derivatives, who suffer from any kind of psychosis, whose heartbeat is less than 60 beats per minute, or whose systolic blood pressure is below 100. It may be dangerous to individuals with low blood pressure, liver disease, or psychosis.

It could result in a reduced ability of the body to adjust to cold temperatures. Common symptoms include runny nose, skin flushing, and headache. Less common symptoms are a slow heartbeat, tingling fingers, and blurred vision. Rare symptoms include fainting, rash, nausea, vomiting, stomach cramps, dizziness when arising, drowsiness, soreness under the tongue, and loss of appetite. Overdosing can cause agitation, headaches, flushing in the face, nasal congestion, nausea, vomiting, a drop in blood pressure, blurred vision, weakness, collapse, coma, and amnesia. Many doctors are not convinced of its efficacy. It is rather expensive.

When combined with other ergot preparations or sympathomimetics, it may result in decreased circulation to the limbs, which could be serious.

It could greatly intensify the effect of caffeine, cause an excessive drop in blood pressure when combined with alcohol, lead to overstimulation when combined with cocaine, and decrease the ergoloid effect when combined with marijuana or tobacco.

Dosage: The recommended dosage in the U.S. is 3 mg/day; in Europe, it is 9 mg/day in three divided doses, but 4.5 to 6 mg/day appears to produce good results. Sublingual tablets are ineffective if swallowed intact. It may take at least half a year before the effects are noticeable, but one study has shown that healthy young people taking 12 mg/day saw greater alertness and mental abilities after only two weeks. It works synergistically with piracetam; when the

two are combined, smaller doses of each are just as effective as a larger dose of one.

ISOPRINOSINE

AKA: Methisprinol.

Two of the ingredients in isoprinosine are inosine, which is used by the body to make RNA, and dimethylaminoethanol (DMAE), which assists the inosine in penetrating the blood-brain barrier. It is chemically similar to DMAE.

Effects: Assists the brain in certain key functions relating to memory formation and promotes RNA synthesis in brain cells. It promotes RNA synthesis in brain cells; is an immune stimulator which may have anti-viral properties; and has been shown to increase the effectiveness of Interferon, render some herpes viruses inactive, and reduce the severity of some AIDS symptoms.

Precautions: It should not be used by those with gout or who are predisposed to developing it.

K.H.3

A procaine formula similar to Gerovital and Vitacel, it comes in gelatin capsule form, where it is coupled with hematoporphyrin, which increases the effectiveness of procaine.

Effects: Allegedly improves alertness, concentration, and recall, along with a host of physical disorders.

Precautions: It is not taken by those allergic to procaine or who are taking sulfa drugs or MAO inhibitors. The precautions that apply to Gerovital also apply to K.H.3.

Dosage: 1 or 2 capsules a day

with meals for five months, followed by a period of two to four weeks of no K.H.3.

MILACEMIDE

AKA: 2-n-pentylaminoacetamide.

Effects: A few studies have shown it to improve certain aspects of memory in normal people, while having no effect on memory on those afflicted with Alzheimer's or schizophrenia. Much more research needs to be done.

Precautions: Possible side effects include elevated liver enzymes, nausea, diarrhea, and disorientation.

It is not combined with any MAO-B inhibitor drug, such as deprenyl, as it may have a negative effect on memory and brain function.

Dosage: The optimal dosage seems to be 400 to 1200 mg/day. Since it apparently has an inverted U-shaped dose-response curve, smaller doses (unless used in combination with other smart drugs) and larger doses may have insignificant, or even negative, results.

NAFTIDROFURYL

A metabolic brain-enhancer.

NDD-094

Effects: A compound said to stop, and even reverse, memory loss, apparently by regrowing nerve cells that create acetylcholine. patients taking NDD-094 have registered improved brain activity levels on PET scans.

Precautions: There may be side effects, including nausea. Much more research needs to be done.

NEFIRACETAM

Effects: Like piracetam, it is derived from pyrrolidone, which is believed to enhance the nervous system's ability to utilize acetylcholine as a neurotransmitter.

NOOTROPYL

AKA: 2-oxo-pyrrolidine acetamide.

An analogue of gamma-aminobutyric acid, a neurotransmitter.

Effects: It apparently stimulates the flow of information between the two hemispheres of the brain in rats and mice.

OXIRACETAM

AKA: CT-848, hydroxypiracetam, ISF-2522, Neuractiv, Neuromet.

An analogue of piracetam that is about two to three times more potent.

Precautions: It appears to be non-toxic, with no ill effects in doses as high as 2400 mg/day. Little research has been done on healthy individuals, however.

Dosage: Doses of 1200 to 2400 mg/day seem to produce the greatest improvement in cognitive function, though some recommend 800 to 2400 mg/day.

OXPRENOLOL

A beta-adrenergic blocking agent prescribed to reduce angina attacks, stabilize an irregular heartbeat, lower blood pressure, and reduce the occurrence of vascular headaches.

Effects: It has been shown to reduce phobias and eliminate anxiety.

Precautions: It is not taken by

anyone with an allergy to any beta-adrenergic blocker; by those with hypotension, as it lowers blood pressure, aggravates any condition of congestive heart failure, produces tingling in the extremities, and light-headedness; by those with asthma, pollen allergies, upper respiratory disease, or arterial spasms; or by those who have taken MAO inhibitors or other psychiatric or psychotropic drugs within the preceding two weeks. It is used by those who have chronic obstructive pulmonary diseases (e.g., asthma, bronchitis, hay fever, or emphysema), diabetes or hypoglycemia, kidney or liver problems, heart disease or poor circulation in the limbs, an overactive thyroid function, or surgery within the previous two months (including dental surgery) that requires general or spinal anesthesia.

For those over age 60, the side effects may be more severe and frequent. Prolonged use can weaken the heart muscles, and it may mask symptoms of hypoglycemia or alter the results of some medical tests.

Common side effects include a pulse rate slower than 50 beats per minute, diarrhea, dizziness, drowsiness, fatigue, nausea, numbness or tingling in the fingers and toes, weakness, cold hands or feet, and dryness of the eyes, mouth, and skin. Less common side effects include hallucinations, nightmares, insomnia, headaches, breathing difficulties, joint pain, anxiety, chest pain, confusion, lack of alertness, depression, impotence, abdominal pain, and constipation. Rare symptoms include rash, sore throat, fever, unexplained bleeding or bruising, and dry burning eyes.

There is an enhanced beta blocker effect when combined with betaxolol eyedrops or Levobunolol eyedrops, and a diminished beta blocker effect when combined with Dextrothyroxine or Indomethacin. It can intensify the effects of antidiabetics, antihypertensives, barbiturates, insulin, and narcotics, and can lessen the effects of antihistamines and beta-agonists. It can decrease the effectiveness of Digitalis if taken for congestive heart failure, but increase its effectiveness if taken for any other medical reason.

There is an increased drop in blood pressure when taken with alcohol, calcium channel blockers, Clonidine, Diazoxide, or Guanabenz. When combined with angiotensin-converting (ACE) inhibitors or non-steroidal anti-inflammatory drugs (NSAIDS), it could increase the anti-hypertensive effect of one or both drugs; with Encainide, it could damage the heart muscle; with Molindone, there could be an increased tranquilizer effect; with MAO inhibitors, there could be a rise in blood pressure if the latter is discontinued; with cocaine, there could be an irregular heartbeat and a decreased beta-adrenergic effect; with daily marijuana use, there could be circulation problems in the hands and feet; and with tobacco, there could be an irregular heartbeat. It may also interact with certain ingredients in over-the-counter cold, cough, and allergy remedies.

PENTYLENETETRAZOL

AKA: Metrazol.

Effects: Stimulates theta rhythms in the brain, which are associated with periods of creative thinking, and may increase learning ability and slow the advance of senility.

Precautions: Causes convulsions.

PHENYTOIN

AKA: Dilantin (extended action), Diphenylan (prompt acting), Diphenylhydantoin (DPH), Ditan (prompt acting), Ethotoin, Mephenytoin, Mesantoin, Peganone, Phenytex, PHT.

The most commonly prescribed drug for epilepsy, it has been the subject of at least 8000 papers. The exact mechanism by which it works is still not understood, but it is believed to influence the electromagnetic fields, polarizing the electrically charged elements of the cells.

Effects: Though it is mainly used as a treatment for epilepsy, it has a number of other various effects: it can normalize electrical activity in the cell membranes; it can stabilize behavior by suppressing obsessive thoughts, fear, anger, violent behavior, and passivity; it can supposedly improve intelligence, concentration, learning, long-term memory, comprehension, and speed of visual-motor coordination; it has some anti-aging effects, including restoring the homeostasis of the neuroendocrine system; in small doses, it increases the "good" form of cholesterol, called high density lipoprotein (HDL).

Precautions: It is not taken by anyone who is allergic to hydantoin anticonvulsants, has liver damage or impaired liver functioning, has had surgery within the last two months that has required general or spinal anesthesia, has diabetes, or a blood disorder. Those over 60 should realize that adverse reactions and side effects will occur more often and much more strongly than they do in younger individuals.

Common side effects include constipation; mild dizziness; drowsiness; gums that are bleeding, swollen, or tender; nausea; increased susceptibility to sunburn; and vomiting. Less common side effects include agitation, breast swelling, confusion, diarrhea, an increase in facial and body hair, hallucinations, headaches, insomnia, muscle twitches, rash, slurred speech, staggering, vision changes. Rare symptoms include abdominal pain, an increased chance of bleeding or bruising, fever, jaundice, and sore throat. Other symptoms cited by some sources include anemia, balding, chest pains, depression, mental confusion and learning disability, conjunctivitis, nervousness, numbness of the hands and feet, nystagmus, retention of water, sensitivity to bright lights, swollen glands, tiredness, irritability, and weight gain, though these also disappear as time goes on and dosage is reduced. A severe allergic reaction could be life-threatening, and could include such symptoms as fever, rash, swollen glands, and kidney failure. Use of phenytoin may even cause liver damage, including hepatitis. If stomach upset occurs, it should be taken with meals. Long-term effects may be weakened bones, gum overgrowth (though this occurs mainly in children and is rare in instances where the lower, cognitive-enhancing doses are taken; still, good oral hygiene is recommended), constant eye movements, liver damage, lymph gland enlargement, and numbness and tingling in the hands and feet.

An overdose can cause problems in maintaining balance, a drop in blood pressure, slow, shallow breathing, coma, drowsiness, spastic eye movements, decreased intelligence, slow reaction time, slurred speech, and staggering. There have been reports of insomnia, tremors and in some cases, liver toxicity in the first month or so of use. It is not habit-forming, but abrupt cessation could trigger severe epileptic seizures.

Phenytoin may deplete the body's stores of B-12, lead to a heightened need for thyroid hormone, interfere with the absorption of vitamin D and folic acid (supplements of calcium should be taken along with vitamin D and folic acid, though calcium will decrease the amount of Phenytoin the body absorbs from the small intestine).

The effects of Phenytoin can be increased when taken with alcohol (small amounts), Allopurinol, salicylate drugs such as aspirin, benzodiazopine tranquilizers and sedatives, Chlorphiramine, Cimetidine, Ibuprofen, Metronidazole, Miconazole, Molindone, Nizatidine, Omeprazole, Phenacemide, succinimide antiseizure medicines, tricyclic antidepressants, Trimethoprim, or Valproic Acid. The anti-convulsant effect can be enhanced when taken in combination with Amiodarone, Carbamazepine, Chloramphenicol, Disulfiram, Fluconazole, Isoniazid, Methylphenidate, Nicardipine, Nimodipine, Oxyphenbutazone, Para-aminosalicylic acid (PAS), Phenothiazines, Phenylbutazone, Sulfa drugs, or Warfarin. The anti-convulsant effect is diminished when Phenytoin is taken with alcohol (habitual use), antacids, anti-cancer drugs, barbiturates, Carbamazepine, charcoal tablets, Diazoxide, Glutethimide, influenza virus vaccine, Loxapine, marijuana (with attendant drowsiness and unsteadiness), Nitrofurantoin, Paroxitine, Pyridoxine, Rifampin, Sucralfate, or Theophylline. When taken in combination with anticoagulants or Propafenone, the effects of both drugs are intensified, and when taken with Xanthines, the effects of both drugs are weakened. Phenytoin can amplify the effects of Estrogen, Griseofulvin, Methotrexate, Propranolol, Quinidine, sedatives, and Warfarin, and curtail the effects of Amiodarone, Carbamazepine, corticosteroids, cortisone drugs, Cyclosporine, Dicumarol, Digitalis preparations, Disopyramide, Doxycycline, Furosemide, Haloperidol, Hypoglycemics, Itraconazole, Methadone, Metyrapone, Mexiletine, oral contraceptives, potassium supplements, Probenecid, Quinidine, Sotalol, Theophylline drugs, and Valproic Acid. Phenytoin can interact unpredictably with Clonazepam, Dopamine, levodopa, Levonorgestrel, Mebendazole, Phenothiazine anti-psychotic medicines, or oral antidiabetic medications.

The severity of side effects and adverse reactions increases when taken with Felbamate, there is an increased risk of toxicity when taken with Cimetidine, and an increased risk of liver toxicity when taken with Acetaminophen. The anti-convulsant dose may need to be adjusted when taken with tricyclic anti-depressants; there may be a changed seizure pattern when taken with barbiturates; there is a greater chance of bone disease when taken with carbonic anhydrase inhibitors; there could be oversedation when taken with central nervous system depressants; the incidence of seizures increases when taken with cocaine or oral contraceptives; corticosteroid drugs could hide any Phenytoin-sensitivity reactions; there could be an increase in drug levels in the blood when taken in combination with gold compounds; and Leucovorin could counteract the effects of phenytoin. When taken with Lithium, it can increase the toxicity of the latter drug; when taken with MAO inhibitors, it could result in an increased polythiazide effect; when taken with Meperidine, it can decrease the pain-relieving effects of the latter while increasing its side effects; when taken with nitrates, it could result in an excessive drop in blood pressure; when taken with Omeprazole, there could be a delay in the excretion of phenytoin with a resultant excess remaining in the blood; when taken with Phenacemide, it could result in an increased risk of paranoia; and when taken with Valproic acid, it could result in seizures.

Dosage: Adult epileptics are generally given doses of 200 to 400 mg/day in two to four divided doses. About an eighth of that, or 25 to 50 mg/day are given for cognitive-enhancing effects, though some recommend as much as 100 mg/day in two to four divided doses.

PICROTOXINE

Effects: May increase learning ability and slow the advance of senility.

Precautions: Causes convulsions.

PIRACETAM

AKA: Cerebroforte, Dinagen, Gabacet, Nootropil, Normabrain.

Its chemical structure is very close to the amino acid pyroglutamate, a substance found in meat, vegetables, fruits, and dairy products.

Effects: Protects the brain against — and helps it recover from — hypoxia; protects against metabolic stress related to low oxygen flow to the brain resulting from intense athletic performance, high altitude conditions, and smoking; steps up the rate of metabolism and level of energy in the brain cells by increasing the production of adenosine triphosphate (ATP) and improving the blood flow within the brain;

improves memory, alertness, and some kinds of learning in normal humans (probably by helping the brain synthesize new proteins); prevents memory loss caused by physical injury and chemical poisoning; and facilitates the flow of information between the two hemispheres of the brain, an important component of creativity, insight, and peak performance. May contribute to the growth of more cholinergic receptors in the brain. It has been used in the treatment of dyslexia, stroke, alcoholism, vertigo, senile dementia, and sickle-cell anemia, among other conditions.

Works synergistically with centrophenoxine, choline, Deaner, DMAE, gingko biloba, Hydergine, or lecithin; for improving memory, the combination of Piracetam and choline is particularly effective.

Precautions: Though piracetam is derived from pyrrolidone, a substance that is believed to enhance the nervous system's ability to utilize acetylcholine as a neurotransmitter, the exact mechanism by which it works is still not fully understood. There is some evidence that it increases the number of receptors in the brain, but it also seems to increase blood flow to the brain. Still other theories suggest that it improves protein synthesis in the brain, improves the function of nerve fibers in the corpus callosum (thereby assisting the flow of information between the two halves of the brain), or that it reduces free radicals.

It is avoided by those with severe kidney failure and those taking anticoagulant drugs.

In rare cases, it may cause gastrointestinal distress, diarrhea, headaches, insomnia, nausea, and psychomotor agitation. It may result in acetylcholine's being used up more rapidly in the body, so a choline supplement may be needed.

It may also increase the effects of such drugs as amphetamines, psychotropics, and Hydergine. It is not believed to be toxic or addictive, and has no contraindications.

Dosage: 800 to 1600 mg/day after an initial daily dose of 1200 to 2400 mg/day taken in the morning for the first two days. Others recommend 2400 to 4800 mg/day in three divided doses, while still others a more modest dose of 500 to 600 mg/day for a healthy person and 1000 to 2000 mg/day for an elderly person with mild to moderate memory impairment.

PRAMIRACETAM

AKA: CI-879, Neupramir.

A variant of piracetam, it stimulates the functioning of the cholinergic system, but at much lower doses (it is approximately 15 times stronger than piracetam). It is not as fully tested and researched as piracetam.

Precautions: Toxicity is rare, and known side effects are few.

Dosage: 75 to 1500 mg/day.

PRL-8-53

Effects: An experimental drug that has been shown to increase recall in subjects by as much as 150 percent.

PROPANIRACETAM

A nootropic drug similar to piracetam.

PROPRANOLOL

AKA: Inderal, Inderal LA (long acting), propranolol hydrochloride.

A beta-andrenergic blocking agent medication prescribed for high blood pressure patients and used in the treatment of angina, hypertension, specific tremors, and certain cardiac arrhythmias.

Effects: Reduces fear and stress by blocking the muscle's receptor sites for adrenaline; it also reduces the oxygen requirements of the heart and reduces the contractions of the blood vessels in the heart, scalp, and other areas. Taking it a half hour before an anxiety- or fear-inducing event may help an individual overcome his or her aversion to that situation.

Precautions: Most studies have been short term (six weeks or so), and more recent evidence does not support the claim that it works consistently over the long run. There is also evidence that it controls the physical symptoms of anxiety, but not the psychological ones.

It is not taken by anyone with an allergy to any beta-adrenergic blocker; by those with hypotension, as it lowers blood pressure, aggravates any condition of congestive heart failure, produces tingling in the extremities, and light-headedness; by those with asthma, pollen allergies, upper respiratory disease, or arterial spasms; or by those who have taken MAO inhibitors or other psychiatric or psychotropic drugs within the preceding two weeks. It is prescribed for those who have chronic obstructive pulmonary diseases (e.g., asthma, bronchitis or emphysema), diabetes or hypoglycemia, kidney or liver problems, heart disease or poor circulation in the limbs, an overactive thyroid function, or surgery within the last two months (including dental surgery) that requires general or spinal anesthesia.

Common side effects include a slow

pulse rate (fewer than 50 beats per minute), a coldness in the hands and feet, diarrhea, dizziness, drowsiness, a dryness of the mouth, eyes, and skin, fatigue, and numbness or tingling in the fingers and toes. Less frequent symptoms include abdominal pain, a loss of alertness, anxiety, difficult breathing, chest pain, confusion, constipation, depression, hallucinations, headache, impotence, insomnia, joint pain, and nightmares. Rare side effects include excessive bleeding and bruising, eyes that are dry and burning, fever, rash, sore throat, vomiting, and emotional instability. Other possible side effects include short-term memory loss, visual disturbances, weakness, and paranoia.

Overdose symptoms include a drop in blood pressure, bronchial muscle spasms leading to breathing difficulties, convulsions, fainting, heart failure, a slow or weak pulse, cold and sweaty skin, and weakness. Toxic psychosis will occur when the dosage is high (i.e., thousands of milligrams a day). Use is discontinued by decreasing the dosage gradually over a period of two weeks, as abrupt cessation could damage the heart.

For those over age 60, the side effects may be more severe and frequent. Prolonged use can weaken the heart muscles. It may mask symptoms of hypoglycemia or alter the results of some medical tests.

There is an enhanced beta blocker effect when combined with betaxolol eyedrops or Levobunolol eyedrops, and a diminished beta blocker effect when combined with Dextrothyroxine or Indomethacin. It can intensify the effects of antidiabetics, antihypertensives, barbiturates, insulin, and narcotics, and can lessen the effects of antihistamines and beta-agonists. It can decrease the effectiveness of Digitalis if taken for congestive heart failure, but increase its effectiveness if taken for any other medical reason.

There is an increased drop in blood pressure when taken with alcohol, calcium channel blockers, Clonidine, Diazoxide, or Guanabenz. When combined with angiotensin-converting (ACE) inhibitors or non-steroidal anti-inflammatory drugs (NSAIDS), Propranolol could increase the anti-hypertensive effect of one or both drugs; with Encainide, it could damage the heart muscle; with Molindone, it could increase tranquilizer effect; with MAO inhibitors, it could raise blood pressure if the latter is discontinued; with cocaine, it could lead to an irregular heartbeat and a decreased beta-adrenergic effect; with daily marijuana use, it may promote circulation problems in the hands and feet; and with tobacco, it could lead to an irregular heartbeat. It may also interact with certain ingredients in over-the-counter cold, cough, and allergy remedies.

Dosage: Some recommend 10 to 30 mg a half hour before the trauma-inducing event, though the usual prescribed dosage is 5 to 10 mg. Propranolol will have a greater effect if taken with meals.

RIBAMOL

AKA: 2-hydroxytriethylammonium ribonucleate.

Effects: May enhance memory and learning.

RIVASTIGMINE

The first in a new class of drugs known as acetylcholinesterase inhibitors.

Effects: A study has shown that it may improve the brain functioning of those with mild to moderate forms of Alzheimer's disease, enabling them to perform normal activities again.

RN-13

AKA: Regeneresen.

Developed by Hans J. Kugler, it is a mixture of RNA from twelve organs (placenta, testes, ovaries, hypothalamus, adrenal cortices, pituitary, thalamus, spleen, vascular walls, cerebral cortex, liver, and kidneys), along with yeast-derived nucleic acid.

Effects: Said to double the life span of dwarf mice, have a rejuvenating influence on the human body, and improve learning, memory, and general brain function.

ROLZIRACETAM

Effects: Like piracetam, it is derived from pyrrolidone, which is believed to enhance the nervous system's ability to utilize acetylcholine as a neurotransmitter.

SABELUZOLE

Effects: Preliminary evidence indicates that it may prevent Alzheimer's from progressing, and may improve memory and learning in normal individuals.

STRYCHNINE SULFATE

Effects: May increase learning ability and slow the advance of senility.

Precautions: Causes convulsions.

SULBUTIAMINE

AKA: Arcalion.

A compound similar to Hydergine, but stronger.

Effects: Promotes alertness, strengthens long-term memory, improves reaction time, fights fatigue, lowers anxiety, and improves resistance to stress.

Precautions: More than three 200 mg tablets a day may result in severe headaches.

Dosage: 400 mg/day with breakfast for 20 days.

SYGEN

AKA: GM1 ganglioside.

Effects: In use in Italy as a treatment for Alzheimer's and memory disorders.

TACRINE

AKA: Cognex, tacrine hydrochloride, Tetrahydroaminoacridine, THA.

Effects: Has a good track record for improving memory in Alzheimer's patients, especially when taken with deprenyl and lecithin, though it does not help other damage caused by this disease. It is most effective for those whose memory problems are the result of too little acetylcholine, as it is the only drug proven to raise levels of acetylcholine in the brain.

Precautions: It is not taken by those allergic or sensitive to Tacrine or acridine derivatives. A doctor should be consulted first if any one of the following conditions are present: heart rhythm problems, ulcers, liver disease, bladder disease, seizure disorders, asthma, or a previous reaction to tacrine that has caused jaundice or elevated bilirubin. Women are likely to retain more of this drug in their blood and suffer side effects.

It could be hepatotoxic (toxic to the liver) and should only be taken under a physician's guidance. It is used as a "smart drug" only by those with Alzheimer's, and even then it loses its effectiveness after only a few months.

Common side effects include headaches, sore throat, dizziness, fainting, chills, sweating, fever, stomach gas, skin rash, lack of coordination, diarrhea, nausea, vomiting, swelling in the legs and feet, a tingling in the hands and feet, difficulty urinating, joint pain and inflammation, spasticity, hyperactivity, nervousness, sinus inflammation, bronchitis, pneumonia, difficulty breathing, convulsions, liver inflammation, conjunctivitis, blood pressure changes, and broken bones. Less common side effects include loss of appetite, changes in taste, drowsiness, eyes that are dry or itching, eye pain, sties, double vision or other vision problems, glaucoma, cataracts, earache, ringing or buzzing in the ears, deafness, infections of the middle or inner ear, a flushing in the face, facial swelling, a sickly appearance, indigestion, insomnia, muscle aches, runny nose, rash, stomach pain, heavy sweating, dehydration, greater chance of tiredness or weakness, and weight gain, heart failure, heart attack, angina pains, stroke, vein irritation, cardiac insufficiency, heart palpitations, abnormal heart rhythms, migraines, slow heart rate, blood clots in the lung, elevated blood cholesterol, inflamed tongue swollen gums, dry mouth and throat, mouth sores, upset stomach, excess saliva, difficulty swallowing, esophagus and stomach irritation, bleeding or

ulcers in the stomach or intestines, hemorrhoids, hiatal hernia, bloody stools, diverticulitis, loss of bowel control, impacted colon, gallbladder irritation or stones, increased appetite, diabetes, anemia, osteoporosis, tendinitis, bursitis, abnormal dreams, speaking difficulties, loss of memory, twitching, delirium, paralysis, slow muscle movements, nerve inflammation or disease, Parkinson's-type movements, apathy, heightened sex drive, neurosis, paranoia, nosebleeds, chest congestion, asthma, rapid breathing, respiratory infection, acne, hair loss, skin rash, eczema, dry skin, herpes zoster (shingles), psoriasis, skin inflammation, cysts, furuncles, cold sores, herpes infections, blood and puss in the urine, kidney stones and infections, sugar in the urine, frequent urination, urinating at night, cystitis, vaginal bleeding, genital itching, breast pain, impotence, and prostate cancer. Rare side effects include heat exhaustion, blood infection, very abnormal heart rhythms, bowel obstruction, duodenal ulcer, convulsions, lack of coordination, thyroid changes, a reduction in white blood cell and platelet counts, muscle disease, some loss of the senses (particularly touch), severe uncontrolled movements of the face, loss of muscle tone, changes in liver function (resulting in yellow skin or eyes, changes in stool color), inflammation of the brain and possibly the central nervous system, Bell's palsy, suicidal thoughts, hysteria, psychosis, vomiting blood, fluid in the lungs, lung cancer, sudden choking, skin peeling, oily skin, skin ulcers, skin cancer, melanoma, bladder or kidney tumors, kidney failure, urinary obstruction, breast cancer, ovarian cancer, inflammation of the male reproductive tract, blindness, drooping or inflamed eyelids, and disturbances or inflammation of the inner ear. Overdose symptoms include a decrease in blood pressure, collapse, convulsions, decreased heartbeat, muscle weakness (leading to respiratory failure and death), severe nausea and vomiting, increased salivation, and heavy sweating.

Cimetidine can increase the amount of Tacrine in the blood, and tobacco can increase the rate at which it is broken down in the liver. Theophylline could intensify the effect of this drug, and anticholinergics could diminish the effect of this drug. It could also strengthen the effects of muscle relaxants during surgery.

Tacrine is taken at least one hour before or two hours after eating.

Dosage: Subjects with Alzheimer's showed the best improvement when given doses of 120 to 160 mg/day, but improvements in memory and the ability to think and reason lasted for only 24 weeks, after which the decline in mental abilities resumed.

2-MEA

AKA: Cysteamine, 2-mercaptoethylamine.

Effects: An anti-oxidant. It bolsters the immune system and may increase life span. It is used as a treatment for radiation sickness in the former Soviet Union, and can remove heavy metals such as cadmium, lead, and mercury from the body.

Precautions: May actually shorten the life span if a very high dosage is combined with a very high dosage of vitamin E.

Dosage: John Mann recommends 200 mg/day for life extension.

VINCAMINE

AKA: Oxicebral.

Made from an extract of the periwinkle plant.

Effects: A vasodilator (improves blood flow to the brain and enhances the brain's utilization of oxygen). Users claim it improves memory and cognition, but sufficient scientific research is lacking for normal, healthy people.

Precautions: It may cause a reduction in white corpuscles and a degeneration of muscle tissue. In rare cases, it causes gastrointestinal problems.

Dosage: 60 mg/day in two divided doses.

VINPOCETINE

AKA: Cavinton.

A close relative of vincamine believed to elicit more benefits and fewer side effects.

Effects: Reportedly a strong enhancer of memory and concentration. It improves the brain's metabolism by increasing the blood flow, speeding up the rate at which ATP is produced by the brain cells, and improving the use of glucose and oxygen in the brain. It is particularly effective for disorders caused by poor or impaired circulation, such as stroke, headaches, recurring dizziness, macular degeneration, and certain ear problems.

Precautions: No toxicity or contraindications. Side effects, which include dry mouth, hypotension, tachycardia, and weakness, are rare.

Dosage: 5 to 10 mg/day. It takes a year for the drug to reach its peak efficiency.

VITACEL 3

The tablet form of GH-3, it has the active PBN ingredient as Gerovital. Vitacel 4 has the addition of bee propolis for its antibacterial and antiviral qualities, and royal jelly for its high levels of vitamins B-5, B-6, and C. Vitacel 7 has replaced the bisulfite and benzoic acid with vitamin-complexing agents to prevent allergy problems; according to creator Dr. Robert Koch, this last formulation helps the procaine hydrochloride stay active in the body for several hours.

Precautions: See the entries under Gerovital and Royal jelly.

CHAPTER 13

Other

BHA

AKA: Butylated hydroxyanisole.

A food preservative added to prevent oxidation and reduce rancidity in oil-containing foods.

Effects: An anti-oxidant. According to Jane Brody, it has been proven to protect the body against certain carcinogens. It is more quickly metabolized by the body and less likely to cause kidney problems than BHT.

Precautions: It is considered a possible carcinogen and, for that reason, most nutritionists warn that it should be avoided. It may cause a mild dermatitis resulting from an allergic reaction, which may be avoided if nutrition is adequate, particularly vitamins A and C.

It works synergistically with most other anti-oxidants, but some research suggests that, when both BHA and vitamin E are taken together in very high doses, their life-extension properties are severely curtailed.

Dosage: John Mann recommends 200 mg/day. When taken in gelatin form, it may not be fully assimilated by the body and could irritate the stomach. Mann recommends lightly warming 16 ounces of safflower oil in a pan and stirring in 2 level teaspoons until all the crystals have dissolved. After cooling for a few minutes, the oil should be put back in the fridge until needed. The oil is used within a week or two so that it does not become oxidized. It is not used for frying.

BHT

AKA: Butylated hydroxytoluene.

A food preservative added to prevent oxidation and reduce rancidity in oil-containing foods.

Effects: An anti-oxidant. According to Jane Brody, BHT has been proven to protect the body against certain carcinogens, to inactive some viruses, and provide some protection against carbon tetrachloride poisoning. According to Pearson and Shaw, it can also extend life and be used as a treatment for herpes.

Precautions: The few studies conducted have yielded contradictory results or have had flaws. It is considered a possible carcinogen and, for that reason, most nutritionists warn that it should be avoided. It is not to be taken by those with a diseased or damaged liver, or who have had a liver test that is abnormal. Those taking it have follow-up tests for liver function, serum lipids, and a complete blood count.

An initial side effect is hypotension and lightheadedness when getting out of bed in the morning, which goes away after a few days. This problem can usually be avoided if a quarter gram is taken at bedtime, with the dosage slowly increased over time. It may cause a mild dermatitis due to an allergic reaction, which may be avoided if nutrition is adequate, particularly vitamins A and C.

It can intensify the effects of barbiturates, other downers, or alcohol when combined with these drugs. There may be possible harmful interactions with steroid hormones or oral contraceptives. It works synergistically with most other anti-oxidants, but some research suggests that when BHT and vitamin E are taken together in very high doses, their life extension properties are severely curtailed.

Dosage: Pearson and Shaw take 2 to 6 g/day for its free radical-fighting and life-extending properties, though Joseph G. Llaurado, M.D., Ph.D., of the Nuclear Medicine Service at the Jerry L. Pettis Memorial Veterans Hospital and the Loma Linda University School of Medicine asserts that 2 grams is very close to the lethal dose. John Mann recommends 200 mg/day. When taken in gelatin form, it may not be fully assimilated by the body and could irritate the stomach. Mann recommends lightly warming 16 ounces of safflower oil in a pan and stirring in 2 level teaspoons until all the crystals have dissolved. After cooling for a few minutes, the oil is returned to the refrigerator until needed. The oil is used within a week or two so that it does not become oxidized. It is not used for frying.

DDC

AKA: Ammonium diethyl-dithio-carbamate.

Effects: An anti-oxidant.

ETHOXYQUIN

AKA: Santoquin.

A food preservative.

Effects: An anti-oxidant. Laboratory rats fed ethoxyquin had a longer life span, fewer tumors, and a lower incidence of obesity than rats in the control group. It has been shown to prevent vitamin E deficiency in the diets of animals (the metabolic activity of the two are identical). It is said to improve memory.

Precautions: Albino rats given 1000 to 4000 mg of ethoxyquin per kg of food showed signs of kidney fibrosis, kidney disease, changes in the structure of liver cells, and possible damage to the thyroid. It has also been linked to liver tumors in mice. It is still in the experimental stage.

Dosage: John Mann recommends no more than 100 mg per meal. Individuals have taken as much as 1000 to 3000 mg/day, though any long-term effects are not known.

NDGA

AKA: Nordihydroguaiaretic acid.

A resinous substance extracted from a variety of plants (such as the creosote bush and Guaiac gum trees) that was once used as a preservative in pie crusts, candy, lard, butter, ice cream, and canned whipped cream.

Effects: An anti-oxidant which may have some life-extension properties.

Precautions: It was banned by the FDA in 1968 when high doses were found to cause kidney damage in rats; since rat urine is much more concentrated than human urine and rats urinate infrequently, this problem may not extend to humans.

PROPYL GALLATE

A food preservative similar to BHA and BHT.

Effects: An anti-oxidant.

Precautions: It is a suspected carcinogen. More studies are needed to evaluate the safety of this substance.

SODIUM BISULFATE

A food additive that prevents discoloration and inhibits the growth of bacteria.

Effects: An anti-oxidant.

Precautions: It destroys vitamin B-1.

SODIUM HYPOPHOSPHITE

Effects: An anti-oxidant.

STRYCHNINE

An alkaloid found naturally in various plants, though contrary to popular opinion, not in most hallucinogenic ones.

Effects: In rats, it produces definite improvements in maze learning and visual and spatial discrimination. In humans, it has a stimulating effect on the spinal cord. It can produce a painful erection, a dangerously high heart rate, excessive body heat, and profuse sweating.

Precautions: It is extremely toxic.

Dosage: Doses high enough to result in measureable improvements in brain functioning (2 mg or more) carry a very high risk of rapid heart rate, convulsions, opisthotonus (a condition where the head is bent back as far as it will go), intense pain (consciousness is maintained until death), and death from respiratory paralysis; doses small enough to avoid these risks do not produce any measureable improvements. As yet, no one has isolated the brain-enhancing component for safe commercial use.

TBHQ

AKA: Monotertiary butyl hydroquinone, tertiary butyl hydroquinone, 2-tertiary butyl hydroquinone.

A food preservative.

Effects: An anti-oxidant.

THIODIPROPIONIC ACID AND DILAURYL THIODIPROPIONATE

A food preservative and its dilauryl derivative.

Effects: Both are anti-oxidants. They are highly synergistic with anti-oxidant vitamins, especially in combination with citric acid.

Precautions: More testing is needed.

Dosage: John Mann recommends 200 mg/day.

Bibliography

Balch, James F., MD, and Phyllis A. Balch, CNC. *Prescription for Nutritional Healing: A-to-Z Guide to Supplements.* New York: Avery, 1998.

Ballentine, Rudolph, MD. *Diet and Nutrition: A Holistic Approach.* Honesdale, Penn.: Himalayan International Institute, 1978.

Berger, Stuart M., MD. *How to Be Your Own Nutritionist.* New York: William Morrow, 1987.

Bloomfield, Harold H., MD. *Healing Anxiety with Herbs.* New York: HarperCollins, 1998.

Brody, Jane. *Jane Brody's Nutrition Book.* New York: Bantam, 1981.

Brown, Judith E. *The Science of Human Nutrition.* New York: Harcourt Brace Jovanovich, 1990.

Callahan, Maureen. *DHEA: The Miracle Hormone.* New York: Signet, 1997.

Carper, Jean. *The Food Pharmacy.* New York: Bantam, 1988.

Chaitow, Leon, ND, DO. *The Healing Power of Amino Acids.* Wellingborough, England: Thorsons Publishing Group, 1989.

Cherniske, Stephen, MS. *The DHEA Breakthrough.* New York: Ballantine, 1996.

Crook, Thomas H. III, PhD, and Brenda Adderly, MHA. *The Memory Cure.* New York: Pocket Books, 1998.

Czop, Judith. "Health Update." Syndicated newspaper column.

Davis, Patricia. *Aromatherapy: An A–Z.* Saffron Walden, England: C. W. Daniel Company Ltd., 1991.

Dean, Ward, MD, and John Morgenthaler. *Smart Drugs and Nutrients.* Santa Cruz, Cal.: B&J Publications, 1990.

Dean, Ward, MD, *et al. Smart Drugs II: The Next Generation.* Menlo Park, Cal.: Health Freedom Publications, 1993.

_____. *GHB: The Natural Mood Enhancer.*

Petaluma, Cal.: Smart Publications, 1997.

Dembling, Sophia. "Melatonin: The Latest Wonder Pill." *Health and Fitness News Service.* October 31, 1995.

Di Cyan, Erwin, PhD. *Vitamins in Your Life.* New York: Fireside Books– Simon and Schuster, 1974.

Dobkin de Rios, Marlene. *Visionary Vine: Hallucinogenic Healing in the Peruvian Amazon.* Prospect Heights, Ill.: Waveland Press, 1972.

Dreyfus, Jack. *A Remarkable Medicine Has Been Overlooked.* New York: Dreyfus Medical Foundation, 1992.

Duke, James A., PhD. *The Green Pharmacy.* New York: St. Martin's, 1997.

Elkins, Rita, MA. *Wild Yam: Nature's Progesterone.* Pleasant Grove, Utah: Woodland Publishing, 1996.

Emboden, William. *Narcotic Plants.* Revised and enlarged. New York: Macmillan, 1979.

Graedon, Joe, and Teresa, PhD. *Graedon's Best Medicine.* New York: Bantam, 1991.

_____. *The People's Pharmacy.* New York: St. Martin's, 1997.

_____. "The People's Pharmacy." Syndicated newspaper column.

Griffith, H. Winter. *Complete Guide to Prescription and Nonprescription Drugs.* New York: Body Press– Perigee, 1996.

Haas, Robert. *Eat Smart, Think Smart.* New York: HarperCollins, 1994.

Harris, Ben Charles. *The Compleat Herbal.* Atlanta: Larchmont Books, 1972.

Hart, Carol. *Secrets of Serotonin.* New York: St. Martin's, 1996.

Hausman, Patricia, MS. *The Right Dose.* New York: Ballantine, 1987.

Hendler, Sheldon Saul, MD, PhD. *The Doctor's Vitamin and Mineral Encyclopedia.* New York: Simon and Schuster, 1990.

Hoffer, Dr. Abram, and Dr. Morton Walker. *Smart Nutrients.* New York: Avery, 1994.

Holvey, Donald N., MD. *The Merck Manual of Diagnosis and Therapy,* 12th edition. Rahway, N.J.: Merck, 1972.

Hutchison, Michael. *Mega Brain Power.* New York: Hyperion, 1994.

Jacobson, Michael F., PhD., *et al. Safe Food: Eating Wisely in a Risky World.* Los Angeles: Living Planet Press, 1991.

Katzenstein, Larry. *Secrets of St. John's Wort.* New York: St. Martin's, 1998.

Khalsa, Dharma Singh, MD. *Brain Longevity.* New York: Warner Books, 1997.

Kilham, Chris. *OPC: The Miracle Antioxidant.* New Canaan, Conn.: Keats Publishing, 1997.

Klatz, Dr. Ronald, with Carol Kahn. *Grow Young with HGH.* New York: Harper-Collins, 1997.

Lieberman, Shari, PhD, and Nancy Bruning. *The Real Vitamin and Mineral Book.* 2nd edition. New York: Avery, 1997.

Lilly, John C. *The Scientist: A Novel Autobiography.* New York: Bantam, 1978.

Lust, John. *The Herb Book.* New York: Bantam, 1974.

Malcolm, Andrew I. *The Pursuit of Intoxication.* New York: Pocket Books– Washington Square Press, 1971.

Mann, John A. *Secrets of Life Extension.* New York: Bantam, 1980.

Marriott, Alice and Carol K. Rachlin. *Peyote.* New York: Mentor, 1971.

Masline, Shelagh Ryan, and Barbara Close. *Aromatherapy.* New York: Dell, 1997.

Mayell, Mark. *Natural Energy.* New York: Three Rivers Press, 1998.

Mindell, Earl. *Earl Mindell's New and Revised Vitamin Bible.* New York: Warner Books, 1985.

_____. *Earl Mindell's Safe Eating.* New York: Warner Books, 1987.

_____. *Earl Mindell's Herb Bible.* New York: Fireside–Simon & Schuster, 1992.

_____, RPh, PhD. *Earl Mindell's Anti-Aging Bible.* New York: Fireside–Simon & Schuster, 1996.

Morganthaler, John, and Dan Joy. *Better Sex Through Chemistry.* Petaluma, Cal.: Smart Publications, 1994.

Murray, Dr. Michael, ND. *Grape Seed Extract and Other Sources of PCOs.* Vital Communications, 1998.

Null, Gary, and Steve Null. *The Complete Handbook of Nutrition.* New York: Dell, 1972.

Ott, Jonathan. *Pharmacotheon: Entheogenic Drugs, Their Plant Sources and History.* Natural Products Co., 1993.

Passwater, Richard A., PhD. *The New Superantioxidant — Plus.* New Canaan, Conn.: Keats Publishing, 1992.

Pearson, Durk, and Sandy Shaw. *Life Extension: A Practical Scientific Approach.* New York: Warner Books, 1982.

_____. *The Life Extension Companion,* New York: Warner Books, 1984.

Pelton, Ross, RPh, PhD, with Taffy Clarke Pelton. *Mind Food and Smart Pills.* New York: Doubleday, 1989.

Perry, Paul J. *Psychotropic Drug Handbook.* 3rd edition. Cincinnati: Harvey Whitney Books, 1981.

Peterson, Lee Allen. *A Field Guide to Edible Wild Plants.* New York: Houghton Mifflin, 1977.

Phillips, W. Nathaniel. *Natural Supplement Review.* 2nd ed. Denver: Mile High Publishing, 1991.

Potter, Beverly, PhD, and Sebastian Orfali. *Brain Boosters.* Berkeley, Cal.: Ronin Publishing, 1993.

Pressman, Alan H., DC, PhD, CCN, with Sheila Buff. *The GSH Phenomenon.* New York: St. Martin's, 1997.

Prevention Magazine. Future Youth: How to Reverse the Aging Process. Emmaus, Penn.: Rodale Press, 1987.

_____. *The Prevention How-To Dictionary of Healing Remedies and Techniques.* New York: Berkley, 1992.

Reavley, Nicola. *The New Encyclopedia of Vitamins, Minerals, Supplements and Herbs.* New York: M. Evans, 1998.

Regelson, William, MD, and Carol Colman. *The Superhormone Promise.* New York: Pocket Books, 1996.

Reiter, Russel J., PhD, and Jo Robinson. *Melatonin: Your Body's Natural Wonder Drug.* New York: Bantam, 1995.

Rosenbaum, Michael E., MD, and Dominick Bosco. *Super Supplements.* New York: Signet, 1987.

Rosenfeld, Dr. Isadore, "A Doctor's Guide to Herbs." *Parade Magazine.* May 31, 1998.

Rudgley, Richard. *The Encyclopedia of Psychoactive Substances.* New York: St. Martin's, 1998.

Rudin, Donald O., MD, and Clara Felix. *The Omega-3 Phenomenon.* New York: Rawson Associates–Macmillan, 1987.

Ryman, Daniele. *Aromatherapy: The Complete Guide to Plant and Flower Essences for Health and Beauty.* New York: Bantam, 1991.

Sahelian, Ray, MD. *Melatonin: Nature's Sleeping Pill.* Marina del Rey, Cal.: Be Happier Press, 1995.

_____. *5-HTP: Nature's Serotonin Solution.* Garden City Park, N.Y.: Avery Publishing, 1998.

_____. *Kava: The Miracle Antianxiety Herb.* New York: St. Martin's Press, 1998.

Schultes, Richard Evans. *Hallucinogenic Plants.* New York: Golden Press, 1976.

Shakocius, Sandy, and Durk Pearson. "Mind Food." *Omni*. May 1979, vol. 1, no. 8, p. 55.

Shamsuddin, AbulKalam M., MD, PhD. *IP6: Nature's Revolutionary Cancer-Fighter*. New York: Kensington Books, 1998.

Siegel, Ronald K., PhD. *Intoxication*. New York: Pocket Books, 1989.

Silverman, Harold M., *et al. The Pill Book*. 7th edition. New York: Bantam, 1996.

Sosin, Allan, MD, and Beth Ley Jacobs, PhD. *Alpha Lipoic Acid: Nature's Ultimate Antioxidant*. New York: Kensington Books, 1998.

Tierra, Michael, CA, ND. *The Way of Herbs*. Santa Cruz, Cal.: Unity Press, 1980.

Walker, Dr. Morton. *DMSO: Nature's Healer*. New York: Avery, 1993.

Weil, Andrew, and Winifred Rosen. *From Chocolate to Morphine*. New York: Houghton Mifflin, 1993.

Woodward, Lucia. *Poisonous Plants: A Color Field Guide*. New York: Hippocrene, 1985.

Young, Lawrence A., *et al. Recreational Drugs*. New York: Berkley, 1977.

MAGAZINES

Energy Times
Health Counselor
Let's Live
Nature's Impact
Men's Health

Index